DATE DUE

The publisher gratefully acknowledges the generous support of the Valerie Barth and Peter Booth Wiley Endowment Fund in History of the University of California Press Foundation.

Down by the Bay

Mount Tamalpais from the Albany dump. Used by permission of the artist, Jonathan Oppenheimer. © Jonathan Oppenheimer, 2012.

Down by the Bay

SAN FRANCISCO'S HISTORY
BETWEEN THE TIDES

MATTHEW MORSE BOOKER

UNIVERSITY OF CALIFORNIA PRESS
Berkeley   Los Angeles   London

University of California Press, one of the most distinguished university presses in the United States, enriches lives around the world by advancing scholarship in the humanities, social sciences, and natural sciences. Its activities are supported by the UC Press Foundation and by philanthropic contributions from individuals and institutions. For more information, visit www.ucpress.edu.

University of California Press
Berkeley and Los Angeles, California

University of California Press, Ltd.
London, England

Library of Congress Cataloging-in-Publication Data

Booker, Matthew Morse, 1968–.
  Down by the bay : San Francisco's history between the tides / Matthew Morse Booker.
     p.   cm.
  Includes bibliographical references and index.
  ISBN 978-0-520-27320-7 (cloth : alk. paper)
  ISBN 978-0-520-95148-8 (ebook)
  1. San Francisco (Calif.)—History.   2. Land use—California—San Francisco—History.   3. San Francisco Bay Area (Calif.)—History.
4. Land use—California—San Francisco Bay Area—History.   5. San Francisco (Calif.)—Environmental conditions.   6. San Francisco Bay Area (Calif.)—Environmental conditions.   7. Nature—Effect of human beings on—California—San Francisco—History.   8. Nature—Effect of human beings on—California—San Francisco Bay Area—History.
9. Human ecology—California—San Francisco—History.   10. Human ecology—California—San Francisco Bay Area—History.   I. Title.
  F869.S357B66   2013
  979.4'61—dc23   2013000528

Manufactured in the United States of America

21 20 19 18 17 16 15 14 13
10 9 8 7 6 5 4 3 2 1

In keeping with a commitment to support environmentally responsible and sustainable printing practices, UC Press has printed this book on Rolland Enviro100, a 100% postconsumer fiber paper that is FSC certified, deinked, processed chlorine-free, and manufactured with renewable biogas energy. It is acid-free and EcoLogo certified.

Contents

Illustrations

MAPS

Acknowledgments

If books had watersheds, this one would drain a vast area. It represents the confluence of so many wise and generous people.

This project began in my first meeting with Richard White. Richard's questions and his criticism shape much of what is good in this book. Together with David M. Kennedy and Kären Wigen at Stanford University, Richard helped me conceive and finish the dissertation that became this book. I cannot imagine better mentors or models than these three scholars.

Several institutions provided financial support. During a period of dramatic cuts in state funding for higher education, North Carolina State University consistently supported travel for research and conferences. The Bill Lane Center for the American West funded a sabbatical year as visiting assistant professor at Stanford University. My thanks to David Kennedy, Richard White, Jon Christensen, Tammy Frisby, and fellows Peter Alagona, Greg Simon and Bob Wilson. The Spatial History Project at Stanford University also contributed to this book. Great thanks to fellow investigators Jon Christensen, Zephyr Frank and Richard White, to lab staff Erik Steiner, Kathy Harris and Whitney Berry, and to researchers Michael De Groot, Gabriel Lee, Alec Norton, Allen Roberts and Andy Robichaud.

The History Department at North Carolina State University provided me with the best job I've ever had and a room of my own to write in. Colleagues who read the manuscript and gave important suggestions include Ross Bassett, Jim Crisp, David Gilmartin, Will Kimler, Kat Mellen Charron and Jonathan Ocko. Chad Ludington offered critical editing and companionship as he finished his fine book on the politics of wine in Britain. Office staff Courtney Hamilton, LaTonya Tucker and Norene Miller made my life easier. I appreciate that my students allowed me to work out ideas in lectures, in seminars, and in continuing friendships. Special thanks to Laura Hepp Bradshaw, Dean Bruno, Shane Cruise, Gabriel Lee, Neil Oatsvall and Rob Shapard.

This book is built on the labor of many archivists and librarians in the San Francisco Bay region and beyond. Special thanks are due to staff at Stanford University's libraries, particularly Maggie Kimball, former director. I owe much to local librarians, most memorably Dean Baird at the Alviso public library. At the Bancroft Library, the great repository of Western history, I recognize Susan Snyder and Michelle Morton. My thanks to staff at the U.S. National Archives in San Bruno; California State Archives and California State Library in Sacramento; Holt-Atherton Special Collections at the University of Pacific; Huntington Library in San Marino; San Mateo County Historical Society; U.S. Geological Survey photo library in Denver; and the North Carolina State University libraries.

I am humbled to add my small trickle to the great stream of work on San Francisco Bay's social and ecological communities. I owe much to Ellen Joslin Johnck, former Executive Director of the Bay Planning Coalition and to Laura Watt of Sonoma State University. Timothy Babalis, Elinore M. Barrett, Gray Brechin, Andrew Cohen, Philip Dreyfus, Philip Garone, Andrew Isenberg, Mark Kurlansky, Frank Leonard, Whitman Miller, Mitchell Postel, Jasper Rubin and Dick Walker provided sources, correctives, or inspiration.

Much of this book is a conversation with people who manage and plan future uses of public land. At the Don Edwards San Francisco Bay National Wildlife Refuge, I thank Eric Mruz, refuge manager, Mendel Stewart, project manager, and former refuge manager Marge Kolar, who let me camp out in the refuge files. Ken LaJoie, retired from the U.S. Geological Survey, strongly influenced chapter one. Art Rice shared his perspective as lead designer of the 1974 master plan for an SF Bay National Wildlife Refuge. Special thanks to Trish Mulvie, former director of Save the Bay, for several years of inspiring conversations.

This book owes a great deal to Robin Grossinger, Erin Beller, Alison Whipple and the other members of the historical ecology program at the San Francisco Estuary Institute. Robin and his colleagues are my models not only for practical application of historical research to land planning and habitat restoration, but also great practitioners of "public" history, by which I mean placing the knowledge and power of the past in the hands of everyday people.

Several experts read and improved the manuscript. Sally K. Fairfax, professor emeritus in environmental policy at the University of California at Berkeley, read and critiqued chapter five. John Cloud at NOAA introduced me to extraordinary maps of the bay past. Dennis Baldocchi at UC Berkeley shared his ongoing research on the Delta. Robert Sommer at UC Davis shared his wonderful work on mudflat art. Food historian Erica Peters read and critiqued chapter four with her keen editorial eye. Stephen Tobriner, professor emeritus in the Department of Architecture at UC Berkeley, first inspired me to think about the city as a natural space many years ago. More recently he read and corrected several mistakes in chapter two. Of course, any absences or errors in the manuscript are entirely my own.

Friends brightened my life and this book. Matt Klingle read the entire manuscript early on and offered helpful advice throughout the writing and publication process. Rachel St. John saved this project at several points. I cannot thank her enough for her advice about the introduction and conclusion. Jared Farmer shared wisdom, counseled perseverance, and suggested the title. Jay Taylor read and gave thoughtful comments on chapter three. Matt McKenzie provided sources and read portions of the manuscript. Michael Allen and Doug Kerr gave key advice early and late. David Igler and Robin Grossinger critically reviewed the manuscript for the University of California Press, offering several important suggestions. I am also grateful to three people who read the entire manuscript: Nancy Langston, Ted Steinberg and Louis Warren.

Many ideas here were tested in conference presentations. I am grateful for audience and panelist comments at meetings of the American Historical Association, American Society for Environmental History, European Society for Environmental History, Food + History Conference at NC State, Organization of American Historians, Society for the History of Technology, and the Western History Association. Portions of chapter four appeared in the *Pacific Historical Review,* February 2006.

Many people helped me get my research into print. I hope this book can meet the high standard set by my writing group: Rachel Jean-Baptiste, Carol Pal, Shelley Lee, and Lise Sedrez. Sharon Sweeney did the index. Bill Nelson made the maps. Thanks to the National Oceanic and Atmospheric Administration, map collector David Rumsey, and the California Historical Society for reproductions. And I am delighted to reconnect with my childhood friend, Jon Oppenheimer, who allowed use of his sketch in the frontispiece. At the University of California Press in Berkeley, I thank former director Lynn Withey for giving me a chance; Jenny Wapner, former editor, for the contract; Hannah Love, her assistant, for keeping me in the loop; Niels Hooper, my editor, for steady guidance and several more chances; Kim Hogeland, his assistant, for keeping me on track; Emily Park, who meticulously copy-edited the manuscript; and not least, Suzanne Knott, who got the book into print.

This project explores how generations of people tried to make the bay into a home. Working on it made me grateful every day for my own community. My daughters Clara Isabel and Ella Grace were born near the beginning of this project. They called this book my "ten-year," and it must have seemed like a prison term at times. For me, living with them makes these the best years of my life. Many other family members provided love and a leavening of humor. My mother, Patricia Morse, reminded me often of the power of art to reimagine the world. She read early drafts and actively listened to many fledgling ideas. My grandmother, Joyce Pfueller Morse, inspired me with her example of disciplined work and joyful living. I appreciate regular moral and financial support from my uncle DC and Jan Fairbanks. My brother Noah introduced me to key scholarship, shared his experience in ecological restoration, and reminded me these are the good old days. My brother Aaron was always there for me in moments of crisis. My sister Anna showed me how to carry on in the face of my grief and her own. The person who bore the heaviest burdens and endured the highs and lows of this decade-long project is Aránzazu Lascurain. Thank you Aránzazu, for everything.

Two of my heroes died while I was writing this book. My grandfather, David Morse, is my model for a life lived well. My great wish is to follow Opa's honest, fair and generous example. My cousin Bill Morse was the perfect academic and father. He encouraged this book at key moments of doubt, especially in our last visit together, and I hope I can pay forward his many gifts.

This book is dedicated to the memory of those who went ahead: John Edward Booker, Judy Davis Booker, Harry Marvin Strauss, William H. Morse II and David Chisholm Morse; to those who carry on, Joyce Pfueller Morse, Patricia Morse and Aránzazu Lascurain; and to those who will inherit the world we've made, Clara and Ella Booker.

INTRODUCTION Layers of History

To visiting tourists, the iconic experience of the San Francisco Bay Area may be viewing orange bridge towers emerging from swirling fog. For locals, however, it is crossing San Francisco Bay to go to work. Every weekday morning a million people leave their homes around the bay and drive, bike, or ride a train or ferry to work. For many, the destination is the city of San Francisco, where some 765,000 people sleep but nearly a million spend their workdays.[1] San Francisco sits at the tip of a peninsula surrounded by water, so for most commuters, getting to work means crossing the bay on one of eight bridges.

The experience is similar at each bridge. Idling in traffic, drivers may see or smell a patch of remnant marsh or fragrant brown mudflat along the water's edge. Most drivers do not see, or choose to ignore, the sprawling, rusting network of railroad tracks between the highway and the water's edge. Driving through the tollbooths, commuters pass giant steel gantries at the busy seaports of Oakland, Redwood City, Richmond, and San Francisco. On roadways elevated high above the water, drivers fly over container ships and oil tankers bound for inland ports: Martinez, Stockton, Sacramento. Cars speed past three international airports and three naval airfields claimed from the brown bay waters. The bridges descend into industrial districts, where commercial products from gasoline to chewing gum to computer games are made and stored. Finally, many drivers enter the concrete canyons of San Francisco's downtown financial district.

As they commute from home to work, traversing a complex landscape, workers also move backward through the economic cycle. They move from places of consumption to distribution to production. They move through the infrastructure of economic life in this region, past and present. The basis of this built environment is largely hidden from view. In the San Francisco Bay Area the bridges, ports, and airports, the warehouse and industrial districts, the freeways, even the downtown itself, are all built on filled land taken from the water. The tidelands—the lands exposed by low tide and covered by high tide—have a unique role in the region's legal, economic, and social history. Enormously productive of fish and wildlife in their unaltered state, San Francisco Bay's tidelands were also among the most coveted real estate in the American West.

San Francisco Bay is the largest and most important estuary on the Pacific coast of North America. It is also home to some of the oldest and proudest cities in the American West. It is both a beloved urban space and a resilient natural space. Nowhere is this more apparent than in the complex history of the bay's tidal margin. The invisible marshes and mudflats now filled in to make real estate or dredged to enhance shipping make possible our industrial society. As this book shows, San Francisco is embedded in and depends upon a hidden natural world.

But for most of the past two centuries, San Franciscans have not seen their city or its bay in this way. Instead they worked hard to remake the bay into a specific kind of urban landscape and, more recently, to preserve an idealized vision of nature. These decisions had consequences not only for the bay, now 30 percent smaller due to a century of fill, but also for its people. As they dug up the tidal shallows or set aside marshes for birds, Californians also granted the bay's riches to some and denied them to others. The region is defined now by two sets of lines: lines on the land setting apart wildlife preserve and paved urbanity, and lines on maps segregating private from public property.

It was not always so. For millennia Ohlone Indians made salt, foraged, and built epic mounds, or middens, from the millions of shells they discarded. At the turn of the last century oyster pirates fought oyster growers over the right to harvest shellfish from the bay. After many battles over who would use the bay, the state and its laws came to San Francisco. The state sold the region's most important real estate to private owners. The law demanded that only those who owned the tidelands and the shore should have right to use them. Prior to the state and the law, the bay was neither private nor public, but a *commons* belonging to all. Declaring property stripped the poor and the powerless of their access to the bay. This helped define them as workers and renters because the bay no longer provided food and independent livelihood. The bay now "belonged" to somebody else. Few understand how this hybrid landscape was constructed, or that it was constructed at all. This book helps us to understand how this came about, why it is a dilemma, and, perhaps, how this situation might be resolved.

Down by the Bay tells a set of connected stories about San Francisco Bay and the surrounding region. It is a story about how a great city developed on a barren peninsula, reliant from the beginning on making land from the sea, and how the 1906 earthquake revealed San Franciscans' inability to escape the natural world no matter how thickly people covered the surface with their constructions and filled its spaces with ideas. This is a story about how draining the Sacramento-San Joaquin River delta to make some of the world's most fertile farmland turned out to have unexpected consequences because we now value the lost water more than the made land. It is a story about how gold miners in the mountains and farmers in the valleys upstream filled the bay with mud and wiped away many native plants and fish. In their infinite creativity Californians imported oysters from across the continent, which thrived until they too passed as industrial society again remade the bay. It is a story about how the oldest form of mining in California—evaporating salt from San Francisco Bay water—eventually swallowed most of the bay's tidelands. Yet even this disaster was not total. Because making salt made money, the salt ponds were not themselves filled for some other use, as happened to most of the remaining shoreline. As a result, in the late twentieth century the salt ponds would become the basis for one of the most ambitious and costly efforts to restore wetlands in all of American history. Those restored marshes would become the centerpiece of a regional strategy to adapt to climate change and rising sea levels in the twenty-first century. Each of these episodes remade the natural world, but in no case was the change "natural." Each was manmade and reshaped power relations in society. Environmental change was social change. And change benefited some and harmed others.

The history of San Francisco Bay's margin is as much about changing ownership as physical transformation. Property meant access to and control over nature's productivity. The quest to make San Francisco Bay pay was a bid to control particular resources, which have included shellfish, ducks, real estate, farmland, salt, and bird habitat. The bay could provide only so much of each, and often extracting one product meant a decline in another kind of productivity. As a result, those who harvested the bay's riches often did so at the expense of other uses and other users.

·   ·   ·   ·   ·

We are often told that we live now in a "postindustrial" age in which consumption is king. The daily news tells us that the jobs and the factories have moved offshore. But production is more often hidden than replaced. Indeed, the ports, the industrial districts and downtown skyscrapers, and the rail network and highways are still very much in use. Together this infrastructure maintains a powerful regional economy that provides wealth and security for seven million people around San Francisco Bay. San Francisco Bay's harbors and airports are the economic engine of this region. Most people rarely notice this infrastructure and fewer recognize that natural places are part of the productivity that society depends upon.

Down by the Bay illustrates this paradox on San Francisco Bay's shoreline. The bay's tidal wetlands are both incredibly productive and often unrecognizable. Few places in the American West have been more modified. Two maps make this clear. In 1999 the San Francisco Estuary Institute recreated the environments of the bay's edge around the time that Spanish explorers first described the bay and contrasted those to the recent shoreline. In the first map, wetness dominated the Bay Area landscape. Salt marshes, brackish rushes, willow groves, and seeps blanketed a vast area between open water and the steeply rising hills of the surrounding mountains. However, a map of present-day San Francisco Bay shows that almost a third of the bay's surface area is missing. What had been mudflats and marshes alternately washed and exposed by the tides are now military bases, airfields, working harbors, and former industrial districts supporting high-end lofts.

Some remnant marshes are still present, perhaps 10 percent of the more than ninety thousand acres surrounding the bay two centuries ago. The other 90 percent have been modified, but they have not disappeared. A veneer of cement hides the shoreline's past. But fill is a recent phenomenon, and it is superficial. Beneath the concrete, behind the seawall, and beyond the freeway, the tidelands remain. Such filled marshes have a disconcerting tendency to reappear. For instance, during the severe earthquakes of both 1906 and 1989, structures built on filled marshes in Oakland and San Francisco slumped as the seemingly solid land beneath quivered and turned liquid. As they reappeared, the ghost wetlands threw down bridges, broke gas lines and water mains, and cracked open streets. Remnants of the old shoreline still existed beneath the cities and their reappearance disrupted newer social arrangements.

Together, the natural and cultural history of these ghost tidelands continues to influence how people live in these places. The ineradicable nature and persistent culture of the bay's edge starkly reminds us that the past shapes the present. At a time and in a place when people constantly claim to reinvent themselves, the tidal margin provides an inescapable continuity. Whether they realize it or not, human societies in this region have always relied on this rich, liminal ribbon where land meets water.

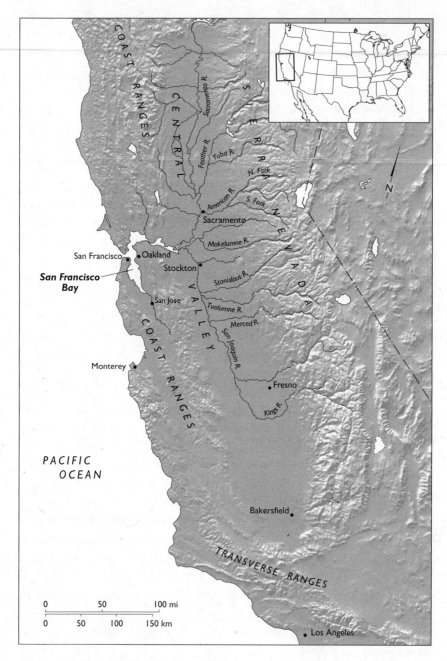

Map 1. San Francisco Bay and its watershed.

Historians, scientists, artists, and poets have previously described and reflected upon San Francisco Bay and its past. These reflections can be reduced to two kinds of stories. In the first story, the bay and its shore are described as an ecological wonderland. The bayshore, they tell us, offered extraordinarily rich feeding grounds, a rich and diverse place for wildlife. In these stories, people often drop away. The dominant species—*Homo sapiens*—usually appears as an unwanted invader and a destroyer of nature. Nature, they seem to say, is beautiful and diverse in inverse relationship to the size and technological sophistication of human society. In the second story, the exciting human history and achievements of San Francisco Bay's cities are emphasized. These are sometimes remarkable and often popular histories of California's native peoples and the succeeding Spanish, Mexican, and American societies. These stories celebrate human accomplishments or expose human failings. But they rarely acknowledge society's dependence on the land itself. For historians in particular, the actual place we live is too often portrayed as a lovely but inert backdrop for human action. Where ecologists tell stories about places without people, historians too often tell stories about people without a place.

When told in this way, these two kinds of stories—ecological and historical—can appear to exclude the other. They suggest that human places are not natural places and that cities cannot be habitat for other creatures. The problem with this view of nature and culture is that it does not fit the realities of nature or culture, past or present. The story left untold is of human habitat, where humanity and nature meet. The trouble with the binary story is that it leaves out the grey areas that connect human beings to the natural world. In this book I discuss this connecting tissue, and I try to describe how human beings live in the world. This book brings together both sets of stories so that we can go beyond seeing the shoreline as some kind of insufficiently pure wilderness or as a blank canvas for human creativity. Seeing the San Francisco Bay region through the area between the tides helps us go beyond those equally myopic tales. For example, the drained peat farmlands of the delta and the walled salt ponds of the south bay result from manipulating a natural habitat to make it more productive for human ends. Reclaimed fields and salt ponds are neither entirely natural nor purely human creations. They are hybrid landscapes in which human beings have manipulated natural habitats in an effort to enhance their productivity, and that also provide substantial ecological benefits.[2]

Seeing hybrid landscapes rather than degraded ones reflects the ecological realities of the twenty-first century. It helps to overcome the persistent view that the only truly worthy habitats are those free of any human influence. John Muir, who helped to found the American environmental movement, lived for decades scarcely a stone's throw from San Francisco Bay, but he and his Sierra Club ignored nearby nature to focus their energies on far-off wilderness. Muir and succeeding generations of environmental activists ignored critically important but partially humanized habitats like the bayshore. They sought purity, and they looked for it far from the city. This attitude is no longer widely shared. In recent decades, many environmentalists, ecologists, and land managers have come to appreciate the critical role played by San Francisco Bay and its remaining wetlands. In fact the valuable wildlife habitat in California is often close to the cities. With 90 percent of California's tidal wetlands long gone, wildlife ecologists look to restore habitat in urban areas. Wildlife ecologists in this region have pioneered a new approach to nature that builds on what is still here. They know that ignoring habitat in or near cities is an attitude we can no longer afford.

There are antecedents from the past to draw on. The subtitle of this book echoes a pioneering example of describing the hybrid urban-natural world. In *Between Pacific Tides*, the biologists Jack Calvin and Edward Ricketts wrote the first guidebook to the Pacific coast's ocean shores. That book included piers and other human constructions as habitat, as places to encounter marine animals. The following year, in 1940, Ricketts and his friend John Steinbeck proposed a second book. This book would do for San Francisco Bay what *Between Pacific Tides* did for the outer coast. Ricketts and Steinbeck intended to introduce visitors, especially high school students, to the shore: to the typical animal communities on rocks, to sand and mudflats, and to pilings and bridges. In proposing to see tidal animals in relation to one another and to their homes, Steinbeck compared human ecology to animal ecology:

"Just as a man's life is surely bound up in the material and social life of his city, with its climate, its water supply, its swamp or altitude, its politics, factories, its food supply and transportation, so is the life of each individual in a tide pool inextricably relative and related to every surrounding environmental factor."[3] Ricketts and Steinbeck never wrote their book on San Francisco Bay: the war came, Steinbeck moved to New York, and Ricketts died at age fifty in 1948. It would be two generations before ecologists once again began to think of the bay as both human and natural. Yet Ricketts and Steinbeck's notes remain, and they remind of us of the power of history. While the past entraps it can also liberate; it can remind us of possibilities we did not know we had.

· · · · ·

Down by the Bay is a book about the ebb and flow of the shoreline itself— its steady disappearance and conversion to factories, farms, and housing, and more recently, the restoration of its drained areas to marsh and open water once again. This is not simply about destruction and loss or decline and recovery. The bay's various landscapes are the products of history, made up of centuries of land use decisions operating in different parts of the region. Therefore, it makes sense to view this past through case studies around San Francisco Bay rather than forcing a strict chronological order. The five chapters in this book move through space as much as time, overlapping in places and leaving gaps in others.

Chapter 1 covers the birth of the bay and its first human societies. This landscape is less than ten thousand years old, a product of sea level rise caused by retreating glaciers. But the surrounding area contains human settlements as old as the bay itself. Ohlone Indians built economies on the shore that adapted to rising sea levels, wet and dry cycles, and shifting animal and plant populations. Native peoples withstood enormous environmental change, but they did not so easily survive the arrival of Europeans.

Chapter 2 describes the rise of urban California. In 1848, the U.S. military occupied Mexican California. As the world rushed in to seek gold, American immigrants built a new city, San Francisco, on this filled bay mud. But this reshaping of nature was followed by catastrophe. Fires and earthquakes revealed the linked fate of natural and urban spaces. In 1906 thousands of people died in one of the nation's worst natural disasters, showing the significant human costs of privatizing and commodifying the bay.

Chapter 3 takes place in the freshwater wetlands of the delta. Beginning in the 1860s, San Francisco's capitalists invested profits from mines, commerce, and real estate to drain the vast peat marshes where the Sacramento and San Joaquin rivers flow into San Francisco Bay. Reclamation created a precarious social and ecological order supported by state and federal subsidies. For Californians, the delta in 1840 had too much water and too little land. Today, the delta has too little water and too much land. Reversing the two made the delta fabulously profitable for some, but it left a dangerous inheritance for all.

Chapter 4 concerns the evolution of food production in San Francisco Bay. During the second half of the nineteenth century, private oyster farms provided inexpensive protein to California's working class. Oyster growers and oyster pirates fought over who would own the bay's riches, but both were helpless against the shifting ecology of the bay. By the 1910s, San Francisco Bay was becoming a place to dump waste and no longer a place to harvest food.

The final chapter describes the rise of environmental activism in San Francisco Bay. In the twentieth century, grandiose plans emerged to replace the bay's marshes and mudflats with industrial facilities and suburbs. But a new political movement also sprang up in opposition to development. After a series of remarkable political decisions that reached from city council meetings to President Nixon's desk, most of San Francisco Bay's margin became the nation's first urban national wildlife refuge. The newly public land, however, wasn't very accessible. Even as habitat began to trump real estate as the top priority for the baylands, social injustice and environmental instability persisted and undermined plans for the bay's edge.

.   .   .   .   .

It might be clear by now that this book grows from my own love of San Francisco Bay. I grew up at a time when the bay's future teetered in the balance between dump site and refuge. I've come to see the bay and its shore as a product of both nature and human action because I lived next to it during the formative years of my life. I am not advocating specific policies in this book. Any plan or prescription addresses conditions that, from a historian's perspective, are simply passing things. Those come and go. Rather, I am advocating for a way of thinking that sees people as essential members of the San Francisco Bay community. Nature and human societies have always been symbiotic. We can see this inescapable linkage most easily in complicated landscapes like San Francisco Bay.

Recently, two factors have forced reevaluation of San Francisco Bay's future. First, ecologists realized that too little habitat currently exists to support the endangered species of the tidal margin. For the bay to continue as a nursery and resting place for millions of fish and birds, habitat will have to be created. Restoring the wetlands became the top environmental priority in the region. Second, tide gauges like the one operating at the Golden Gate since 1854 proved that the seas are rising. In the next century the bay is projected to grow by at least a third, returning to approximately the same extent it had in the 1840s. In the process, rising tides will wash over the most expensive and important infrastructure in the region: airports, water treatment plants, water pumps, seaports, rail yards, and freeways. The salty sea may destroy the brackish marshes so carefully restored over the past decade, making the future of many species uncertain. Together, restoration and rising seas require us to acknowledge human beings as participants—neither victims nor masters—in shaping the future of the region, as we have its past.

I hope that readers of this book will see that physical realities underpin human settlement in the San Francisco Bay estuary. Accretion and erosion, the great opposing forces wrought by water, created and maintain this landscape. Sand and mud carved from the land and moved by the rivers and tides settled at the edge of the water. Over millennia this sand and mud accreted, forming marshes, shorelines, and finally solid ground when not eroded away by floods and currents. We can also use accretion as a metaphor, a way to understand the human history of the changing margin. Sediments accrete like a layer cake, burying the past. Accretion builds, hides, and covers, but it does not destroy.[4] Beneath each new layer is the previous one, concealed but not erased. Human beings are geological agents, too. In this place, they have mined, filled, dammed, and dredged the bay margin. And these actions have also left a residue, a history often invisible beneath layers of concrete. In the low places where we live, the past has been covered up but it has not been destroyed.

Cities are like old houses that have been painted many times. Each new layer of paint covers those below, making the past invisible. Yet the hidden layers persist. Similarly, each layer of history in the San Francisco Bay Area—each transformation of the natural world, each rebuilding of the cities—simply covered over a previous past. Too often building a new future meant ignoring or denying the past. This often led to injustice. Denying land use and occupancy justified stripping Indians of access to the shore and Mexicans of their ownership of land. More recently, it has meant denying the poor access to the bayshore. Disclaiming the past also meant that Californians repeatedly made the same mistakes, building on unstable fill and pushing out to the very deepest water. So while the people of the bay may have thought that they were erasing or burying the past, in fact they were simply accreting new layers onto the old. Those natural processes that made the bay and made it valuable to people were not destroyed by human efforts to engineer nature. Instead, each set of changes put people in danger or created headaches for future generations. That is the legacy of the history between the tides in San Francisco Bay.

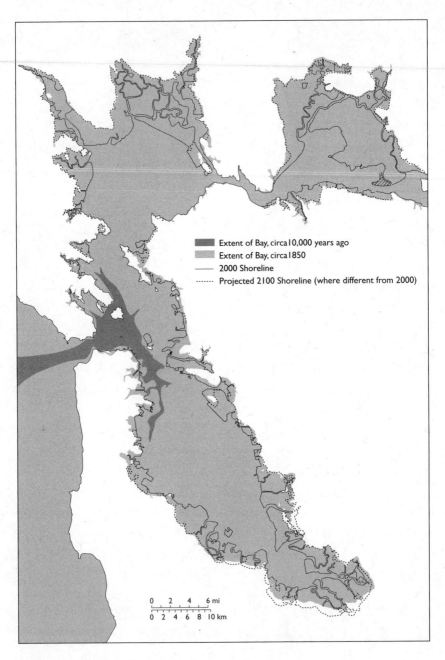

Extent of Bay, circa 10,000 years ago
Extent of Bay, circa 1850
2000 Shoreline
Projected 2100 Shoreline (where different from 2000)

0 2 4 6 mi
0 2 4 6 8 10 km

Map 2. San Francisco Bay, past and present.

ONE Rising Tide

Seen from space, California's coast is a thin white line between the deep blue ocean and the green and brown of a seasonally arid land. In a thousand miles of pounding surf and steep cliffs, only once does the ocean enter deeply into the land. Three great, kidney-shaped bays spread inland and eastward from the ocean, meeting ribbons of water draining snow-capped mountains to the east. The three shallow bodies together form San Francisco Bay, arm of the sea and estuary of the Sacramento and San Joaquin Rivers. From about five miles up—the altitude of a commercial airliner—cities, highways, and farmland come into view. They suggest the widespread presence and influence of human beings on the landscape of the San Francisco Bay Area. Seen from a descending airplane or the hills that ring the bay, the baylands come into focus. At low tide, dark brown mudflats and shallow channels dominate much of the bay surface. A swath of green salt marsh and bulrushes covers the shores of the northern bays, and the ridgetops around the bay are open grassland parks. From this height, a human landscape dominates the bayshore. Cities, suburbs, airports, vast seaport shipping facilities, industrial areas, garbage dumps, salt ponds, and diked farmland extend to the horizon. But from water level, the cities recede and the bay is revealed as an enormous open space largely free of human constructions. If our camera eye drops still lower, beneath the surface of the turbid water, we can see that the foundation of this human landscape is the thick mud of the bay bottom. The cities, the airports, and the farmland all rest on a drowned river valley's silts.[1]

Our descent from the stratosphere to the bay floor reveals a unique natural feature: the only major break in the Pacific coastal wall between Mexico and the Columbia River. This is western North America's most important estuary. Forty percent of the rain and snow that falls on California drains through this estuary into the ocean. Winds blow through the narrow gap in the rampart of the coastal mountains, cooling the interior valleys and producing unique microclimates, fog belts, and windswept hilltops. Water also flows through the gap. Twice each day, the ocean's great tides, heaving up and down in response to the pull of the sun and moon, sweep up into the interior of California and then, with power greater than any river, rush out again. As the tides move through the bays, they mix cold, salty ocean water with warmer, fresh river water. Swirling sediment-laden currents carry this nutrient-rich brew back and forth, upstream and down under the California sunshine, gradually but inexorably toward the sea.[2]

This richness is the product of enormous and ongoing geological change. San Francisco Bay as we know it is a recent and ephemeral phenomenon. The water's edge today laps against a shoreline dozens of feet higher than when human beings first entered the region. At the height of the last ice age, approximately twenty thousand years ago, so much of the earth's water was locked into miles-high glaciers that the ocean beaches lay beyond what are now the Farallon Islands, more than thirty miles from the Golden Gate. About ten thousand years ago the rising sea first pushed through the Golden Gate into the river valleys beyond. For more than five millennia the water swallowed the land and created San Francisco Bay.

San Francisco Bay, then, is a very recent landform. Geologists tell us that the bay's presence is cyclical. During the ice ages, the ocean retreats offshore. And during the interglacial periods—warming periods like the one we are in now—a bay briefly appears. Sea levels have reached present heights only once before, and rarely have they been high enough to come through the Golden Gate at all. The bay we have now is the largest and longest lasting ever recorded. We live at a time of unusually high water, near the top of the tide.[3]

Life on earth ultimately takes its energy from the sun. But sunshine alone does not guarantee life, as any visitor to the desert knows. More than four-fifths of the surface of the earth is open ocean, desert, and ice. These are sunny places. Yet the open oceans, deserts, and polar ice caps are among the most barren habitats on earth. For plants to grow, they must have sufficient moisture as well as light. All celled creatures depend on a handful of key chemicals that are found on the continents. These nutrients are constantly washing away into the sea. The continents are nutritionally poor, and they get poorer all the time. The sea, on the other hand, is too diffuse. The great stocks of minerals eroded from the land are dissipated in the immense volume of seawater covering two-thirds of the planet. Life is most abundant when limiting chemicals—particularly nitrogen and phosphorus—occur in the presence of plentiful sunshine and water.[4] This happens most often on the edges between land and water. And it happens most effectively where rivers carrying their precious cargo of eroded terrestrial nutrients meet the sea. At these estuaries, freshwater and salt water mingle, and rivers drop their loads of rich silt and sand.[5] Thanks to this unique combination of light, nutrients, and topography, as geologist and marsh scholar Nathaniel Shaler observed more than a century ago, "the undersea portion of the beach becomes, of all the water-covered areas, the fittest seat for life."[6] Shaler referred to the tide-washed shoreline. Around the edges of the estuary, shallow-water communities of plants take up the nutrients from the fertile sediments. These are the tidelands, the area of land and water existing between high and low tide.

Life moves with the water. Microscopic plants travel in the water column, blooming in the nutrient-rich, sun-soaked shallows. Diatoms encrusted on flecks of mud and free-floating plankton alike capture the energy of the sun and make it available for creatures small and large. This productivity is concentrated on the edge of the bay. On the margin, salt-tolerant marsh grasses colonize soft mud. The partially submerged grasses break up the tidal currents and shelter myriad creatures. Young salmon come downstream and use the salt marshes and shallows as rearing areas. The young fish grow quickly in these sheltered puberty pools. Crabs and other ocean species move into the brackish bay to mate, giving their young the benefit of the nutrient-rich estuary and its protection. Terrestrial animals feed on the plants and fish in the marshes. Human beings, terrestrial animals ourselves, rely on the estuary's fertility and productivity in many ways, but most directly for the shallow water fisheries. Historically, California's most consistent and most valuable fish species were found in San Francisco Bay.[7]

All of this spectacular richness rests on something quite prosaic. Rivers and streams carry nutrients into San Francisco Bay, and the tides recirculate them. A speck of silt entering the bay from the delta does not continue onward, in stately fashion, to the ocean. The tides, pushing and pulling the bay's water in currents more powerful than any river on earth, carry every cup of river water back and forth from delta to deep bay, up and down in the water column. Between the moment that a drop of muddy water enters the estuary and the instant that it finally leaves the bay for the Pacific Ocean, it may whirl hundreds of miles through the bays and delta. The tides recirculate the water twice daily. This mixing is the key to the bay's fecundity. Thanks to the tides, bay marshlands receive a constant flow of nutrients. The tidal plants never lack, because the bay brings more with every tide.[8]

San Francisco Bay's tidal wetlands, like tidal marshes worldwide, are extraordinarily productive of vegetation. According to scientists, the largest "above-ground standing crop in North America" may belong to bulrushes in the freshwater tidelands of the Sacramento-San Joaquin delta. Growing nine to twelve feet in a year, these rushes annually produce over half a pound of plant matter per square foot, a density nearly unparalleled in nature. Because of the rivers and tides, this amazing richness is not trapped in place. Tiny pieces of plant stems break off and are circulated by the tides. The delta's freshwater tidelands, together with the salt marshes fringing the bays, annually contribute 2.2 billion pounds of fixed carbon to the San Francisco Bay estuary. Carbon compounds are the building blocks of all life on earth. Dissolved in water or mixed in the atmosphere as carbon dioxide gas, available carbon measures how much plant growth can occur. It is a measure of productivity.[9]

Only modern agriculture, assisted by fertilizers and machinery, can match the output of salt marshes. Tidal wetlands exist at the bottom of rivers and top of the ocean, where they build up from fertile soil washed off the land by rainfall. They are sustained by the constant push and pull of the tide, which brings in nutrients and animals and carries away waste. Acre for acre, tidal wetlands convert more sunlight, air, and water to plant matter and animal flesh than any grassland or tropical rain forest. Salt marshes are nature's furnaces, stoking a rich food web that sustains biological communities all over the world.

Despite all this movement, the communities of the tidal margin are relatively stable compared to those of central California's upland habitats. Climate cycles made the valleys and hills sometimes very fecund, but these areas were also prone to extended drought. The bayshore, on the other hand, could be depended upon for food resources during all seasons and in all years. The marshes and shellfish beds did not dry up, burn down, or wash away; they were rare reliable food sources in a feast-or-famine landscape. As a result, these were the places where California's native peoples congregated.

A CROWDED AND CULTIVATED LAND

In 1793, His Britannic Majesty's Captain George Vancouver crept into San Francisco Bay in command of a small flotilla of vessels. Entering the territory of a traditional enemy without permission, Vancouver was relieved to discover that the Spanish fort commanding the imposing south shore of the bay entrance, the Presidio de San Francisco, was defended by only a small band of troops manning a handful of decrepit cannons. After a tense exchange of formal greetings with the Presidio's proud but outgunned commander, Vancouver went ashore with his ship's surgeon, naturalist Archibald Menzies. Menzies was eager to compare the plants and animals of this unknown coast to his collections from elsewhere in the north Pacific, but he contented himself with exploring the long lagoon behind the sandy beach near the Presidio. Vancouver, meanwhile, began a busy round of social activities and surreptitious spying. He dined with the officers of the Presidio, ogled their wives and daughters, and visited the nearby Mission San Francisco. Vancouver and his lieutenants borrowed horses from their hosts to visit Mission Santa Clara at the south end of the bay. The party picnicked in a grove of oaks that reminded Vancouver of an English park. Surveying the brown autumn hills and plains, dotted with majestic oaks and occasional streams, the Englishman saw a landscape that recalled familiar European places, and that seemed equally imbued with promise. But, Vancouver judged, the Spanish were neglecting this potential. After a quarter century of Spanish religious instruction and economic guidance, the Indians, the laborers of the region, "still remained in the most abject state of uncivilization." Only the introduction of "foreign commercial intercourse" could "stimulate the Indians to industry," asserted Vancouver.[10]

Neither Vancouver nor his lieutenants recognized that human hands had already shaped the shores of San Francisco Bay. Archibald Menzies was a professional naturalist and a keen observer of Pacific coastal habitats whose name graces many of the region's plant species, including the most common conifer, the Douglas fir, *Pseudotsuga menziesii.* Yet Menzies had little to say about the salt marshes and shoreline plants of San Francisco Bay. Partly this was due to his unfortunate timing. November is among the least rewarding times to see San Francisco Bay's rich diversity of flowering plants. And the salt marshes, in any case, are not laden with bright flowers. Their beauty is found more in shades of green, grey, and brown: the sort of beauty revealed by winter, a beauty of the bone. Menzies's eye wandered past the salt marsh and up toward the brown hills, which he so badly wanted to see in bloom.[11] Like other nineteenth-century European visitors to San Francisco Bay, Vancouver and Menzies hardly noticed the marshes lining its shore. These men saw the bay as a world apart from the land, and it was the land that interested them for its potential agricultural bounty.

When we read Menzies's, Vancouver's, and other Europeans' descriptions of San Francisco Bay, we can be fooled, as they were, into thinking that neither Ohlones nor the Spanish and Mexicans who lived among them manipulated their natural surroundings. It would be a grave mistake to repeat this error. The Indians and Spanish did change the landscape, just not in the ways that English visitors expected. In recent years, a group of historical ecologists has shown that San Francisco Bay's tidal margin contained a remarkable diversity of habitats ranging across a spectrum from salty and marine to freshwater and terrestrial. Many of these habitats were made or maintained by human beings. The bunchgrass prairies and parklike oak savannahs, for instance, that so captivated Vancouver's men on their ride to Mission Santa Clara, would have been overgrown by brush without frequent fires set by Indians. Ohlones maintained these grassy plains with their widely spaced majestic oaks.[12] Native peoples surely also modified tidal and aquatic habitats. Like other coastal peoples of the Pacific, Ohlones used the shoreline intensively. They harvested fish, shellfish, and other food resources from the marshes and bay waters. They built fish traps and shot and netted waterfowl. Historians and ecologists have also speculated that native peoples enhanced naturally occurring salt evaporation ponds to improve their harvests of the precious mineral, which they traded with inland peoples.[13] Ohlone oral tradition recalls some of these practices and their purposes in a social world whose heart was the water's edge.[14]

A LANDSCAPE OF SHELLMOUNDS

California's first humans arrived during the final millennia of the last ice age. They probably came by water. The oldest archaeological sites are from islands off the central California coast and from inland sites not far from the coast.[15] It is very likely that people lived in the river valleys before San Francisco Bay covered them. Their campsites, their villages, and their burials are now themselves buried by thousands of years of tides and silt. What is certain is that the bayshore has been home to thousands of people for thousands of years. As late as the twentieth century, hundreds of mounds dotted the bay's edge.

Much of what modern scholars know about San Francisco Bay's native peoples derives from the waste they left behind. Native peoples built hundreds of mounds around San Francisco Bay from the shells of mollusks they collected from the bayshore. These mounds, which ranged in size from a few yards to dozens of yards in diameter, were more than just middens, or kitchen garbage. Most of the few large mounds excavated contained human remains buried in ritual fashion, and they clearly served multiple purposes for the peoples who built them over long centuries. Archaeologists excavating the shellmounds have constructed a cultural history of human use of the bayshore for at least three millennia and thousands of years longer farther inland. As Joe Eaton notes, "There are places in California with the time-depth of Troy or Jericho." Scholars can only speculate on how such intensive harvest may have influenced favored shellfish species, but it is clear that Indian people were huge consumers of marsh and mudflat animals.[16]

The Ohlone economy was local, personal, knowledgeable, and communal. It was part of a flexible economy adapted to unpredictable cycles of rain and drought. These were people who knew intimately the productive places and seasons of the baylands.[17] Native peoples harvested so many shellfish that they built hundreds of huge mounds around the bay. In 1906, University of California scholar N. C. Nelson found that, despite decades of destruction by farmers and road builders, several hundred mounds still remained.[18] The shellmounds held deep cultural meaning for Ohlone people. Some mounds held hundreds of burials, with bodies carefully oriented and accompanied by special objects. It is one of the great tragedies of California history that so much of the meaning of these spaces has been lost. Yet even stripped of their context the shellmounds are testimony to the tremendous productivity of the tidelands and their central place in the indigenous economy. Far from subsisting solely on the acorn, deer, and salmon that anthropologists once assumed were the basis of all California native economies, Ohlones used resources from every part of their landscape, from peaks to bay. At the center of their lives lay the bay's edge. As Europeans colonized California, they destroyed native economies by limiting Indian access to the most important resources, which lay along the bayshore.

War and epidemic disease broke the back of independent Ohlone communities in the decades after the Spanish arrived in the bay region. Shattered by sickness and warfare, and perhaps attracted by the material wealth and spiritual power of the Spanish god, Indian villages surrounding the bay broke up and their members joined the Franciscan missions.[19] All over California, missions absorbed Indian communities, but nowhere more so than in the San Francisco Bay region. Between 1776 and 1820 Spanish missionaries constructed five missions to serve the dense native population around San Francisco Bay. By 1821, missionaries had successfully removed native peoples from their villages and family groups along the entire coast from San Diego to San Francisco. These people were reconfigured as members of mission communities, where their identity was based on labor. Indian workers made a wide range of products for local use and sale, from soap to wine to pottery; they managed mission gardens, planted and harvested mission fields of wheat, and oversaw mission livestock herds that totaled nearly four hundred thousand cattle, sixty thousand horses, and over three hundred thousand pigs, sheep, and goats. This new wealth came at a tremendous cost. California's indigenous population had once been among the highest in North America. During the fifty years between the founding of missions in Alta California and the end of Spanish rule in 1821, the missions buried tens of thousands of acolytes. The province's native population fell by 75 percent, from about seventy-two thousand to eighteen thousand.[20]

Mission life was brutal, and where possible, native people rebelled. Spanish military power, concentrated along the bay shoreline and directed against tightly controlled, linguistically divided Indian populations, meant that outright armed resistance was never successful in San Francisco Bay missions.[21] Native peoples more commonly ran away, returning to family groups. Yet ethnic divisions between native groups at the missions made even escape difficult, as a visitor observed at Mission San Jose in 1806: "Every now and then attempts at escape are made. On such occasions, no sooner is any one missed than search is made after him; and as it is always known to what tribe the fugitive belongs, and on account of the enmity which subsists among the different tribes, he can never take refuge in any other (a circumstance which perhaps he scarcely thought of beforehand), it is scarcely possible for him to evade the searches of those who are sent in pursuit of him."[22]

After the 1790s, as independent Indian communities disappeared from the area immediately surrounding the bay, runaways fled farther east into the marshes and grasslands of the San Joaquin valley. Here mission runaways joined other tribes, such as the Yokuts, or created new communities based on raiding and rustling mission stock. Spanish and later Mexican military expeditions crushed these runaway communities when they could find them.[23] In 1828, hundreds of mission runaways founded a fortified village in the San Joaquin valley, from which they carried out raids against mission herds. A series of Mexican military expeditions against the rebels, who were led by a Mission San Jose acolyte called Estanislao, eventually forced the runaways back into the missions. But runaways and valley Indians so frequently raided mission herds that mission livestock numbers actually declined during the nineteenth century despite the great expansion of ranches into Indian lands.[24] California's native peoples, like those of other North American borderlands, responded and adapted as best they could to the triple whammy of European invasion, epidemic disease, and environmental transformation. This was a new world not just for Europeans, but for Indians as well.[25]

As colonial military expeditions aided missions to shatter and then remake Ohlone society, European animals also changed the land. In 1828 a French merchant visiting Santa Clara mission estimated that Santa Clara and San Jose missions grazed twelve thousand cattle and fifteen thousand sheep in the south bay hills.[26] These herds had a profound and lasting effect on the landscape, from ridgetop to bayshore. Spanish livestock trampled or consumed bulbs, seeds, and fields of greens managed by native villagers, helping to destroy Indian economies and making them dependent on missions for food.[27] Too many livestock also changed the land itself. The enormous herds sheared off California's perennial

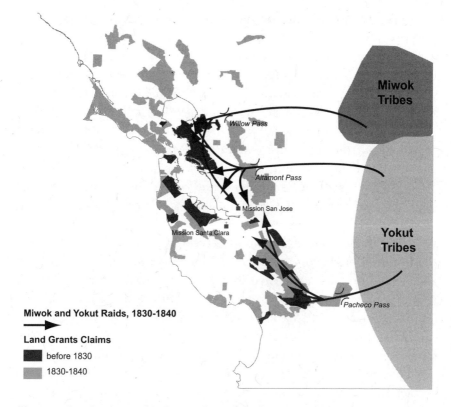

Miwok
Tribes

Willow Pass

Altamont Pass

Mission San Jose

Mission Santa Clara

Yokut
Tribes

Pacheco Pass

Miwok and Yokut Raids, 1830-1840
→

Land Grants Claims
■ before 1830
■ 1830-1840

Figure 1. Land grants and Indian raids. Michael De Groot and Matthew Booker, Spatial History Project, 2009, www.stanford.edu/group/spatialhistory/.

bunchgrasses and pulled them up by the roots. Slow-growing perennial grasses rather than grazing-resistant annuals, bunchgrasses were unable to recover. Winter rains washed the naked soil off in great sheets. Erosion was most concentrated in those areas where cattle were thickest and had been present longest, particularly on the mission lands of the south and east bay. On the extensive marshy plain near the mouths of Coyote Creek and Guadalupe River—not far from what is now downtown San Jose—swollen streams annually piled up fresh deposits of mud. Years later, a cowboy on the Alviso rancho described the continuing mudflows. Harry Wade explained that "high waters" had made "deposits of sand" so extensive that the bayshore road could no longer be traced and had to be abandoned.[28] Storms dumped sheets of mud as much as eighteen inches thick that wiped out roads and filled in the bay.

Disaster planted the seeds that later yielded the fruits of survival. By joining the missions, San Francisco Bay's Indian peoples passed into a familiar category, one with legitimacy in the Spanish and later Mexican community. By 1848 Ohlones were sufficiently acculturated—dressing, speaking, and eating like the mestizos around them—that to American eyes, at least, they often merged into the "Mexican" category. This may have saved their lives. In general, Americans arriving during the gold rush did not practice mass murder on the former Mission Indians as they did the less-acculturated native peoples of northern and eastern California. The bayshore Indians survived by becoming Mexican. They mixed with the Spanish and mixed-descent Mexican population.[29]

In practice, "becoming Mexican" meant fitting into the Mexican economy. Indians' labor gave them a place in the strange hybrid of American California and therefore a kind of future. In 1847, California's military governor, Richard Barnes Mason, and his secretary of state, Henry Wager Halleck, created a code regulating Indian behavior.[30] The document paralleled the Black Codes that ruled the actions of blacks in the American South. Historian Albert Hurtado argues that the code, which restricted Indian movement, did not make Indians into slaves. But in other ways, the parallel with the Black Codes is striking. Indians' only protection came from their status as laborers. In February 1847 the naval commander John B. Montgomery proclaimed that Indians in the district of San Francisco should not be held as slaves. Every Indian would instead have a contract—but one that could be revoked only if the Indian could prove abuse. Indians without contracts were liable to forced labor in public works.[31] The result of the code was that Bay Area Indians were again denied the chance to choose their own places of residence and economic activity. Indians who been forcibly removed from their lands by the missions, then cheated in the Mexican dispensation of the mission lands, now found themselves barred from any return to the bayshore. Yet some Indians did manage to return, and the story of one man and his land brings that relation into sharper focus.

When Mexican Californians closed California's Franciscan missions in the 1830s, they thought they would make Indians into Mexican citizens by granting them individual farms. This Enlightenment ideal of citizenship had particular resonance for Spaniards, who had long struggled to break down and incorporate Indian peoples throughout the Americas. Spanish administrators in New Spain and their Mexican successors alike obsessed about their failure to fundamentally change communal Indian villages. Whether granting land to California's Indians might have actually made them "citizens" of Mexican California is unknowable because so few Indians received any land.[32] Of five missions around San Francisco Bay, with several thousand Indian inhabitants, historians have positively identified only one Indian who received a land grant.

Iñigo (or Yñigo) Lope was born around 1800 in an Ohlone village near the southwestern shore of San Francisco Bay. Together with the remnants of his family group, Lope abandoned his village and moved into nearby Mission Santa Clara, where he was baptized and given the Spanish name "Iñigo," the name he would use publicly for the rest of his life. As a mature man, Iñigo worked as a scout for the Spanish and Mexican military. He guided expeditions to recapture runaways from the missions and to pursue Indian stock thieves, who took refuge in the tule swamps and grasslands east of the bay. In the 1830s, Iñigo appealed for and was granted a parcel of land formerly part of Mission Santa Clara stretching inland from the bayshore near present-day Sunnyvale, California. Scholars Randall Milliken and Lawrence Shoup speculate that Iñigo's unique success in receiving mission land derived from a combination of powerful patrons and his service as a Mexican soldier. Perhaps it did not hurt that Iñigo asked for land that, from the Mexican perspective, was the least valuable property in the region. Iñigo's grant, which became known as Posolmi, was a rough square two miles on each side. Posolmi included a few hundred acres of seasonally flooded meadows, at least one artesian spring, and large expanses of marshlands bordering on San Francisco Bay. Shoup and Milliken deduce from archaeological and documentary evidence that Iñigo sought this particular land for good reason. Shellmounds on the property contained the bones of Iñigo's own ancestors. Iñigo's home village most likely sat on this very land before his family moved into the Santa Clara mission and the village rotted away.[33]

The fate of Iñigo, his family, and their property is poignant. Disease swept away his wife and children. After his death Iñigo's powerful patrons divided his land and sold it. Farmers plowed over the site of his shellmound, exposing the graves of his ancestors and many of their possessions. Both bones and tools became souvenirs for the curious. A newspaper story in the 1920s mentioned that a skull from the shellmound had been put on public display. Destroying the shellmound scattered Iñigo's own history and the history of his people. Little record remained of their millennia-long occupation of this site. Similarly, the fate of the land since Iñigo's death has made its past invisible. Settlers cut the willow groves that once graced the property. In their thirst for irrigation water farmers drained the aquifer that fed Posolmi's springs. Without the springs, wetlands that had attracted clouds of waterfowl dried up.

The fate of Mexican Californians and their productive landscapes is almost as forgotten as that of Iñigo and his people. Spanish and Mexicans remade the Bay Area as a more fertile version of Castile with cheap Indian labor. Their economy centered on grazing and small-scale irrigated agriculture, where Indians had relied on a variety of seasonal resources. The Americans who replaced Mexicans as the owners of the bayshore would bring with them a very different idea of productivity: one that valued the intersection of land and water as a key element in an economy based on exchange.

Americans took California as the prize of a war fought largely on far distant battlefields. Around San Francisco Bay, the Mexican-American War was a brief affair. In early January 1847 Americans and Mexicans fought briefly in the area around Mission Santa Clara in the south bay. The "Battle of the Mustard Stalks" was the only sizeable engagement fought in northern California, and it ended Mexican rule in the northern part of the province.[34] Ownership of the lands around San Francisco Bay was never again in doubt. American military commanders now assumed the role of an occupying army and provisional government. U.S. law applied only to American territories, while Mexican California was an occupied land. U.S. military governors thus found themselves enforcing Mexican laws, including those regulating the sale of public lands.[35]

By 1847, Spanish and Mexican governments had long since granted most land located within striking distance of navigable waterways like the bays, ocean, and rivers. Americans who swarmed into California at the news of the war, and in far greater numbers following the discovery of gold in the foothills of the Sierra Nevada, soon discovered that American governance did not mean access to free land. This was a surprise. After the Louisiana Purchase of 1806 and subsequent purchases of lands from Indian tribes and European nations, Congress had swiftly placed the new lands in the hands of the General Land Office for sale to settlers. Now, in 1847, Americans in California expected to purchase land. At the least, given that no surveys had yet been done, Americans hoped to be able to hold land for later purchase by "preemption," or homesteading. Instead, land-hungry Americans discovered a mess. California did not become a state until 1850. In the meantime, its land surface was the property of the federal government, which acted slowly in organizing a territorial government. Absent state or federal land surveyors, land could not be legally mapped, divided, or sold. More importantly, the 1848 peace treaty signed by Mexico and the United States—a treaty whose negotiations had dragged on for more than a year after fighting had ceased in Mexico, and nearly two years after the end of hostilities in northern California—guaranteed that Mexican law would be respected regarding landownership. American negotiators promised that Mexican landowners would keep their land.[36]

California was the most remote province in both the Spanish New World empire and later the Mexican Republic. Its remoteness gave it some distinctiveness, but the basic pattern of landownership and use was similar to other regions of northern Mexico. Control of labor, not landownership, was the overriding concern. Franciscan missionaries, supported by Spanish soldiers, coerced Indian peoples into providing that labor. Mission Indians worked fields and herds in a pastoral and agricultural economy intended largely for local consumption. After the Mexican government passed the Secularization Act of 1833, mission lands in California were supposed to be granted to individual Indians, but instead a handful of men, often cronies of the Mexican governors, received immense estates.[37] These private properties seemed like a significant departure from the communal practices of the missions. Yet these landed estates relied on the same pastoral economy and Indian labor that had supported the Spanish missions.[38]

On the eve of the American conquest, therefore, most land surrounding San Francisco Bay was held in enormous ranchos, owned by immigrants from Mexico or their descendants and worked by Indians. The ranchos claimed land from the edge of the bay upward. The most valuable lands for a grazing economy were not those lying along the bay, with their access to salt marsh and bay resources, but rather the grasslands of the surrounding uplands. Ranchos were mapped by simple, almost abstract representations called *diseños* that gave only vague descriptions and usually based boundaries on prominent natural features ("the edge of the bay"; "the top of the valley") or by referring to a neighboring property. Mexican-era land grants closely matched the former mission boundaries they derived from, and the divisions between grants were designated by creeks, the edge of the bay, or occasionally straight lines corresponding not to a survey but rather from point to point.[39] Mexican law required the grantee to live on the land and prohibited land transfer through donation, sale, or use of land as collateral for a loan. This republican notion of land was intended to attract and keep settlers in California, not to make them wealthy through speculation.[40] But these restrictions and the vagueness of Mexican-era property boundaries were not problematic in a society whose notion of property was based on using rather than selling land. Ownership for Mexican Californians rested more on occupation and use of land than on deeds or legal description.[41]

The 1848 treaty meant that Mexican rancheros could keep their land, since their title was legal. But there was a complication. Mexican-era land grants were vaguely defined, with boundaries marked by trees, mountains, or bodies of water. This imprecision presented legitimate Mexican land grantees with the opportunity to fraudulently expand their holdings. Even more serious, entirely false grants might be fabricated. In reaction, Congress created a land commission to determine legal ownership of the Spanish and Mexican land grants. But the commission created as many problems as it solved. It proved very difficult for grantees to prove their title. U.S. land commissioners forced Mexican landholders into court to prove the legality of their titles. Legal fees piled up. In the long run, most grantees won their cases, only to lose their land to the lawyers who represented them. More immediately, the litigation over land titles threatened to halt sales of any land in California. This encouraged squatting. It also led to the enormous expansion of the only clearly American-owned land in all of California, tiny Yerba Buena on San Francisco Bay.

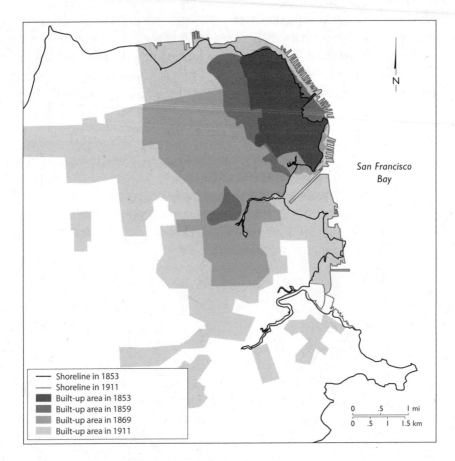

San Francisco
Bay

N

— Shoreline in 1853
— Shoreline in 1911
■ Built-up area in 1853
■ Built-up area in 1859
■ Built-up area in 1869
■ Built-up area in 1911

| 0 | .5 | | 1 mi |
| 0 | .5 | 1 | 1.5 km |

Map 3. Bay fill and growth of San Francisco, 1853–1911.

TWO

Ghost Tidelands

A traveler walking south of San Francisco's Market Street on any summer or fall day in 1869 would have seen something both very odd to modern eyes and yet typical of that time. Men slowly rowed an open boat along the waterfront, pausing every few yards to record the depth of the water. On the beach, another group of men equipped with chains and poles traced the meanders of the shoreline, their boots squishing through sticky mud, spongy pickleweed, and knee-high cordgrass. Later, the data from the boat and the sketches from the shore were combined into a map. The map depicted the shoreline and bottom of San Francisco Bay, divided into perfect rectangular blocks broken by rights of way for streets. The map showed real estate where there was water and mud. These men worked for the state of California, and they were making property.[1]

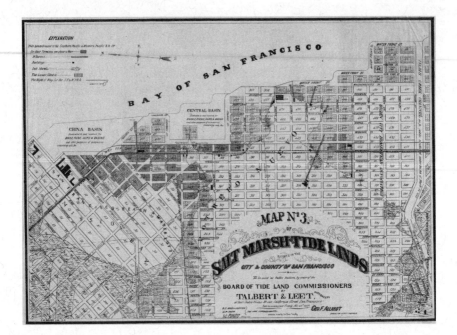

Figure 2. Nature made property. Tide Lands Commission, Map No. 3 of Salt Marsh & Tide Lands, 1869. David Rumsey Map Collection, www.davidrumsey.com.

The story of the surveyors and their map reminds us how the present often hides its past. We think of San Francisco as a city built on hills by the ocean. In fact, San Francisco was first built on muck and mud. Nineteenth-century San Franciscans built their city on the mudflats and salt marshes that once ringed the shoreline of its namesake bay. To build the city, they reshaped the bay's tidelands both materially and legally. They transformed the land physically to make it more productive. But this quest had unintended consequences both for their time and for our own.

The making of San Francisco's waterfront illustrates how Americans struggled with unstable nature and uncertain property as they made a nineteenth-century harbor city. Instability is a shared problem of both property law and natural habitats like tidelands. Uncertainty of legal title to property, like ever-changing landscapes, blocked the development of

American society toward the world of republican freeholders and commercial progress championed by Thomas Jefferson and Henry Clay. While these men found much to disagree about, they shared a fundamental vision of the United States as a nation built on improved land. The nineteenth-century American project was to improve the Western wilderness and to construct a productive society. But standing in the way were American society's own contradictions, including a common-law legal heritage sometimes at odds with progress, and a natural world whose rich and fecund landscapes were not yet adapted for human industry and commerce. Instability, whether in law or nature, was a problem for nineteenth-century Americans. The search for stability gave birth to some of the young nation's most influential and enduring institutions: the General Land Office (which surveyed and sold the public lands); the Department of Agriculture; the U.S. Coast Survey (which charted the nation's coasts for commerce); and the Army Corps of Engineers, which drained, dammed, diked, and dredged, improving nature for American commerce.

By 1847 large portions of the twenty-nine United States were already well on their way to stabilization. The states along the Atlantic coast seemed "built up" to many Americans. Land prices were high, and much of the usable farmland was already in production or had begun to lose its fertility due to decades of intensive agriculture. The question that consumed the nation was what to do with the new western territories recently taken from Indian nations, European empires, and the Republic of Mexico. Southerners and northerners alike agreed that these lands were integral to the future of the nation. In 1847 the western territories remained only partly settled and their future was uncertain. Most crucial was the fate of California. This massive Mexican province had just been seized by American soldiers and sailors in a war fabricated by an American president publicly and privately determined to possess the Pacific coast of North America. The Mexican-American War succeeded in making California into American property.

Property is one of those words, like *nature,* whose meaning at first seems straightforward, even obvious, but turns out to be complicated and untidy. Like many complicated and contested things in our time, the meaning of *property* is usually left to lawyers, not historians. Yet property is not a timeless fact but a historical process, one that has significant influence on society and on the nonhuman world that society depends upon and interacts with. Property is neither easily constructed nor simple to wrest from changeable nature. In the modern United States, property in land—what we know as "real estate"—is the source and symbol of wealth, security, and stability. It is also the preeminent tool that Americans wield to organize and modify the world around them.[2]

Private is as complicated a word as *property,* and the joining of the two deserves discussion. Raymond Williams has traced the development of the English word *private* to the Latin verb *privare,* to bereave, a term later applied to members of separatist religious orders. This meaning is still echoed faintly in the English word *deprive.* By the sixteenth century, *private* had acquired a sense of secrecy, concealment, and privilege, a sense we associate with the word *exclusive.* This sense of privileged privacy was developed specifically in opposition to *public,* so that we speak of private education, private clubs, and private property. As Williams puts it, "Private . . . is a record of the legitimation of a bourgeois view of life; the ultimate generalized privilege . . . of abstraction and seclusion from others (the public), and lack of accountability to them." In the modern period, *private* has become closely associated with individual freedom and personal independence.[3] This etymology is a reminder of the fluidity of words and the things they stand for. *Property* is no exception.

Private property is a paradox in that it is defined in opposition to but dependent upon the larger society. Securing private property requires two things. Individuals must recognize other people's exclusive rights to property, and they must agree not to steal or damage it. Property is inherently public in that the community grants and enforces rights. It is a kind of grant from the public to individuals. Legal scholar Robert Ellickson points out that informal property agreements may be as common and certainly as effective as formal, legal agreements, precisely because whether formal or informal, property is only as private as the community is willing to permit.[4]

Effective ownership of private property also requires a cooperative natural landscape. A dynamic natural world must be made static. This is more difficult in some places than others, and San Francisco's waterfront was one of the more difficult places to make stable and secure. In the nineteenth century, few places in North America were more valued or more modified than San Francisco Bay's tidal margin. The tidelands, one of the most modified yet most productive environments in North America, also have one of the most complicated legal histories on the continent.

San Francisco Bay's edge was valuable because of its location and vulnerable because of its nature: part of the ocean and part of the continent, the mudflats and marshes could be made into water by dredging, or into land by filling. This was a landscape that, with effort, could be made into waterfront real estate or ship channels. In this sense it was a blank slate for Americans to write upon. Yet the tidelands also had a dense cultural history. Tidelands had been common property in English tradition and for more than a century American Englishmen had exercised commons rights to the salt marshes and tide flats of the Atlantic coast of North America. Law and custom marked these places as distinct. Now, in a newly conquered province, the law was not so clear. The tidal margin was as unstable legally as it was unruly physically.[5]

Tidelands were a unique legal space. Mexican law followed Spanish custom (in turn based on Roman practice) in declaring the area between high and low tide to be the sovereign property of the nation as a whole. Theory became practice in California when in 1835 Mexican official Francisco de Haro laid out a new pueblo on Yerba Buena Cove, the future eastern edge of the city of San Francisco. De Haro instructed the surveyor, naturalized Mexican citizen William Richardson, to reserve two hundred varas (yards) inland from the water's edge as the property of the federal government. The town of Yerba Buena began uphill from that line, and no individual could own or occupy the shore. As his surveyor's payment, Richardson took the lot closest to the water, but his property remained far from the water's edge.[6] Mexican insistence on the sovereign status of the shoreline meant that tidelands, unique among the lands near the bay, were not transferred into private hands in the frenzy of land grants. Instead they remained inviolable, intact, the property of the nation and therefore of no single individual.

Mexico was not alone in claiming tidelands by virtue of its sovereign status. In the early years of the American republic, jurists held that the individual states inherited sovereignty from the British crown. The states were literally the people. Thus states rightfully possessed those lands formerly held by the king, most notably the beds of rivers and the tidelands of the ocean shore. American law differed from Mexican law in assigning sovereignty and therefore possession of tidelands to the states, not to the federal government. But seeming clarity vanished in the face of American occupation. What exactly was California's legal status between the de facto end of Mexican rule in 1846 and statehood in 1850? Did Mexican law remain in effect? Should officers of the U.S. government impose federal laws on the conquered province as if it were a federal territory? Or was California in fact a nascent state, with military officials merely guardians of its future lands? The temporary interregnum, the absence of a sovereign, confused the legal status of property. American officials in early California contributed to the legal confusion by acting in arbitrary ways, sometimes claiming authority under Mexican law and sometimes under U.S. law. Legal uncertainty was abetted by greedy and hasty city officials and real estate speculators in San Francisco who took advantage of the absence of state authority to sell as much of the tidelands as possible without regard for its legal status. The result was decades of conflict in the courts and on the waterfront between competing claimants.

The waterfront was also physically unstable. Superficially, the salt marsh and mudflats that made up the shoreline of the future city in 1846 were entirely wiped away within a few short years. First by constructing buildings on long wooden poles pounded into the mud, and later by filling in the bayshore with sand, garbage, and rubble and placing buildings on top, San Franciscans obliterated most evidence of the tidal landscape. Yet the material landscape was not gone; it was merely covered up. The domesticated surface hid an unstable and unreliable mix of water and mud.

CITY ON THE MARGIN

In building their city on tidelands, San Franciscans built on a peculiar part of the earth. At high tide, these lands are covered with water and appear to be part of the ocean. At low tide, they are exposed and thus visibly land. Storm surges, deposition of eroded soils, and long-term sea level changes make defining tidelands even more complicated. They are fuzzy landscapes, hard to pin down. San Francisco Bay in the nineteenth century was wider, deeper, and far less defined than it is today. The edge between land and sea was blurred by vast tide flats that merged into salt marshes and brackish wetlands filled with reeds. Tidal channels wound far up into the land. Water was everywhere. In what is now the city of San Francisco, rocky points bracketed curving bays with sandy beaches, brackish lagoons, and wide swaths of salt marsh leading off into mud-flats and finally deeper water.[7] This was a landscape in which sea graded into land almost imperceptibly. This extensive tidal shoreline contrasted starkly with the land above high tide. On shore, sand dunes marched down from the ocean, miles to the west. Strong winds kept the dunes in ceaseless motion, making the city site a land of shifting sands broken by occasional rocky heights. A worse place for a nineteenth-century city can scarcely be imagined.

But San Francisco offered other advantages, advantages so significant that they would give the tiny settlement a boost over its rivals and make it one of the great port cities of the nineteenth century. For those with vision, the shallow waters and tidal wetlands fronting on Yerba Buena Cove were filled with latent possibility. The tidelands could be made into real estate and that real estate would front on the West's greatest harbor. The problem was simply to fill in the water and create land. Nineteenth-century Americans believed that they not only could but also should remake complicated natural places into productive landscapes. Within a few years those who carried this vision would unrecognizably alter the Mexican town of 1846.

Placed at the junction between navigable rivers and the ocean high-way, San Francisco became the port and hub of a waterborne transportation network that linked mines in the Sierra Nevada, farmers in the central valley, and investors and consumers in Asia, Europe, and Europe's overseas colonies. San Francisco Bay was merely one shore in a Pacific world, a littoral society that stretched from Chile to China, Alaska to Australia.[8] The great city had its humble beginnings as a depot in the trade that sent California cowhides on Boston ships to New England workshops to be made into shoes for southern slaves. In 1835, when a young Harvard dropout named Richard Henry Dana visited the settlement on Yerba Buena Cove, it consisted of little more than a handful of ramshackle huts serving as storehouses.[9] Just one home was visible from the bay, that built by the expatriate English trader William Richardson and his Californio wife on their surveyor's lot. But the youthful Dana recognized the settlement's bright future. In 1841 his prediction was confirmed when the Hudson's Bay Company established its California warehouse at Yerba Buena Cove.

As late as 1844 only fifty people lived in Mexican Yerba Buena.[10] Fueled by the hide trade and whale processing and outfitting business, Yerba Buena became the only settlement on the Pacific coast where Americans outnumbered natives or citizens of other imperial powers. A year after the American seizure in 1847, the sleepy village was turbocharged by the rush to mine gold in the Sierra Nevada. The gold rush, remarked one of San Francisco's early historians, was exactly what the first generation of land speculators had hoped for and expected; it confirmed the merchants' wildest speculative dreams.[11] The key to all of this hoped-for wealth was the great harbor of San Francisco Bay. That harbor required a great deal of "improvement," in the language of the day, in order to support the city's economic dreams.

As every visitor from Captain Vancouver to Richard Henry Dana noticed, San Francisco Bay was magnificently suited to be the center of transportation and therefore of settlement in California. San Francisco Bay, alone among Pacific embayments, offered safe year-round moorage with access to the interior via the Sacramento and San Joaquin Rivers. Less obvious was which site within the bay would come to dominate the region's trade. Geographer Jay Vance argued that Yerba Buena Cove, the closest protected harbor to the open Pacific, was destined to become the warehouse for American California.[12] Vance noted Yerba Buena's geographical advantage, but he ignored the site's many disadvantages. Other fine port sites existed around the bay, and some, like the later cities of Vallejo and Oakland, seem like better choices than the windswept sand dunes at the Golden Gate. Both Vallejo and Oakland had better access to water, pasture, and firewood, and both enjoyed better weather.

Harbors on the continental side of the bay were better situated for the eventual terminus of a transcontinental railroad. Most of all, almost any other site around San Francisco Bay offered more and better buildable land than the pinched confines of Yerba Buena. But Yerba Buena possessed something that no other site had. At the time of the American takeover, of the possible harbor sites within the bay only Yerba Buena was a pueblo, a legal entity capable of granting land. Only at Yerba Buena, then, could American citizens buy and sell building lots. Beyond geography, property in land—real estate—helps explain this site's subsequent growth.

PUEBLO AND PORT

Yerba Buena, the settlement that would later be renamed San Francisco, was the northernmost pueblo or secular settlement in California. Pueblos were ancient Spanish legal entities possessing the legal right to grant land to citizens. A basically medieval construct, the pueblo retained large common areas for residents to graze cattle and to cut wood. The mayor (*alcalde*) and council were empowered to grant small town lots to full-time residents, but residents could not own multiple lots, were required to improve and live on their property, and were forbidden to sell their land; pueblo lots could only be inherited. The pueblo created great legal and social stability, but it restricted urban growth. While rancheros received enormous grants, thousand of acres in size, applicants within the pueblo of Yerba Buena received only small lots, typically either 138 or 275 feet square. These were spaces just large enough to contain a house or shop.[13]

Americans coveted San Francisco Bay as a great harbor in the Pacific for more than a decade before war brought California into the United States. In 1835 President Jackson ordered the head of the American delegation in Mexico to try to buy the port of San Francisco, reportedly for five million dollars. In 1842 Commodore Thomas ap Catesby Jones, believing war had broken out with Mexico, sailed into Monterey harbor, marched marines into town, raised the American flag, and claimed possession of California before realizing his mistake. Mexicans were not amused.[14] President Polk made acquiring San Francisco a major aim of his presidency. At first he, too, sought to purchase Mexico's far-northern provinces, for as much as forty million dollars. But a month after war began in May 1846, Polk told his cabinet that he hoped to seize all of Mexico north of the twenty-sixth parallel, but that "in any event we must obtain Upper California." The American military in the form of a naval squadron arrived in Monterey in July 1846, just in time to annex California for the United States before internal rebellion led to an independent republic.[15]

In July 1846 American troops occupied Yerba Buena Cove, with its cluster of buildings used mostly by smugglers and inhabited by a few dozen deserters and sailors. When early in 1847 Captain Joseph Libbey Folsom proclaimed that the United States would establish its supply headquarters at Yerba Buena, not Monterey, the settlement received its first, critical federal aid. The historian John Hittell explained that the federal presence spurred commerce: "Although Monterey was still the political capital of the territory, and had twice or thrice as many people as San Francisco, the latter was the point where the enterprise and surplus money of the American population collected."[16]

During nearly three years of occupation, U.S. military commanders left Mexican laws substantially in place in California. The major exceptions had to do with harbors, commerce, and the ownership of waterfront property. Commodore John Drake Sloat's initial proclamation from the customs house at Monterey, in addition to declaring California a part of the United States, promised lower revenue charges in the port and an increase in the value of real estate. Sloat's successor posted a detailed list of customs charges and appointed customs inspectors, matters of urgent interest to commerce.

With the exception of customs, Mexican law continued to govern California between military conquest in 1846 and Mexico's cession of California to the United States in 1848. Indeed, until the new California legislature officially adopted English common law in 1850, Mexican laws continued to be the basic standards of the territory.[17] In San Francisco, swollen with newcomers from the United States, this created a peculiar situation in which American civilians were ruled by American military officers acting under Mexican law that no one understood. Special agent T. Butler King reported to the U.S. secretary of state on this anomaly when he visited California early in 1849: "As our own laws, except for the collection of Revenue, the transmission of the mails, and establishment of post offices, had not been extended over that Territory, the Laws of Mexico . . . necessarily remained in force; yet, there was not a single volume containing those laws, as far as I know or believe, in the whole Territory, except, perhaps, in the Governor's office, at Monterey."[18]

King urged Congress to intervene, noting that the lack of consistent legal doctrine was particularly damaging to the development of the territory. King grimly reported that no one in California could be sure who owned what, since "the greatest confusion prevailed respecting titles of property." Because U.S. law was not in force, King wrote, "the sale of the Territory by Mexico to the United States had necessarily cut off or dissolved the laws regulating the granting or procuring of titles to land; and, as our land laws had not been extended over it, the people were compelled to receive such titles as were offered to them, without the means of ascertaining whether they were valid or not."[19]

The series of American military governors who controlled California from 1846 to statehood in 1850 might have directed local officials as to what legal standards to enforce. But the governors in fact changed their minds and applied whichever law seemed appropriate to meet their goals in each situation. As a result, the legal instability that so worried King continued to plague California's most important land titles, those to the tidelands of the growing port of San Francisco.

UNDERWATER LANDS

One particularly arbitrary decision serves as a case study in miniature for the legal transformation of the tidelands in the nineteenth and early twentieth centuries. In March 1847, General Stephen Watts Kearny, military governor of a conquered province of Mexico, granted tidelands belonging to the future state of California to the town of San Francisco.

More than a simple grant, Kearny's action was an assertion of control over land. It was a declaration of authority, and it had immediate and far-reaching material consequences. It was also the opening salvo of a war over control of the tidelands that has never really ended.

The American merchant community in the city attempted to gain this critical space shortly after Americans conquered the town in 1846. In October, three of Yerba Buena's prominent American merchants wrote to then-military governor Robert Stockton. The three merchants announced their intent to form a "Yerba Buena Wharf Company" to build the town's first commercial infrastructure. They requested that Stockton grant "a piece of land, fifty Yards wide, and extending out to the Channel, being at some convenient place, on the Sea Side of Montgomery Street," upon which the company could build its private wharf.[20] Stockton, however, rebuffed the attempt to grant waterfront lands to a private firm.

But in March 1847, powerful forces began to line up behind Yerba Buena. The steamer *Oregon* arrived, carrying a commission of army and navy officers who would select the sites of permanent forts and military warehouses in California. Federal money would flow to these places. They would become real and lasting, and those towns not chosen would wither. Hoping to sway their decision, the Yerba Buena town council changed the town's name to San Francisco, forever identifying their settlement with the famous bay. A contemporary observed: "These officers, after a most careful study of the whole subject, selected Mare Island for the navy yard, and Benicia for the storehouses and arsenals of the army. The Pacific Mail Steamship Company also selected Benicia as their depot. Thus was again revived the old struggle for supremacy of these two points as the site of the future city of the Pacific. Meantime, however, San Francisco had secured the name. About six hundred ships were anchored there without crews, and could not get away, *and there the city was, and had to be*."[21]

Armed with this fact, San Francisco's merchants tried again, sending town *alcalde* Edwin Bryant to convince Stockton's successor, Stephen Kearny, to grant the city its "beach and water lots." The grant would give the cash-strapped community a financial foundation and provide buildable property. Kearny made a point of doing very little as governor. His most important act would now be to grant, without precedent in American or Mexican law, all of the waterfront and tidelands lying in front of Yerba Buena Cove to the town of San Francisco. Kearny approved the sale on March 10, and it was announced on March 16, 1847. A few months later the town council of San Francisco, a Mexican city occupied by American troops, surveyed and sold 219 underwater lots belonging to the people of the future state of California.[22]

Kearny may have known that he lacked the authority to grant away the tidelands. It is possible that Bryant convinced the governor that the development of an American port in the Pacific—necessary for defense, as well as in the public interest—required private investment. Granting the waterfront to the town promised to accomplish several goals shared by Kearny and San Francisco's leading men: attracting immigrants, prompting improvement of the port, and heading off future squatters or litigation over the waterfront. But Kearny's action was at odds with his own and other military governors' policies toward public lands. In his official notice, published in the Monterey paper on March 16, 1847, Kearny claimed that his authority to grant San Francisco its waterfront and beaches came from the president of the United States, with himself as local representative. His grant renounced the United States's right to the tidelands. But Kearny must have known that the president of the United States had no claim to nor right to dispose of public lands. Congress disposed of federal lands. And he might have known that even Congress could not grant away tidelands, which were not federal land at all, but belonged to the future states.

Struggles over ownership of tidelands were central to American urban growth. In both New York City and Boston, filled tidelands formed the heart of the port districts and were among the cities' most valuable real estate. "Water lots," as New Yorkers called the tidal lands along their shore, were the city's most disputed and important public property in the eighteenth century.[23] Assumptions about ownership and even fill techniques in San Francisco were probably learned in these two great eastern port cities. In Boston, from the seventeenth century forward, private and municipal authorities "gained ground" by extending wharves into shallow tidal waters and then filling in between the wharves with garbage, building debris, and other waste.[24] This precise method of filling in the bay to create buildable land was followed in San Francisco in the 1850s. Ownership of tidelands was uncertain, since they possessed certain characteristics of both sea and land. This liminality often led to disputes over ownership of tidal areas, particularly in lands won from nations with their own traditions of landownership. Americans wrestled with the disposition of public lands in new states taken from other nations. The states of Louisiana, Florida, Alabama, and Mississippi had all entered the union in the decades before California and had all witnessed contests over their tidelands.

The questions Kearny faced had recently been addressed by the United States's highest court. In 1845, following years of confusion over land titles in the new southeastern states, the U.S. Supreme Court heard a tidelands case. In *Pollard's Lessee v. Hagan,* the high court ruled that the federal government held tidelands in trust for future states; the federal government's only legal role in the tidelands was the right to safeguard navigation and regulate commerce. The United States, ruled the court, held no jurisdiction over tidelands, whether in existing states or in newly acquired territories. The court affirmed the "equal footing" doctrine: since the original thirteen states inherited their tidelands upon admission to the Union, new states should also own their tidelands.[25] By the clear decision of the Supreme Court, General Kearny's action was illegal under existing U.S. law.

Kearny's decision was also out of step with decisions by California's other military governors. Colonel Richard Mason, who took over from Kearny in May 1847, cited U.S. law in refusing to grant land to individuals. When James Marshall discovered gold at a mill site early in 1848, Marshall and his employer, John Sutter, sent an emissary to Mason. The two men asked Mason to apply Mexican mining law, which permitted discoverers of precious metals to own the land. But Mason refused them the title, saying that U.S. law permitted only Congress to grant titles to land in the territories.[26] Kearny himself had previously shown little respect for Mexican law. As conqueror of New Mexico in 1846, Kearny presided over the creation of a "Kearny Code" in which Mexican laws were modified to conform to U.S. constitutional law and to the law of the model state of Missouri. Kearny rushed to declare New Mexico a territory of the United States, despite the fact that only a treaty with Mexico—which would not occur for more than two years—could transfer territory.[27]

Whatever Kearny's reasons, the sale of the water lots had a lasting impact. The sale led to the first modification of San Francisco Bay on a large scale and the expansion of the actual port and city of San Francisco. Within weeks of the sale in July 1847, men and machines went to work to pound pilings and dump sand and garbage into the mudflats. An 1849 map of San Francisco was outdated within a year because of the speed with which the city authorities surveyed and sold the land lying under Yerba Buena Cove. By 1850, all 444 lots surveyed three years previously had been filled. A second survey in 1850 platted another 328 lots, which sold immediately. These lots were as much as thirty-five feet underwater and already in use as anchoring grounds. Five more public sales took place before the new California legislature stepped in to stop the sales.[28]

There is nothing surprising about the frenzy of land speculation that gripped San Francisco after the U.S. takeover. Speculation, particularly in western lands, was a long-standing American tradition dating from the Atlantic colonies' break from Britain.[29] Foreigners and even some Californios speculated in land in Mexican California too. But those speculations were in farm or grazing land, not in urban real estate. They derived from a simple calculus that increasing population would drive prices of wheat and beef upward, and therefore also the value of productive farm or ranch land. What sets San Francisco's water lots apart from land speculations of the Mexican era was the commodity being valued. The water lots produced no wheat or cattle hides nor any saleable product. They returned nothing to those who might work on them, except perhaps some shellfish readily available anywhere on the bayshore. San Francisco's water lots were totally worthless in and of themselves. What made tidal frontage valuable, as speculators knew full well, was its *potential*. Water lots represented a new kind of productivity in California in which the value of land derived from its future use, not its present use. Speculators bought and sold a future vision in which the mudflats would transform into waterfront real estate in the commercial capital of California.

Historian Bruno Fritzsche argues that *property* in the modern sense of the term—as a freely traded commodity whose value is based not on use but on the expectation of future demand—developed in San Francisco only after the American conquest. Fritzsche notes that during the eleven years that Yerba Buena was a Mexican pueblo, only a dozen real estate transactions occurred. There was no need to buy land when it was available for free. Under Mexican law, any Mexican citizen could apply for a grant of land from a pueblo in which he planned to reside. Up to 1846, only a few dozen citizens applied for building lots in Yerba Buena. The settlement was, after all, a fairly miserable place from the perspective of a grazing economy. The sixty-four applications for lots in Yerba Buena before 1846 were all granted, with the only payment a nominal fee.[30] This lackluster interest in Yerba Buena during the Mexican period contrasts sharply with the frenzy of the following year.

In the year and a half between the U.S. takeover in July 1846 and Mexico's cession of California by treaty in March 1848, San Francisco's city government sold 780 building lots. Many of these were sold and resold repeatedly during that period.[31] Bruno Fritzsche argues that many of these lots sold for little more than the original pueblo fee and therefore were not strictly speculative. Real speculation began with the survey and auction of underwater real estate during the summer of 1847. Between July and September, San Francisco's town government sold more than two hundred of these "beach and water lots" at public auction. These lots, comprising the most valuable waterfront real estate in western North America, became the focus of a raging speculative land market.[32]

San Francisco's path to wealth and power may have been clear to the merchant community in 1847, but it turned out to be slow going. Legal confusion plagued San Francisco's waterfront for decades, making the work of improving the harbor tedious. The confusion sown by Kearny's illegal grant was exacerbated by city officials who, between 1847 and 1850, sold the same water lots several times, sometimes innocently and sometimes, as in the case of Justice of the Peace G. Q. Colton, for personal gain.[33] The legal heritage of Kearny's illegal grant constantly dogged the city's land sales. Because the water lots were under city control, but the state had never released its title, owning tidelands became a risky business encouraging speculation but discouraging long-term investment. Furthermore, as the city's most valuable properties, the tidelands were constantly under attack by San Francisco's many creditors. In 1851, Peter Smith, who was owed $64,000 for caring for the city's indigent sick, won a judgment against the city. Smith's claim was a relatively trifling amount considering the great value of the remaining city properties, and the city was expected to raise the money easily by auctioning a few tideland lots. But when city officials bitterly and publicly stated that lands sold in this manner would have no legal title, only a few speculative buyers attended the auctions. Poor attendance kept bids low, and speculators bought for a song some of the most valuable city tideland properties remaining, including a six-hundred-foot strip along the outer waterfront. Eventually courts ruled that titles to the so-called "Peter Smith" sales were legal, and buyers resold the undervalued lots for huge profits.[34] Most of the city lots auctioned in 1851 had never been intended for sale. They were to be public spaces. The auctioned tidelands included rights of way for future streets and moorage space for vessels tied up at existing wharves.[35]

Contemporaries often remarked that real estate was both rewarding and risky in early San Francisco. William Tecumseh Sherman, later a Civil War general and commander of the U.S. Army, witnessed the city's speculative frenzy in his four-year career as a San Francisco banker. Sherman arrived in April 1853 in the midst of a real estate boom. His journey had been difficult, capped off by not one but two shipwrecks. Sherman's first sight of San Francisco came as he clung to the side of an overturned lumber schooner drifting through the Golden Gate. He recalled the moment in his memoirs: "Satisfied she could not sink, by reason of her cargo, I was not in the least alarmed, but thought two shipwrecks in one day was not a good beginning for a new, peaceful career." The shipwrecks were in fact good preparation for life as a San Francisco banker in the 1850s. "At the time of my arrival, San Francisco was on the top wave of speculation and prosperity," wrote Sherman. Speculators gladly borrowed money at high interest rates, plowing the money back into tidelands real estate in the booming city. As Sherman put it,

"Everybody seemed to be making money fast; the city was being rapidly extended and improved; people paid their three per cent a month interest without fail, and without deeming it excessive."[36] But the high tide of financial good times was regularly interrupted by panic when money flowed uncontrollably out of Sherman's bank. The young banker was left literally gasping for air with stress-related asthma. Real estate was volatile, and no one, least of all newly arrived Sherman, knew where the city's growth would go. The city paid scrip to fund projects to plank the streets and extend the wharves; the scrip became a favorite collateral for bank loans, enabling further speculation. When much of the scrip turned out to be forgeries, nervous depositors demanded cash and many banks failed. Sherman pulled out of San Francisco for good in 1858, after real estate prices plunged by more than 50 percent from 1853.[37] Later in life, Sherman remembered his time in speculation-mad California. Recalling his capture of Atlanta during the Civil War, Sherman wrote, "I can handle a hundred thousand men in battle, and take the City of the Sun, but am afraid to manage a lot in the swamp of San Francisco."[38]

It took nerves of steel to weather the vagaries of waterfront development in San Francisco. But for those who had the requisite patience and capital, the rewards were great. Creating a deepwater port city on the Pacific required improving the characteristics of Yerba Buena Cove as it existed in 1846. The goal was to have access to deep water yet have dry land to build upon. Options included building a beach levee, as was done in the area subsequently known as Leidesdorff Street;[39] suspending structures over the water on wooden pilings, as were many of the warehouses in the 1850s;[40] building on top of beached sailing ships, which became basements;[41] or filling in the marshes and mudflats with sand and earth, the eventual fate of the shallows of Yerba Buena Cove. Fill was the final answer to the need for access to deep water from stable, solid ground. Fill seemed to solve the problems of building a city on pilings over the water.

How much did San Francisco's tidelands matter to the city in 1851? The little settlement's first official survey, drawn in 1849 by William M. Eddy of the U.S. Navy, was dominated by a curving red line that showed the *former* shoreline of the city as it had been in 1847, before filling began.

Beyond the sinuous red line was a blocky, geometric line showing the extent of the surveyed water lots. San Francisco's leaders in 1851 understood that what mattered to those who might want a map of the city—potential investors, merchants, or future residents—was the city's waterfront, and the Red Line Map was a map of the city's future waterfront, its economic engine and most valuable real estate.[42]

By the 1850s San Francisco had become a humanized landscape, but the city remained inescapably tied to the natural world. Its location on the tide flats of San Francisco Bay gave access to the ocean highway and, once filled, provided the city with the large areas of water frontage that commerce demanded. Yet turning tidelands into the infrastructure of a city made San Francisco both profitable and dangerous for its inhabitants. Infectious diseases were a daily threat. San Francisco was a microbial breeding ground where sewers, if they functioned at all, discharged beneath the streets into the former bay edge, now deep within the advancing city. Even walking was perilous in a city built on stilts. San Francisco in 1851 was an uncommonly hazardous place for pedestrians. Numerous persons drowned after falling through the city's unfinished and treacherous plank streets and wharves. An unsuspecting walker might suddenly find the sidewalk giving way, or a sailor weaving drunkenly back to his ship would slip and plummet to his death through a gap in the planking.[43]

Many of those who came to San Francisco in these heady days described the odd town built over the bay margin. Among these was Mrs. D. B. Bates, a new arrival in April 1851. Mrs. Bates was terrified by the prospect of walking through the city's commercial district, with its unfinished plank streets doubling as wharves for ships. Describing the scene of her arrival years later, she recalled that "the interstices between some of these streets were not yet filled. I grow dizzy even now, thinking about it." Her first day in San Francisco included a terrifying walk above water. "In our haste to reach Happy Valley, and avoid, as far as lay in our power, those interminable sand-hills, it was proposed to cross one of those interstices on a hewn timber, which, at least, must have been nearly one hundred feet, and at a height of twelve feet, I should think, from the green slimy mud of the dock." Halfway across the forbidding gangway,

Bates found herself clinging to the plank for dear life. "After much crying on my part, and coaxing and scolding on the part of the gentleman, I succeeded in reaching the terminus of the timber. That was my introduction to the town of San Francisco in 1851."[44] Mrs. Bates's experience was a daily part of living in a city suspended in air above the soggy edge of the sea.

Property itself seemed as tenuous and insecure as sidewalks in early San Francisco. Bates arrived in San Francisco just before the destructive fires of 1851, when the planked streets and sidewalks burned along with most of the rest of San Francisco. Bates noted the destruction and loss of life, but she emphasized a curious thing: merchants seemed more concerned about the security of their immobile, rubble-strewn building lots than their piles of goods lying scattered about the streets. Early in the morning after the fire, she observed, some property owners "had already commenced fencing in their lots, although the smoldering ashes emitted an almost suffocating heat. These hasty proceedings were at that time expedient, to prevent their lots from being jumped; for these were the days of squatter memory, when possession was nine-tenths of the law."[45]

Bates saw that the fire of 1851 threatened not just movable property, but the essence of property itself: the control of useful space. To modern Americans this seems improbable, even bizarre. How can real estate be made insecure? Isn't it by definition permanent, unchangeable, real? In fact, both land and its meaning in nineteenth-century San Francisco changed dramatically between 1851 and the end of the century. The landscape was transformed as grading smoothed the steep hills, and the city grew bayward as soil taken from the hills filled the waters of its neighboring bay. What had once been uncertain, even communal, space—the tidelands fronting Yerba Buena Cove—became speculative real estate and ultimately the heart of the American West's most powerful city.

The paradox of this construction was that while title to the tidelands became more certain, these lands gained legal stability but not physical stability. As Bates had noticed, the filled tidelands sprouted impressive and solid-looking structures. But appearances were deceptive. The new buildings sat on a thin layer of sand and garbage dumped onto the mud and marsh grasses of the bay edge. Over time, buildings settled and listed. Beneath the fill the earth was made of as much water as soil and was prone to liquefaction, a process by which soil particles consolidate and water floats upward.[46]

The fire of May 1851 marked the fourth time in just eighteen months that California's largest city lay in ashes. Yet as the editor of San Francisco's *Daily Alta California* predicted, the city's favored location, with its access to trade and oceanic shipping, would cause the city to rise again.[47] It would also burn again. The rising and the burning were related. Each time the city was rebuilt it would extend its control further over the tidelands, and each time it was destroyed, the tidelands were part of the reason for the destruction.

Wooden San Francisco, resting on pilings driven into the bay, was also vulnerable to voracious burrowing marine animals. Collectively called "shipworms" by nineteenth-century English speakers, these animals were in fact not worms at all but rather several species of mollusks.[48] The shipworms burrowed into pilings and weakened the wharves. In 1856, the *San Francisco Daily Herald* despaired that the wooden waterfront was rapidly being eaten to bits: "The dilapidated condition of the lower part of the city is known to every dweller within the corporation limits. Man-traps everywhere abound, and a general caving in cannot by any means be regarded as an impossibility. The worms have hastened the work of destruction. The piles in every part of the city which formerly was under water, have been completely honey-combed by these indefatigable insects, and so extensive has been the work of destruction, that it is a wonder that a general caving in has not occurred before now."[49] Shipworms menaced the daily workings of the city by consuming its structures nearly imperceptibly, burrowing from within. Their menace was invisible and slow moving, and it required constant maintenance.

Another even more terrifying kind of danger threatened suddenly to obliterate the wooden city. When San Franciscans built streets on top of wooden pilings, they erected supremely combustible structures that functioned like wind tunnels. Flames were fed by oxygen sucked in from below the streets, and the very streets themselves were flammable. The effect was something like a sideways chimney with a combustible flue. This wood and brick city built over water was prone to catastrophe. Fires in 1848, 1849, 1850, and 1851 collectively did more than sixteen million dollars in damage and forced the continual rebuilding of the city. The worst of these was the conflagration that swept the city in May 1851.

On May 4, the sun rose through clouds of black smoke billowing from the city of San Francisco. Smoke from the burning city was so dense that residents could not see the waterfront from five blocks away, yet others claimed to see the reflection from the towering flames in Monterey harbor, nearly one hundred miles to the south. Pushed eastward by a powerful wind, fires swept through tightly packed canvas tents, wooden warehouses, shops, and banks, jumping from one flammable structure to another, heading for the bay. Fire consumed stacks of goods recently unloaded onto the wharves, and sparks showered over the ships anchored offshore. Heat radiated from the elevated wooden sidewalks and plank streets as they burned and collapsed. Hundreds of people, awakened from sleep by the roar of the fire, fled in their nightclothes. Although handicapped by lack of water and equipment, volunteer fire-fighters managed to keep the fire from burning uphill past Dupont Street, but they could not protect the more densely built waterfront and business districts. The fires burned all night. By 5:00 A.M., when a reporter for the city's surviving newspaper described the spreading blaze, the conflagration had already consumed a thousand buildings and killed at least seven persons. "It is sufficient to say that more than three-fourths of the business part of the city is nothing but smoldering cinders," the reporter wrote, listing as casualties the U.S. Custom House, the Wells Fargo building, all of the city's newspapers save his own, and nearly all the banks in the city.[50]

The next day, May 5, 1851, chaos ruled. Over eighteen city blocks had been entirely destroyed, five or six more blocks partially so. Charred and smoking planks poked from heaps of rubble. Unidentifiable bits of twisted and melted iron lay among the ashes. Disconsolate shopkeepers, suddenly homeless laborers, and ruined bankers all sifted through the ruins for some residue of their property. Streets and public squares were nearly blocked by heaps of furniture rescued from burning buildings.

Open spaces were jammed with piles of merchandise saved from the doomed warehouses along the water's edge. The all-important waterfront was badly damaged. Looking eastward from San Francisco's social and financial center at Portsmouth Plaza, one saw thousands of charred stumps marching out into the waters of the bay—all that remained of the Pacific West's great commercial and port city. The very tip of the city's longest wharf perched on its unburned pilings, separated by ash-strewn waters from the devastated city.[51]

The destructive fires helped accelerate the transformation of a city built on stilts to one built on fill. San Francisco moved from being largely a city of wooden planked streets and one- or two-story wooden warehouses and rooming houses suspended on pilings over the bay's edge to one built on filled water lots on apparently more solid foundations. The fire created land for the new city by producing a vast quantity of garbage and rubble to fill the bay.[52] The process of filling in the bay had begun even before the fire, in the areas closest to land, and usually in the rights of way set aside for streets. Rights of way became piers. Buildings covered piers, and then streets were filled up to the level of the buildings resting on piles around them. The *Daily Alta California* commented favorably on the trend in April 1851, mentioning another benefit of the process: "FILLING IN.—Sansome Street, between Jackson and Washington Street, is being filled in with stones and earth. This is a much better plan than piling and planking, as it entirely destroys the disagreeable smell which rises from the flats at low tide."[53]

Fill came from rubble and garbage, but the major source remained the sand that blanketed the peninsula. The shifting sand dunes, impossible to build on and source of the blinding sandstorms that daily scoured the city, turned out to be a nearly inexhaustible material for filling the mudflats and shallows of the bay edge. Getting the sand to water's edge was the hard part. The possibility of profit spurred great effort. The first railroad in California, brought in by ship and reassembled in San Francisco, ran on temporary rails from the retreating sand hills to the expanding waterfront. The *Elephant*, the West's first steam shovel, tore down the sand hills as it loaded carloads of dune sand to fill the mudflats and shallows.[54] Remembering his first view of the city, one writer recalled the shovel in action in 1864: "A little beyond, at the corner of Third Street, is a huge hill of sand covering the present site of Claus Spreckels Building, upon which a steam-paddy is at work loading flat steam cars that run Mission-ward." As the steam shovel excavated new building spaces in the dunes it simultaneously "made ground" from marshes.[55]

California philosopher and historian Josiah Royce noted that fill was a part of daily life in San Francisco throughout the nineteenth century. "Scurrying rail-cars" toted loads of sand to fill in the water lots. Royce thoroughly approved this remaking of the city's shoreline: "The city meanwhile transformed the appearance of its most important parts by rapidly carrying on the work of extending its water-front towards deep water, through the filling in of the old Yerba Buena Cove. This was done by carrying sand over temporary tracks, in cars drawn by small engines. . . . From the 'Happy Valley,' which lay to the south, the railway track, in July 1851, ran along Market and Battery streets, transporting the sand to the rapidly filling water-lots."[56] California's first railroad carried sand, not passengers or freight. It accomplished two tasks at the same time: filling up the unstable tidelands while removing the unstable dunes. Fill seemed a perfect solution to the problem of making land for real estate while avoiding the hazards of the wooden city built on stilts.

But San Franciscans soon discovered that making land from the bay created new problems. As heavy brick and stone buildings pressed down on the newly filled marshes and mudflats, they compressed the soft soils and depressed the level of the streets. Sags in the street could be temporarily remedied by simply adding more sand to the surface, but the buildings also pressed down on the bay mud beneath the city front. This mud squeezed away from the advancing city like toothpaste from a tube, creating a submarine wave of mud that slowly pushed out into the bay. The mud wave filled up the spaces between piers and filled in the deep-water approaches to San Francisco. This aggravated another threat to navigation. Bay currents deposited sediments against the web of wooden pilings that supported the city's wharves. The pilings acted as a kind of net, trapping the sand that shifted constantly with the current along the bay bottom. Ships began to run aground just offshore, beyond the reach of the wharves. Engineers and water lot owners argued about how best to solve the problem, with some advocating a bulkhead, a solid stone jetty that would create a kind of retaining wall that would protect the city, on the one hand, and prevent mud from leaving, on the other. The bulkhead, or seawall, as it came to be known, would fix the unstable edge of the city and preserve the city's natural advantages, its waterfront real estate and its access to the ocean highway. Inside the wall would be dry land, a space for work and rest. Outside would be water, safely banished. Human labor and engineering facilitated the exchange of goods across the filled tidelands. The seawall would maintain the city's control over the shoreline.[57]

HOLDING BACK THE BAY

The new seawall fit easily into the established pattern of scraping San Francisco's sand hills and dumping them into the bay. Transportation of stone and sand was easiest and cheapest if the materials were taken from nearby. When the municipality graded new streets in the sand dunes or flattened the hills of the city, the displaced sand and rock provided abundant fill material. In the early years this displaced matter helped fill in Yerba Buena Cove, San Francisco's downtown core. Later, the seawall too became a major consumer of material from San Francisco and from islands around the bay. As the city expanded, it became more difficult to extract fill material from an already densely built-up city. Telegraph Hill, one of the few sources of stone close to the waterfront, was a favorite quarry site. In 1885 the state labor commissioner noted $30,000 in damage to homes and property from quarrying on Sansome Street between Filbert and Green. "Property owners, in fear of their lives, were driven from their little homes and firesides," he wrote, due to "the blasting and tearing down of said Telegraph Hill." The seawall contractors defended their right to take stone from the hill, citing an 1884 city resolution granting them material excavated during construction of several streets on the hill. William English, the subcontractor for the project, reported that his men had blasted the hill down by between 110 and 150 feet. The dynamite demolished homes and workshops to get at the underlying rock.

California's state labor commissioner condemned the contractors for "taking poor peoples' property, without compensation, driving and carting it down to and dumping it into the Bay of San Francisco." The investigator observed that constructing the seawall benefited the public—indeed, it made an unusable part of the bay into solid land—but this benefit came at the expense of great suffering by a few property owners.[58]

In 1878 San Franciscans completed the first section of the seawall that they fervently but incorrectly hoped would forever settle the tidelands issue. That same year the city's Pioneers Club published the first comprehensive history of their town. In his *A History of the City of San Francisco*, which he subtitled "and Incidentally of the State of California," John Hittell lauded the contributions of individuals and families in transforming a desolate, sandy peninsula into a vibrant and powerful city whose story overshadowed that of the rest of the state. Dedicated to the American merchant pioneers of the town, Hittell's book singled out the community's ongoing domination of its shoreline as the key to its success. The seawall was only the latest in a string of efforts to beat back the tide and convert the tidelands into real property. In Hittell's telling this was a story of triumph, leavened only by his castigation of a speculative impulse—a tendency toward avarice—among the citizens of the city.[59]

But Hittell neglected the real costs of the remaking of the waterfront, both in terms of a simplified landscape of power and wealth and also in terms of the lost ecological complexity that ultimately undergirded all human presence in the region. Most of all, Hittell missed the point that Americans, like the earlier Ohlones and Mexicans, depended on what nature provided. The tidelands directed human settlement in San Francisco as surely as location and legal accessibility made it the destination of Americans in the first place. San Franciscans did not dominate tidelands, as Hittell claimed, but instead displaced them. Americans constantly destroyed real intertidal wetlands, but the new waterline retained the tidelands' role as the edge between land and sea. Though transformed, the waterfront remained a transitional place between the terrestrial and oceanic realms.[60] And in human terms it was still a place of labor, where people worked and in working gained their livelihood.

The tidelands offered a kind of devil's bargain to nineteenth-century San Francisco. In 1864, a perceptive American wrote that his countrymen, having gained control over the forests and valleys of the entire continent, would next seek to exercise their dominion over the "unstable waters" as well. George Perkins Marsh gave as an example Venice, the ancient city on the marshes, forever struggling to stay above the waves. But Marsh's reference to Venice exemplifies the promise and peril that San Francisco Bay's tidelands held for Californians. On the one hand, the bay shallows offered potential real estate and access to deep water that allowed a small and scruffy village to imagine itself as a new Venice of the Pacific Ocean. The tidelands could make San Francisco into a great port city and center of commerce. On the other hand, the tidelands were "unstable waters" indeed. Filling in the bay created new perils for San Francisco.

San Franciscans, like all city dwellers, continually replaced old buildings with new ones. This process of tearing down to build up was particularly dramatic in the nineteenth century, when private developers and city officials alike saw the city's landforms as a blank canvas upon which to paint their city. San Francisco's sand dunes, rocky eminences, and marshy shores resembled the city walls that graffiti artists constantly repaint today. Temporary buildings spotted the few flat areas during the gold rush but were quickly razed by fire or by more ambitious construction. The city extended roads and building blocks through its high places more slowly. Rincon Hill, in the 1860s the fashionable home to bankers and political figures, was partially leveled in the following decades, its rock carted away to fill the bay. By the 1880s the area around the flattened hill had shifted to working-class residences.[61]

By the turn of the twentieth century, San Francisco's waterfront finally appeared legally secure and physically stable. Decades of lawsuits, state and federal legislation, and acrimonious public debate ensued before ownership of the waterfront was finally resolved. The material waterfront had been no less difficult to construct. In 1906, the seawall was already the single most expensive engineering construction in California history, and still a dozen years from completion. Decades of fill had been required to make the former tidelands and shallows the sites of buildings

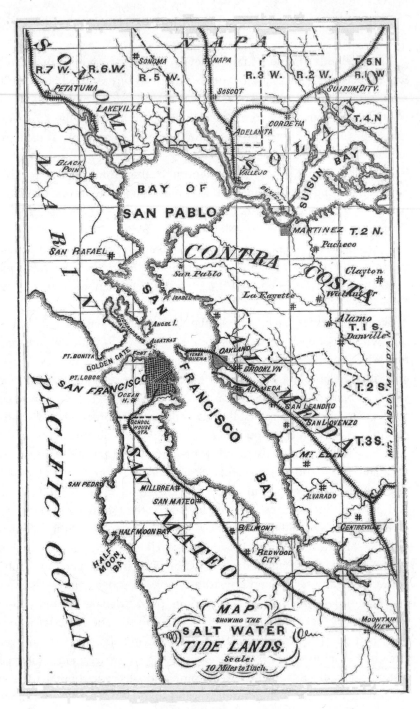

Figure 3.   San Francisco, capital of the tidelands. U.S. Department of
Agriculture, 1873.

and warehouses. Real estate and commerce had triumphed in San Francisco, capital of the tidelands.

The city's great fame and wealth rested on its commercial success as a port and on the power of its financial district. Both rested on the tidelands, now vanished beneath increasingly permanent and magnificent buildings. In 1880 California had nearly a million residents, eight times the population of 1850. More than a quarter of the state's population lived in the four square miles of San Francisco.[62] The city's harbor commission radiated the optimism of the times when it predicted in 1899 that the city's port would soon pass both London and Liverpool in tonnage. "The commercial future of San Francisco cannot be overestimated," the commissioners boasted. "The increase in trade that will surely follow the completion of the Nicaragua Canal, and the greatly enlarged traffic . . . that now seems assured, will in the near future advance this port many points on the list of the great commercial marts of the world's commerce."[63] Maps of San Francisco emphasized the city as the port for the entire region, an open doorway carrying California's bounty to the world. All of this success and optimism rested on almost nine hundred acres of filled tidelands.[64] What had been an impediment to navigation and a legal quagmire for decades was now, at the close of the nineteenth century, the economic engine of the West's great port. The finished nature of the waterfront, which was buried beneath layers of fill, seemingly offered a stable basis for a bright future.

GHOST TIDELANDS

The shaking lasted just two minutes, but the destruction caused by the earthquake in the early morning of April 18, 1906, was just beginning.[65] All along San Francisco's former shoreline, buildings shuddered, swayed, and sank into the suddenly liquid ground. Sewer, water, and gas lines snapped, spewing their contents into the soil and air. Broken gas lines burst into flames in at least two locations, joining dozens of smaller fires caused by overturned lamps and cookstoves, collapsed chimneys, and ruptured furnaces. Within minutes after the shaking had stopped, sixteen fires were reported in to the central fire station. Smoke billowed over the waking city.[66]

Charles Cullen was one of the first to confront the fires. As the captain of the San Francisco Fire Department's Company Number Six, Cullen was on duty at their firehouse at Sixth and Howard Streets. His company guarded the area south of Mission Street, an area of densely packed wooden rooming houses built on marshy and filled ground near the mouth of the former Mission Creek. Captain Cullen later testified about the harrowing next two days for an insurance commission, providing a first-person view of the earthquake and fires of April 18 to 23, 1906.

Like most buildings south of Market Street, the firehouse at Sixth and Howard was a multistory wood-frame building. As the earth shook, the back wall sank more than three feet into the ground and the floor cracked down the middle. The men inside were instantly deprived of the use of their heavy fire engine. "Immediately after the first shake," Cullen recalled, "the doors of our engine house shook open and our horses ran into the streets and escaped. It was with great difficulty that we got our apparatus out of the station." Rushing into the street, Captain Cullen and his six-man engine crew saw that most of the wooden buildings on their street had collapsed. The firefighters responded to the cries of trapped people all around them. The company's first rescues were of five adults and three children from the building next to the fire station. At the end of the block, a three-story hotel had sunk two full stories into the filled marsh. The firemen desperately chopped downward through the exposed roof of the hotel toward screams from deep within the soggy earth. "At this time my crew helped rescue a man and a woman from the Corona House," Cullen recalled, but "approximately forty people were killed by the collapsing of this hotel. The two survivors rescued were pinned on the top floor near a sky-light."[67]

Quake damage was most severe in the filled tidelands and paved-over salt marshes along the former shoreline. Marshes and tidal channels that had been invisible for decades suddenly reappeared. The area devastated in 1906 had experienced subsidence before. Earthquakes shook the city in 1865 and 1868, damaging buildings on the made ground and requiring further fill of sand boils and sinkholes.[68] In 1868, earth movement created a depression near Sixth and Howard Streets dubbed "Pioche's Lake." This reappearance of the former Mission Creek estuary was filled in and built up, only to reopen again in 1906 with terrible loss of life. At least fifty people died near the intersection of Sixth and Howard Streets within two hours of the earthquake.[69] An expert observer later compared the quake's effect on such filled areas to "shaking a bowl filled with jelly."[70]

The earthquake disproportionately affected some San Franciscans and spared others. Destruction was concentrated in the waterfront areas and the tenements built on marshy ground south of Market Street. The wealthy residential districts perched on the rocky heights experienced little damage. At first, the earthquake seemed almost a lark to the better off. Eleanor Watkins, wife of the San Francisco physician James T. Watkins, reported her initial relief that her "Buhl furniture, Louis XIV chairs and cabinets, rarest bric-a-brac" escaped unscathed. Leaving instructions for their servants to sweep and dust, Mrs. Watkins and her husband decided to go downtown to breakfast and see the excitement. They had a thrilling, adventurous trip from their home on the slopes of Russian Hill to the Saint Francis Hotel, where they were forced to serve themselves coffee and rolls, the waiters being "too excited" to offer breakfast.[71]

Disaster underscored the geography of class difference in San Francisco. Wealthy San Franciscans lived on the relatively stable terrain of the hills, and the poor lived on the filled mudflats and marshes south of Market Street. As she sipped her coffee, Mrs. Watkins slowly began to notice suffering: "Union Square was full of poor people, who had fled from the fire south of Market Street, where the poorest people lived. Around them were piled trunks and bundles, parrots and babies. A woman had fainted at the corner and was lying on the grass in the crowd." The coffee helped brace her, Mrs. Watkins wrote, "for I was on the verge of tears over the homeless people in Union Square, little thinking that I should soon be one of them."[72] Eleanor Watkins would flee with the crowds of poor as the fire from south of Market devoured the tony Saint Francis Hotel. Her exclusive neighborhood, barely damaged by the earthquake, would be utterly destroyed by the raging fires.

In the first hours after the earthquake, fires burned out of control in several parts of the city. Eventually a number of fires joined in one huge conflagration spreading southward from the city's center. By the third day after the earthquake, towering flames had not only consumed San Francisco's business and financial core but had gutted most of the residential city. Fires burned a huge, nearly circular path south, then west, then north again, destroying everything between Van Ness Avenue and the waterfront. Ironically, the filled tidelands where the fires began were largely spared. The waterfront, while hit hard by the earthquake, was protected from fire by a combination of favorable winds, abundant seawater for those fire engines able to use it, and wealthy landowners who provided their own firefighting forces.[73]

Past transformation of the tidelands yielded other ironies. Perhaps cushioned by bay mud, the city's docks were largely unaffected by the temblor. As a result, much of San Francisco's transportation infrastructure survived the initial destruction that so crippled firefighting efforts. When the earthquake began at 5:12 A.M. on that Wednesday, the morning rush hour had not yet begun. The ferries that daily brought tens of thousands of passengers from the suburbs of Sausalito, Berkeley, Alameda, and Oakland—mostly professional and "white-collar" employees who worked in the financial and commercial districts—had not yet begun discharging people onto the wharves at the base of Market Street. These ferries instead carried people out of San Francisco, perhaps saving the lives of tens of thousands of people trapped by the fires. The ferries were free to evacuate the city and to bring in National Guard and U.S. Army troops to fight the fires and prevent mayhem. As a result, San Franciscans could leave their burning city. Ferries participated in the largest maritime rescue in American history, an event comparable to the evacuation of British troops at Dunkirk during World War II. Almost thirty thousand people trapped by the fire were rescued by boat from wharves and docks between Lombard Street and Fort Mason. Another 225,000 escaped the burning city on Southern Pacific Company ferries from the lightly damaged ferry terminal at the foot of Market Street and on Southern Pacific trains from the terminal built on filled tidelands at Third and Howard Streets.[74] Between ferries and trains, more than half of the city's population of 410,000 left San Francisco as it burned around them. It was perhaps the single largest evacuation in American history, and it was made both necessary and possible by filling in the tidelands.

The fires of 1851 and the earthquake of 1906 marked the shifting physical and legal contours of San Francisco. In 1851 tidelands had just begun the transition into real estate. By 1906 that process was complete. But making property secure did not make the land stable. In 1851 fire destroyed the emerging waterfront and the flimsy structures along its edge, threatening a fragile landscape of property based on possession, not legal title. Landowners scrambled to defend their uncertain boundaries and ignored the threat of looting or loss of movable property. In 1906 earthquake and fire threatened personal but not real property; buildings fell, furniture burned, and people and animals were killed, but the property beneath the buildings remained legally secure.

In both 1851 and 1906 disaster struck unequally. The distribution of property insured that fire and death were not randomly distributed over the city. The disasters began in the same places, in the part of the city built over and upon the bay. In 1906 the fires following the earthquake burned far inland, but the damage from the earthquake itself was largely restricted to the filled marshes and mudflats along the former shoreline. When engineers later mapped the damage from seismic activity, the curved lines they drew closely followed the former shoreline.[75]

In these devastated areas, buildings rested on former tidelands long since filled in. These filled marshes were only superficially transformed. Made ground was a most unstable mixture of earth and water. A few feet of added garbage, sand, and burned brick rested uneasily on deep layers of loose mud. Disturbance could roil the mix of soil and water, like coffee with milk, making solid unstable. When the earth shook, as it regularly has in San Francisco, made ground literally dissolved, the surface layers settling into the earth and collapsing buildings above. San Francisco in 1851 was largely built *over* the tidelands, not *on* them. In 1906, however, hundreds of people were crushed, suffocated, and buried under rubble by buildings that sank and crumbled in the suddenly liquid soils south of Market Street. The same ground displacement cracked gas lines and

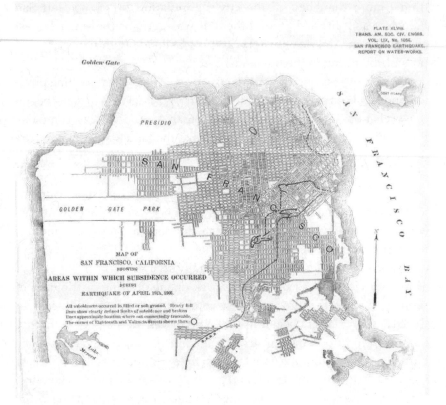

Figure 4. Fill and earthquake damage, 1906. California State Earthquake Investigation Commission, *Map of Portion of San Francisco, Showing 1906 Apparent Earthquake Intensity.*

knocked over furnaces and cooking stoves, sparking the fires that killed hundreds more in the following three days.

Disasters did not discourage San Franciscans from building on the tidelands after 1906 any more than they had after 1851. The shattered rubble of the old city provided solid matter to make yet more new land. During 1906 and 1907 thousands of carloads of burned brick and twisted steel were carted from downtown to fill in the last marshlands on the northern end of the city. The new neighborhoods built on filled shoreline near Fort Mason were rechristened the "Marina District."

This made land too would face a reckoning. In 1989, when the earth shook again in the Loma Prieta earthquake, the filled marshes liquefied, as they had in 1906. Buildings collapsed and burned, people died, and property was destroyed.[76] Ghost landscapes returned to haunt the living.[77] Fires and earthquakes once again followed fill on the bay edge.

The 1906 disaster underscored that abstract legal property—real estate—in San Francisco was more secure than physical property constructed upon the land. Uses of tidelands were always temporary, even fleeting in the case of the gold rush city built over the water lots. The physical city constantly changed. But legal property came to possess extraordinary power, even the power to survive the total destruction of the physical space it described. While buildings rose and fell, lot lines drawn on city plat maps proved more durable. We generally take legal property for granted, just as we take physical reality for granted. The 1906 earthquake challenged both assumptions. The earthquake harshly reminded San Franciscans of the tenuous nature underlying their city. Physical property was destroyed. Legal property in San Francisco's waterfront survived because people maintained it with their belief and force.[78]

Two transformations made San Francisco into a waterfront city. The first was cultural: legal change in property. The second was material: physical fill of tidelands. Together these changes created the foundation for rapid growth and tremendous wealth. But they also led to unexpected consequences: environmental and physical instability were the by-products of efforts to create greater legal stability and to replace a complex watery margin with solid land. Drawing lines between water and land failed to guarantee separation.

Between 1847 and 1906 San Franciscans, in creating their city, had created a paradox. With their success in establishing legal title to the former commons, San Francisco's landowners were able to literally make new land from the sea's edge. They poured sand, garbage, and rubble into the mudflats to create stunningly valuable real estate. They could touch their new land, feel it, and see it, but it was less stable than the abstract boundaries originally laid over water and preserved on paper. Their very achievement in creating land led to the disaster of 1906, when fill failed. But by 1906 San Francisco was a formidable fact. The persistence of marked space—legal property—meant that even when the city was destroyed it could come back in a similar form. The city was rooted in a set of social and economic arrangements that had the paradoxical effect of endangering the city but also insuring that it would rise again. The property was far too valuable to be abandoned and in the wake of each disaster was the possibility of new property from more fill. But with every effort at rebuilding, the property remained physically and environmentally unstable.

Thanks to the continuing transformation of the city's waterfront, those who controlled San Francisco's tidelands became very wealthy in the nineteenth century. They made the city's tidelands work by converting them into solid land. Fill made real estate from the wetlands that had once occupied the same physical space, and that new property produced enormous wealth. This process was at once mundane and yet revolutionary. Making tidelands into real estate changed both the physical and economic character of the land. Mud became solid, and land was valued for its potential rather than for what it actually produced. How this capital was put to transform the city's hinterlands is the topic of the next chapter in the bay's history.

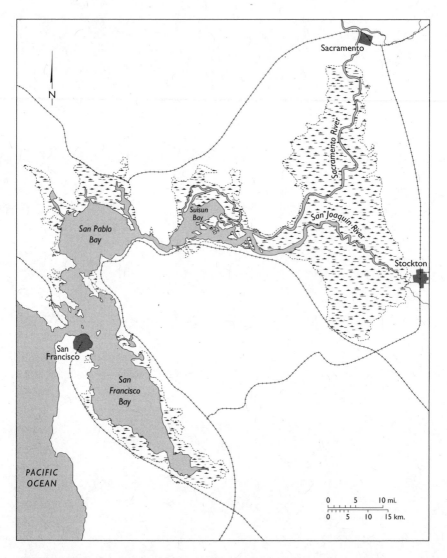

Map 4. Marshes of the San Francisco Bay delta in the nineteenth century.

THREE Reclaiming the Delta

In the late nineteenth century, flush with capital earned in commerce, urban real estate, and the mines, San Francisco's capitalists sought new arenas for investment. Their appraising eyes were drawn to the undeveloped tidal swamplands at the confluence of the Sacramento and San Joaquin Rivers. The Sacramento-San Joaquin delta's vast marshes and floodplains held both natural and legal advantages for market cropping. Delta soils were cheap, rich, and directly accessible to ocean shipping from San Francisco Bay. Ocean tides backed up the sluggish lower reaches of the Sacramento and San Joaquin Rivers, making the delta an extension of the bay. The delta marshes were close to urban and international markets, yet bordered by freshwater. Farmers and land speculators envisioned the delta wetlands as a more productive place, one that grew crops rather than bulrushes.

Making farmland from marsh required vast sums and tremendous effort. "Reclamation," as practitioners termed their work, was a form of gambling open only to high-stakes players. The initial cost of building levees and especially the continuing cost of maintaining them against the inexorable power of water created vast acreages owned by absentee investors. Thousands of Chinese workers helped their white employers create an agricultural landscape that by the early twentieth century was at once economically productive, ecologically impoverished, and socially oppressive. Production came at a great cost. California's practice of granting away huge tracts of state lands and federally subsidized control of the delta's waterways helped legitimate an agricultural landscape and society reminiscent of the plantation south at its apex. Yet this outcome was ever in doubt; the social extremes that arose on the reclaimed marshlands fostered opposition from small farmers and one of the era's most capable social critics, Henry George.

Controlling the freshwater tidelands turned out to be even more difficult than remaking the water lots in San Francisco. The agricultural lands of the delta were repeatedly subjected to disastrous floods after hydraulic gold miners filled the river channels with sand and gravel from the Sierra Nevada. Ironically, the mining debris was as helpful to levee builders as it was harmful to farmers. Without the hard mineral sediments liberated by miners and washed downstream by floods, the flood control levees that protected delta farmland could not have been built. At the heart of the delta story lies this second paradox: California's reclaimed farmlands, the source of such vast wealth, were tremendously costly to create and to maintain. Possessing unique advantages for modification and use, the freshwater tidelands were also uniquely susceptible to natural disasters. They were literally in harm's way.

FRESHWATER TIDELANDS

As both land and water, tidelands mark a blurry boundary between ocean and upland. Nineteenth-century Americans came to see tidelands in less ambiguous ways, as potential real estate or port facilities, but their attempts to pursue these visions ironically made the tidelands even less stable. The tidelands, so biologically fecund, could be made economically productive, but economic productivity came only at the expense of other kinds of productivity and trapped landowners in a cycle of constant maintenance and physical instability. The same inescapable cycle that played out in San Francisco also occurred in the farthest tidal landscapes of the delta.

As the area farthest from the sea still affected by tidal influence in San Francisco Bay, the confluence of the Sacramento and San Joaquin Rivers underwent extreme change during the second half of the nineteenth century. The delta changed in three key ways. First, in a few decades workers transformed an uncultivated marshland into one of the most productive agricultural landscapes on the planet. Second, this rapid physical development gave rise to an agricultural society so industrial, so divorced from the national agrarian myth, and so starkly unequal that by the 1930s an observer referred to delta farms as "factories in the fields." Finally, reclamationists both overcame and exacerbated environmental disasters of several kinds—debris flows, flooding, soil loss, and subsidence. Ultimately, reclamation made a new kind of social and ecological landscape. By area, the greatest transformation of San Francisco Bay's tidal wetlands was diking and draining of marshlands for farmland.[1] The consequences of reclamation reverberated far beyond the San Francisco Bay Area. Between 1870 and 1930 the region was so dramatically reworked that two soil scientists called it "the largest human alteration of the earth's surface" in history.[2] Understanding the historical landscapes of the San Francisco Bay delta demands coming to terms with these extensive ecological and social transformations.

The Sacramento and San Joaquin Rivers spread and shallow as they enter San Francisco Bay, making this confluence a riverine place equally influenced by the sea. Indirectly, the ocean influence extends deep into the land through the push of the tides. The freshwater that falls as snow and rain upon the Sierras comes from clouds of vapor evaporated from the Pacific and carried inland on the winds. This water from the skies is a primary agent in the ongoing formation of the delta. Beginning some millions of years ago, rivers carved deep canyons in the Sierras, carrying rock and sand from the heights into the valley below. Much of the precipitation falling on California eventually made its way toward the rocky dike we know as the Carquinez Strait. There, the Sacramento and San Joaquin Rivers, swollen by numerous tributaries, carved a channel through the coastal mountains. As the rivers flowed into the strait, they were met by unstoppable ocean tides moving up through the Golden Gate and San Francisco Bay. Blocked by the tides, the rivers pooled far upstream. As they slowed, much of the sand and silt chiseled from the mountains settled to the river bottom. These excess sediments created ever more sinuous channels, which in turn further slowed the movement of water. The result was a dizzying maze of winding channels and cut-off river meanders called sloughs, a landscape where water merged seamlessly into land and back again.[3]

All estuarine environments receive energy from both upstream and downstream. Below the tidelands lies the surging ocean. Upriver, the dominant natural force is flooding. Floods are a constant in tidelands: the tidal cycle brings two periods of higher water and two of lower water during each twenty-four-hour day. In addition to daily tides, the delta region also experiences seasonal floods. During winter storms and spring snowmelt, rivers frequently fill the streambeds past their capacity and spill out onto the surrounding lands. The delta is alternately flooded by brackish water from downstream and sediment-laden snowmelt from upstream. These natural forces—moving water, moving earth—contribute unpredictability to the delta, but they also generate great productivity, making the delta an attractive place for animals, including human beings.

Our modern confusion about the identity of the delta—our tendency to give precedence to the power of the rivers over that of the ocean—is hardly new. Visitors from other lands have always struggled to describe the strange plants, animals, and terrain they found in California. Spanish sailors and soldiers, the first Europeans to travel around San Francisco Bay, groped for precedents to describe the enormous "pines" (Douglas fir), "larches" (coast redwood), and fields of "larkspur" (lupines) they saw. They were nearly at a loss for words to characterize the open water and emergent marshes of the Sacramento and San Joaquin Rivers as they merge into the salt marshes of Suisun Bay.[4]

For many years, European visitors disputed whether what we know as the delta was a great river, an extension of the ocean, or a lake so large that it created its own tides. In 1772, the first European to visit the area, Franciscan priest Juan Crespi, thought that the region east of the Carquinez Strait was a single vast river, perhaps extending far into the North American continent, which he called the "Rio de San Francisco." Four years later, a second Franciscan visitor expressed doubt that a river flowed through the dense marshes at all. Father Pedro Font criticized Crespi for his simplemindedness. Font thought that the delta area was no river but rather a "stagnant fresh water gulf or *pielago*," an antiquated Castilian word with Greek roots meaning "sea with islands." Father Font's military escort, Lieutenant Colonel Juan Bautista de Anza, was unsure what to call a body of water with breaking waves and visible tides that was yet fresh to the taste.[5] Crespi, Font, and Anza's confusion is understandable: the confluence of the Sacramento and San Joaquin Rivers is both a riverine and marine environment.[6] The two friars' disagreement points to the fundamental complexity of these uppermost tidal reaches of San Francisco Bay.

The extensive tidal wetlands of the delta region universally struck early visitors as marvelous, no matter how they understood them. Seen from the bordering hills, vast freshwater and brackish marshes stretched away to the horizon, broken only by lines of trees along the ridge of higher ground next to stream channels. In winter, the entire delta plain was frequently covered under a sheet of water or obscured by a dense, ground-hugging "tule fog." In summer, strong winds blew unceasingly from the ocean, and daily high temperatures reached one hundred degrees for months. The water retreated, exposing open areas filled with lush grasses. Native fish, millions of waterfowl, antelope, beavers, and elk all found the landscape congenial. Few places in North America, let alone in Europe, resembled this alternately wet, dry, windy, and scorching place.[7]

Facing a landscape unlike any in North America, Americans, like their Spanish and Mexican predecessors, struggled to find a familiar precedent. Often they arrived at the metaphor of an ocean. Traveling along the Sacramento River in the winter of 1828, trapper Jedediah Smith described the lands bordering the river as a vast sea of grasses. The waves of this ocean were made by the wind blowing rhythmically through the tops of grasses.[8] But unlike the grasslands of the great plains between the Mississippi and Missouri Rivers, the tule marshes were not prairies. They were wetlands, dominated by emergent vegetation. Across much of the delta and the central valley, where seawater mingled with river runoff, *Scirpus acutus,* the common tule, dominated. *Typha latifolia,* cattail rush, covered adjacent freshwater marshes.[9] All bulrushes, including the famous papyrus rushes of the Nile River, "like to have their feet wet," as botanists say. They thrive in soils flooded for all or part of the year. Bulrushes survive in water because they can exchange gases through their leaves rather than their roots.[10]

Despite their technical error, early travelers were not far off in identifying the tules as oceanic grasslands. The tules carpeted hundreds of miles of river channels with uniformly high vegetation. The play of breezes over the grasses was reminiscent of the sea. And in fact the delta region is oceanic, in the sense that the sea plays a central role in creating and maintaining its unique character. The delta, like the rest of San Francisco Bay and its margin, was an estuary, a place between land and sea. When newcomers saw the delta as a river choked with grasses, and its swamps as potential farmland, they imposed a future on the land that did not reckon with the forces that made and controlled the delta. The power of the tides and the proximity of the sea could not be diminished, even if they were ignored.

Europeans, and later Americans, were conceptually confused about the delta, and that confusion had consequences. When Americans imagined the delta as a fertile agricultural landscape, they worked to make the freshwater tidelands into the place of their dreams.[11] The dream was to harness the delta's fertile wetlands as agricultural fields, to turn natural fecundity into economic productivity. This combination of imagination and effort foreshadowed a continuing pattern and is best captured in a series of questions: Was the delta land or water? Was it unimproved farmland or a series of navigable channels? Was it an extension of the ocean, an area legally off-limits to private investment, or a wet wasteland that could be reclaimed as farmland? Who owned and should own the tule marshes? Were the marshes federal or state property? Was the delta the top of the bay or the bottom of the watershed—an arm of the sea or a river threatened by saltwater intrusion?

The first human inhabitants of San Francisco Bay's brackish wetlands had embraced the diversity of habitats rather than puzzling over their disposition. Native people valued the delta's complex of seasonal habitats for the rich products they provided. They found the delta's mixture of water and land to be a fertile source of wild foods. As they have along the shores of San Francisco Bay, archaeologists have excavated a series of Native American mounds dotting the valley floor. Often these mounds formed conspicuous high points in the low-lying landscape. These inland mounds consisted largely of shells from brackish water mussels and clams. But many also contained bones of birds, fish, and mammals, suggesting that residents opportunistically harvested available foods.[12] What remains unknown are the intentions of native people as they systematically raised the level of the mounds. Were the native peoples building land? Were these permanent sites for residence or simply seasonal encampments? We do not know the answer, but it is clear that native peoples adapted their lives to flooding. Later arrivals would attempt to live permanently in the marshes.

OCEAN OF GRASSES

Walking south and east from San Francisco Bay to Yosemite, an ecstatic John Muir described his first view of the tidal wetlands of the southern delta in high spring of 1868:

> When I first saw this central garden, the most extensive and regular of
> all the bee-pastures of the State, it seemed all one sheet of plant gold,
> hazy and vanishing in the distance, distinct as a new map along the foot-
> hills at my feet. Descending the eastern slopes of the Coast Range
> through beds of gilias and lupines, and around many a breezy hillock
> and bush-crowned headland, I at length waded out into the midst of it.

All the ground was covered, not with grass and green leaves, but with radiant corollas, about ankle-deep next the foot-hills, knee-deep or more five or six miles out.[13]

Muir described a vast carpet of flowers stretching from the coast ranges to the foothills of the Sierra Nevada, an ocean of flowers. But the delta was a changeable place. This dynamic character had a distinct seasonal element. Winter rains and spring snowmelt flooded the valley, and summer heat baked it dry. How he perceived the valley depended on when he arrived. Had Muir come through this part of the upper delta a few months earlier, he would have seen a single enormous sheet of water where wildflowers now bloomed. The two cycles—wet and green—reflected the delta's special mixture of water and soil and that mixture's rich results.

From the beginning, newcomers noticed the rich productivity of these wet grasslands. Spanish explorers and later military men often commented on the interior wetlands' great potential for pasturing cattle and horses, as well as for harboring Indians escaping the brutal routine of the Franciscan missions. Large herds of feral horses and cattle grazed in the unfenced central valley during the first decades of the nineteenth century. John C. Fremont, ostensibly mapping prospective railroad routes through the Rocky Mountains, detoured over the Sierra Nevadas into California in the late winter of 1844. Fremont and his men spent nearly a month recuperating at Sutter's ranch near present-day Sacramento, California. Fremont finally departed Sutter's with his motley band of French Canadian voyageurs, Missouri trappers, a free black volunteer from Saint Louis, a captive California Indian boy, and 150 horses and cows. The animals found good feed as they moved southward along the margin of the valley floor, but Fremont had eyes only for the excellent agricultural prospects of the foothill margin. "Our road was through a level country," he recalled, "admirably suited to cultivation, and covered with groves of oak trees."[14] Fremont highlighted features he knew would appeal to American settlers: abundant water, gentle slopes, and plenty of wood for building, cooking, and heating.

Like Fremont, most American and European visitors focused less on the grazing possibilities than on the soil's apparent suitability for growing grain. But that soil first needed to be cleared of its native vegetation. After news of 1848 gold finds in the Sierra foothills made its way outside California, thousands of would-be miners passed through the delta on boats, bound for the mines upstream. One such passenger, Edward Gould Buffum, commented favorably on the soil underlying the "thick, rank growth of tule": "The low, alluvial bottom lands along the shore appear susceptible of the highest cultivation," he wrote, "and I doubt not, when the gold mania shall have partially ceased, the rich bottoms of the Sacramento will be clothed with farm-houses."[15] Buffum was not alone in turning an appraising eye on the delta marshes. He and many others could envision a future in which tule marshes would be replaced with grain fields and livestock pastures. The great nineteenth-century chronicler of California, Hubert Howe Bancroft, wrote that the state had three essential resources: grass, gold, and grain. The state's development, he argued, was an upward progression from primitive accumulation to stable productivity. Mexican stock raisers had relied on grass for their cattle. Rough but hardy miners had built a rich but unjust society on gold. Agriculture would civilize the state and make it great. Like Bancroft, most European and American arrivals seem to have seen farmland as the delta's highest purpose.

Before California's grasslands could become productive grain fields, though, they required some modification, or, in Thomas Jefferson's words, "finishing." Finishing was a familiar concept for nineteenth-century Americans. God might have made the earth for his people, but it usually needed some work before it could be made productive.[16] While Americans found tules unfamiliar, "reclaiming," or improving them through drainage, was a familiar task. But "finishing" implied a static landscape, and the delta was anything but static. Sometimes the grasslands were flooded, other times parched. In autumn, after several months without rain and long after the mountain snowpack had melted, the valley floor was brown and dry. John Bidwell encountered this dry, seemingly lifeless phase when he and a small party of Americans crossed into California in 1841. But the tule region rarely stayed dry for long. After a hostile reception in Mexican San Jose, Bidwell and his companions decided to ride northward to Sutter's Fort on the far side of the

Sacramento-San Joaquin delta. Unfortunately, they left during the first storm of the winter rainy season. A dismayed Bidwell saw the land change from a dry plain to a shallow lake: "Streams were out of their banks; gulches were swimming; plains were inundated; indeed, most of the country was overflowed." Bidwell and his companions were forced to follow winding animal paths, which were sometimes submerged. "The moment our animals stepped to one side down they went into the mire," he recalled. It took Bidwell eight torturous days to travel some sixty-five miles across the delta, a trip that reputedly required just two days of steady riding in summer.[17]

Americans who wanted to transform California's marshy central valley into farmland did have models. In the early nineteenth century, large Spanish and British land grants occupied the lowlands around Mobile, Alabama, and parts of Louisiana. In the marshes of these southern river floodplains, a similar evolution from cattle grazing toward cash-crop agriculture took place decades before California entered the United States. The difference was that, whereas in Alabama and Louisiana sugarcane and cotton came to dominate, in California wheat farms replaced horses and cattle.[18] Seen in the national context, California's agricultural development was merely the latest in a series of newly acquired and drained agricultural landscapes, in which speculators and large-scale commercial agriculture played a dominant role.[19]

SWAMPLANDS: "THERE NEVER WAS A CAT ROLLED WHITER IN MEAL"

After a grueling journey that included crossing the Isthmus of Panama, T. Butler King, special assistant to the U.S. secretary of state, arrived in California in June 1849. King was charged with reporting on the political conditions in the newly acquired territory, but he turned his report into a general survey of the social and economic conditions of California. Arriving at the height of the gold rush, King noted the near-complete breakdown of civil authority in the face of massive migration from the United States and around the world. But King also cast a shrewd eye on the economic prospects of the state. Among the most valuable land, he wrote, were the sodden freshwater marshes at the head of San Francisco Bay. This land cried out for organized management of water. "A system of drainage, which would also secure irrigation, is absolutely necessary to give value to the great plain of the Sacramento and San Joaquin," King wrote. "Such a system," he insisted, "can only be established in the survey and sale of the land." Surveyors should reserve areas for drainage canals and set aside areas along rivers, "that they may have plenty of room to increase their channels when their waters shall be confined within them by embankments." The cost of drainage should be built into the price of the swamplands. But the natural productivity of the land, unleashed by a program of drainage and irrigation, "would, when agriculture shall become a pursuit in California, make this valley one of the most beautiful and productive portions of the Union."[20] King's idea foreshadowed other drainage and irrigation plans, but his suggestion of a centrally guided reclamation plan was not to be. Instead, Congress transferred the nation's swamplands to the individual states.

The Swamplands Act of 1850 granted federally owned "swamp and overflowed" lands to new states entering the union.[21] The premise was that states would sell these flood-prone lands to individuals, raising money for flood prevention and drainage programs. The law promised to raise money for cash-starved new state governments, reduce flooding, and promote the reclamation of worthless marshlands for the lasting benefit of tax rolls. The new law was consistent with a federal policy to quickly transfer public lands to the states, and ultimately to private individuals, for the benefit of both.[22] In practice, the act had unexpected results. At first, California's swamplands moved slowly from the public domain into private hands. But soon, desperate for funds, state legislators rushed to sell the remaining swamplands even before the General Land Office could survey the state. State officials thus allowed local county surveyors to map the "swamp and overflowed lands" within their borders, and because these men used a looser definition of "swamp and overflowed" than the federal agency— some considered it a corrupt definition—California claimed and sold much more land than the land office thought fair. In the eyes of the federal agency, Californians stole large areas of the federal domain under the guise of swampland.[23]

In 1856, state legislators offered 320-acre blocks of swampland for $1.00 per acre, for cash or easy credit. Buyers who bought on credit had to drain half their land within five years or the unreclaimed remainder reverted back to the state. But in 1856 few buyers were interested, perhaps in part due to the uncertainty of state title to the land. Despite the confusion already hampering swampland sales, in March 1864, California's legislators increased the acreage limit on swamplands to 640 acres. California's legislators passed an even more dramatic amendment in March 1868. The so-called Green Act, named for its sponsor, Will Green of Colusa County, removed all acreage limitations. Combined with corrupt practices by county surveyors like Green himself, this legislation permitted a few men to purchase enormous acreages of tule lands in the delta for $1.25 per acre, with no money down. Among the most egregious abuses of public trust in state history, the Green Act was a truly massive transfer of public land to private citizens. In the two years after the act's passage, California transferred over 790,000 acres of swampland to less than two hundred persons.[24] The state's public lands had rapidly passed into the hands of land speculators.

In December 1869, California governor H. H. Haight sent his biennial message to the state legislature. Haight mightily disapproved of the legislators' rash attitude toward California's public lands. Referring to the disastrous effects of the Green Act, Haight thundered, "Our land system seems to be mainly framed to facilitate the acquisition of large bodies of land by capitalists and corporations, either as donations or at nominal prices." An enthusiastic citizen of a nation where government existed largely to transfer land to private individuals, Governor Haight was nevertheless shocked at the inequalities wrought in California. "It would probably have been much better for the State and country if the public lands had never been disposed of," the governor lamented. "As it is, our system in California is in a confused, loose and unsatisfactory condition, productive of much difficulty and litigation."[25]

While passionate, Haight's speech and his position were mild in comparison to the opinions of many Californians. As a few powerful individuals locked up large parts of California's freshwater tidelands, increasing numbers of Californians protested large-scale land monopoly by land speculators. A groundswell of public indignation at land monopoly assailed California's political leaders. San Francisco antimonopolist Henry George demanded to know how it was possible that in a state with so many acres of empty land, average men could not afford to buy a farm. The problem, reformers argued, was that a few men, aided by misguided or corrupt state legislation, maintained a virtual monopoly of California farmland. George and others focused on the state's giveaway of delta tule lands. Commenting on the 1864 swampland act, George charged, "The central idea seems to be making easy of land monopolization, and the favoring of speculators at the expense of the settlers."[26] If the state's most valuable remaining farmland was given away in enormous parcels, how would smaller men have the chance to make their own farm? Would not a handful of the rich and well-placed monopolize the fruits of California's soil?

George had previously spelled out what he saw as the inevitable consequences of land monopoly. California in the era before the railroad (and before the concentration of land that accompanied the railroad era) was a place where "there [had] been a feeling of personal independence and equality, a general hopefulness and self-reliance, and a certain large-heartedness and open-handedness." These positive elements of California's society "were born of the comparative evenness with which property was distributed, the high standard of wages and of comfort, and the latent feeling of everyone that he might 'make a strike,' and certainly could not be kept down long."[27]

George argued that rising land prices—likely to be worsened by land monopoly—would ultimately hurt laboring people. "As proprietorship is thus rendered more difficult and less profitable to the poor," he predicted, "more are forced into the labor market to compete with each other, and cut down the rate of wages—that is, to make the division of their joint production between labor and capital more in favor of capital and less in favor of labor."[28] Great concentrations of wealth would mean greater inequality. Greater inequality would threaten the basis of California's society by leading to greater differences between workers and employers, "less personal independence among the many and the greater power of the few."[29] Giving the state's swamplands away made the rich richer and denied the landless poor the opportunity for advancement.

Henry George was not alone in worrying about who would harvest the products of California's public lands. Outside California, others joined in decrying speculators' theft of swamplands from the public domain. Horace Greeley, the fiery publisher of the *New York Tribune* and a former congressman, bitterly recalled his service on the House Committee on Public Lands. California legislators quoted Greeley at length in their 1872 report. Greeley recalled how he and his fellow congressmen were duped into recommending the Swamplands Act of 1850, which transferred flooded federal lands to the states:

> Various fair-seeming bills and claims came before us, some of which had passed the Senate, yet which we put our heels on as barefaced robberies. . . . At length there came along a meek innocent-looking stranger, by whom we were nicely taken in and done for. It was a bill to cede to the several new States (so called), such portion of the unsold public lands within their limits respectively as were submerged or sodden, and thus rendered useless and pestilential—that is, swamps, marshes, bogs, fens, etc. . . . There never was a cat rolled whiter in meal, and I, for one, was completely duped. . . . The consequence was a reckless and fraudulent transfer to certain States of millions on millions of choice public lands, whole sections of which had not muck on their surface to accommodate a single fair-sized frog, while the appropriation of the proceeds to draining proved a farce and a sham.[30]

Greeley charged that much of the swampland granted to the states was in fact not wet at all, but actually first-class farmland fraudulently mapped as swampland by corrupt state surveyors. In fact, Greeley underestimated the extent of the corruption: the fifteen states covered by federal swampland acts eventually claimed three times more swamp and overflowed land than federal land officials believed to exist.[31]

Spurred by an angry public, California's state legislature directed the State Lands Commission to investigate the charges. In 1877, the land commissioners interrogated Will Green. Green combined in his considerable self the important positions of Colusa County surveyor (1857–1867), local newspaper publisher, and assemblyman from the Colusa district.[32]

Green had authored California's notorious swampland act of 1868, which removed all acreage limitations on purchasers of state lands, which critics blamed for land monopoly. Called to testify before the state land commissioners, Green claimed that removing the acreage limitation was simply an oversight. Incredulous, the commissioners hammered at Green to explain the bill's intent:

Q. *In the preparation of that law, why was the clause eliminated from the law restricting the purchase of State lands to three hundred and twenty acres?*
A. It was an inadvertence.

Q. *Not intended at all?*
A. No, sir.[33]

The land commissioners ultimately concluded that the 1868 swampland act was the "first in the State that sanctioned and legalized land monopoly." Before the legislature could act to reinstate acreage limitations, speculators had "loaded up to the extent of nearly a million of acres," said the commissioners.[34]

Under intense questioning by State Land Commissioner Ball, Will Green admitted his involvement in selecting lands for speculators while also serving as county surveyor. Green described how he helped speculators apply to purchase thousands of acres of swamp and overflowed land. Green kept the incomplete applications on file for years, effectively granting title without payment to the state. After sparring with a cagey Green over his past, Commissioner Ball tried to understand Green's underlying philosophy:

BALL: How do you regard the practice of obtaining title to large bodies of land—as an evil to the State—what is your opinion?

GREEN: I don't think I would like to swear to my opinion. Well, I think large purchases of swamp lands is not an evil. I think it is best for the State to have them reclaimed. I hold that only by allowing capitalists to purchase them in large bodies can they be reclaimed.[35]

Green defended his decision to allow speculators to purchase unlimited quantities of swamplands as a necessary step in developing the state. "At the time of the passage of the law," Green went on, "all the best pieces of swamp land had been entered by small holders, and all the State had left was the bottoms and the tules."[36] Green believed that only powerful capitalists had the money to enclose and drain these soggiest areas.

In 1872, California's senate and house of representatives convened a joint committee to investigate abuses of state and federal lands in the state. The committee found that the state had sold nearly eight hundred thousand acres of swamp and overflowed lands between 1868 and 1872. All but a tiny fraction of these wetlands drained eventually to San Francisco Bay. Four delta counties—Contra Costa, Sacramento, San Joaquin, and Solano—accounted for 205,859 acres, or 26 percent of all wetlands sold. And many of these lands were sold to a relative handful of speculators, as the legislators made clear by listing buyers and their acreage.

Heading the list of buyers was George D. Roberts, a San Francisco mining speculator, with 81,681 acres of swampland, more than twice as many as any other purchaser.[37] Roberts's properties embraced the entire extent of the delta, from above Sacramento down to the edge of salt water at Sherman Island. Together with a group of fellow San Francisco investors, Roberts founded a company to develop these lands and make them productive. The Tide Land Reclamation Company, founded in 1869, was among the first to apply corporate principles and vast capital to reclamation. Its directors and investors, all San Franciscans, included some of California's wealthiest and most powerful men: banker Lloyd Tevis of Wells Fargo; attorney Archibald Peachy of Halleck Peachy & Billings; California State Controller Robert Watt; land speculator George D. Roberts; and investors Charles H. Burton and William Doolan.[38] Their story illustrates how private enterprise imposed its own vision of a productive landscape on the freshwater tidelands.

MAKING THE DELTA PAY

On November 10, 1871, California railroad promoter and civil engineer William Bierlie Hyde met with the man he called the "King of the Delta." Personally and through his partnership in the Tide Land Reclamation

Company, George D. Roberts controlled hundreds of thousands of acres of tule lands near the top of the tide in the Sacramento and San Joaquin River delta, nearly 10 percent of all the privately owned swampland in the state.[39] On this November day, Hyde proposed a breathtakingly ambitious scheme to make "fresh water tidelands" into prime agricultural land. Roberts already had grand expectations for his marshes; his company had employed as many as two hundred Chinese men at one time, digging ditches and building low walls of peat soil on swampy Sherman and Twitchell Islands, near the confluence of the Sacramento and San Joaquin Rivers with San Pablo Bay.[40]

Hyde now proposed a completely new method of managing the reclaimed land. Hyde suggested that Roberts divide his newly drained property into square parcels up to several thousand acres in size. Small numbers of expert technicians riding new steam-powered tractors—machines that Hyde just happened to be inventing—would efficiently plant and harvest enormous fields of wheat on the reclaimed land. With the aid of machines, white farmers would no longer need the assistance of Asian laborers.

To head off complaints about land monopoly, engineer Hyde urged the King of the Delta to undertake a radical new social experiment: to grant homesteads to his steam plow operators. In enthusiastic prose, Hyde explained:

> In the execution of the plans of this Cultivation Company which it is now to be seen has a scope as great as that of our railroad system, it would be well to consider the good policy of forestalling the usual cry of "grinding and oppressive monopoly of poor men's birth rights" by using its influence with owners of very large tracts to make an actual gift out of every 1,000 acres of a homestead of 40 acres to reliable families—securing thus residents upon the lands, the extensive production of small fruits and garden produce—and the presence of contented and efficient laboring element when needed at seed time and harvest.

But Hyde went even further. Not only would workers get homesteads but also every worker would be given additional plots of land within the company holdings, and the profit from those lands would be their own.

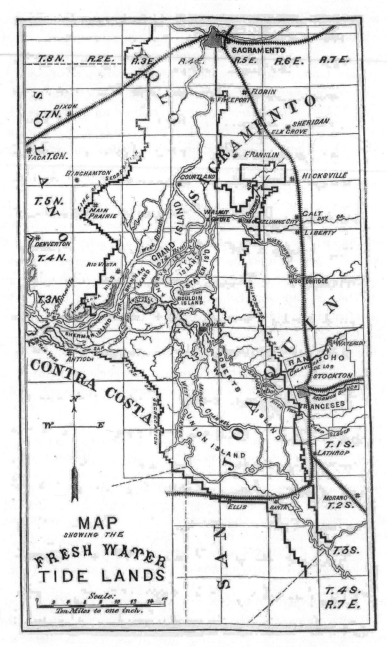

Figure 5. The freshwater tidelands of California. U.S. Department of Agriculture, 1873.

The company's directors would have central control over farming and transportation, but workers, managers, and stockholders would all share in the profits.[41] Hyde also suggested that it would be wise to pay the technological elite, the men who ran the steam plows, an additional production bonus per acre cultivated. Hyde's extraordinary proposal was a kind of privately run Homestead Act, but with a very different vision of society. These homesteads would keep Roberts's agricultural machine humming: houses in the fields would guarantee a supply of workers to tend the machines of industrial-scale agriculture in the drained tidal wetlands of the delta.[42]

Hyde's subsequent letters suggest that the meeting with Roberts did not go well.[43] Hyde was a dreamer others described as difficult, pretentious, and prickly. He rarely appreciated criticism of his often-unrealistic plans. Roberts, too, was a difficult man. Ambitious, stretched thin financially, and wielding near-autocratic control over his gangs of Chinese workers, Roberts appears to have been little interested in social experiments or in sharing any profits, potential or actual. Nor was Roberts committed to any long-term project of building communities in the San Francisco Bay delta. Roberts wanted to flip his investments, make a quick profit, and slide that money into further land and mining speculations. Ultimately, Hyde needed Roberts more than Roberts needed Hyde, as their subsequent relations made clear. Hyde's second draft, written the day after he met with Roberts, proposed far less social engineering. The company would control everything. Later in 1871 and 1872, as Hyde turned away from Roberts and unsuccessfully promoted his project to a succession of other powerful California barons, it lost all elements of economic democracy and became a straightforward project to squeeze money from the delta marshes.[44]

Hyde's initial proposal sought to address tension between settlers, laborers, and large landowners, tensions that the King of the Delta knew very well. Just a month after Hyde proposed his plan for reducing social tensions in the reclaimed lands, Roberts experienced the full wrath of those who did not benefit from reclamation. Earlier in the year, Roberts had hired workers to construct a private levee on property he owned on the Yuba River near Marysville, California. Neighboring farmers believed the levee protected Roberts's land at the expense of their own, and when floodwaters rose in December 1871, a gang of angry and desperate men overpowered Roberts's night watchmen and cut through the levee with pickaxes and shovels. The raging waters utterly destroyed the weakened structure and flooded Roberts's land.[45] Where landowners were relatively equal, communities acted in a long tradition to abate nuisances like Roberts's levee.[46]

Unlike Roberts's property upstream in Marysville, most of the Tide Land Reclamation Company lands were on delta islands close to San Francisco Bay. These islands were massive, single-owner properties. They were more like plantations than farm communities. The United States in the years after the Civil War was shaken by labor struggles that bordered on open class warfare. In California, farm workers and their employers constantly battled over wages and working conditions.[47] Labor strife and financial uncertainty meant that agriculture in this era, while extraordinarily profitable, was also extremely unpredictable. Delta islands offered the possibility of social control unknown since the age of slavery. This was partly due to geography. The tidal rivers and their bordering marshes made the delta islands inaccessible except by boat. In effect, California's delta islands were private fiefdoms in which landowners could send their products out at will while controlling who got in.

George Roberts and other large delta reclamationists increased their control by employing Chinese workers. Roberts contracted with Chinese labor bosses to provide gangs of Chinese men to dig ditches, pile dirt into levees, and grade and maintain the finished embankments. Roberts described a machine-like routine: "We go to the Chinese merchants or business men, and tell them we want to give a contract for a certain number of miles of levee. . . . Sometimes the contracts are for five, six, seven, or eight hundred or a thousand yards, and sometimes less, with one individual, as the case may be. We pay so much a yard, and measure the work after it is done, and they receive their pay."[48] By 1876, Chinese laborers had reclaimed thirty to forty thousand acres of Tide Land Reclamation Company land, and Roberts had at least three thousand Chinese men employed building levees in 1876. Trapped by poverty, these men drained tule lands despite malaria, dysentery, and bone-crushing tasks.[49] Roberts found the Chinese willing to work under conditions and for wages that other workers would not tolerate. Rising at 5:00 A.M., Chinese laborers were on the levees by 6:00 A.M. With just a fifteen-minute water break and an hour for lunch, the men worked steadily through summer heat for twelve hours. The schedule was industrial, measured by bells and enforced by fines for missed work.[50] Testifying in favor of continued Chinese immigration before Congress, Roberts insisted that his company could not reclaim its land without Chinese workers: "I do not think we could get the white men to do the work. It is a class of work that white men do not like. . . . Very few of them come here to do cheap labor. . . . We could not afford to pay three or four dollars a day to white men to do our work."[51] Chinese men carried out the essential labor of reclaiming tule lands for agriculture, and their labor was tightly controlled. They were paid little, worked in gangs, and fed themselves.

The workers turned the delta islands into a landscape that promoters sought to control as rigidly as the social environment. Due to their low-lying topography and the daily tides, reclaimed marshes could be irrigated with freshwater by simply opening a hole in the levee wall at high tide. This spared delta crops from the cyclical droughts that already by 1871 had destroyed several California wheat crops.[52] Reclaimed delta islands promised social and environmental security of a kind not available elsewhere. The islands did not need to be fenced; access was controlled because no one could get to the islands without a boat and even then only by landing at the company wharf. The delta islands were unusually controlled spaces. They offered the possibility of mastery that excited and eluded nineteenth-century business. These spaces, seemingly blank slates socially and ecologically, seemed like the perfect places to produce wealth.

The Tide Land Reclamation Company was in business to make money. This was a kind of business that George Roberts, a former mining speculator, understood. Historian Sucheng Chan has estimated the profits reclamation brought to Roberts and his company. Roberts paid $1 to $4 per acre to California for swampland, and another $6 to $12 to drain it and build levees. In the case of Twitchell Island, the Tide Land

Reclamation Company quickly sold the reclaimed land for between $20 and $100 per acre, a minimum gain of $4 and a maximum of $93 profit per acre. Chan estimates that Roberts and the company cleared between $1 million and $2 million in profit on the Twitchell Island reclamation work alone.[53] With state land prices so low, Chinese labor so cheap, and demand for farmland so high, reclamation could sometimes be a very profitable business.[54]

More commonly, however, reclaiming land did not pay so well. Like mining, farming drained land was a speculative activity that required great investment and used up a finite natural resource. Before the first crop could be planted, workers had to drain water off the land, hack down and remove the existing tule rushes, plow up the roots, and burn the highly organic soil down as much as two feet. Planting a dense monocrop of annual grass (wheat) produced enormously in the short term. But it did so through radically simplifying an existing wet-grassland ecosystem. From an ecologist's perspective, it used the accumulated soil nutrients from hundreds or thousands of years and burned up the soil in the process. Given the high flooding and levee failure rate, we should see this kind of agriculture as gambling rather than as farming: if the crop survived, the yield and profit were huge; if the levee broke, the crop was a total failure.

Environmental forces created economic uncertainty, but they also threatened to take back the reclaimed "islands" in the delta permanently. Floods constantly threatened farms, especially after the 1860s, when upstream miners filled the delta with sediment. Mining debris flowed down the rivers, filled in the channels, exacerbated seasonal flooding, and scoured away topsoil or dumped inches of sand on farmlands. Fierce currents often destroyed levees. Big floods in 1871 and 1878 swept away years of labor and tens of thousands of dollars in improvements.[55] A second danger to reclaimed lands came from the nature of the delta soil itself. As the marsh soils dried, they shrank like dried-out sponges. When rivers rose against them, levees constructed of stacked peat blocks literally floated away. Water ran underneath the levees into the islands, forming channels called "cracks" by the reclamationists. Water also boiled up unexpectedly in the middle of fields far from the river's edge, flooding crops that seemed secure behind protecting walls. Reclamation workers

faced both human-caused and natural dangers. Their labor was an end-
less struggle to keep water off the land.[56] Eventually, hydraulic
mining debris dredged from the waters would provide the materials to
finally build effective levees.

DREDGING

Dredging as a technology dates back to ancient times. Archaeologists have
found ancient vessels on the Nile River that were adapted to remove mud
from river bottoms, and there was a fully articulated theory and practice of
dredging to reclaim land and deepen shipping channels in the Netherlands
by the fourteenth century.[57] In California, the first dredges were in use by
the early 1860s in San Francisco harbor, sweeping away sand and mud that
piled up along the city front. But dredging for the purpose of land reclamation began later, in the 1870s, as speculators turned their eyes to the flooded
soils of the Sacramento-San Joaquin delta region. According to scholars,
the California dredge was a hybrid based on a steam-powered scoop
dredge used in New York harbor and adapted to San Francisco Bay.
Essentially a self-propelled barge with a giant timber A-shaped frame on
deck, the "California dredge" sported an enormous boom, as much as
three hundred feet long, with a giant hinged scoop at the end. The boom
could be swung side to side and the bucket hoisted or lowered by means
of cables. A single scoop of the bucket could lift as much as six cubic yards
of soil, more than a man could shovel in an entire day.[58]

California dredges were designed to remove sand and gravel from the
bottom of a river. They enabled engineers to deepen the channel of a
river, hence increasing its capacity to carry water and reducing flooding.
But California dredges also built levees. The genius of the California
dredges was that they carried out both flood prevention and land reclamation at the same time. When a dredge removed sand from the bottom
of the river, it reduced flood danger. When it placed that sand on the
bank, it made a levee, promoting reclamation.

The widespread adoption of hydraulic gold-mining technology in
the late 1850s made dredging a necessity. At first gold miners worked

primarily alone or in teams, panning or sluicing gold from streambeds. But as the easily available deposits were exhausted, and as capitalized mining corporations arrived, miners increasingly sought to tap the richer supplies of gold captured in ancient stream channels. These ancient channels were often high on the sides of Sierra canyons, where tectonic uplift and faulting had left them.[59] Miners sought to remove the layers of trees, soil, and rock that overlaid these so-called "auriferous gravels." Starting in 1852, Anthony Chabot invented a new technique to work his hillside claim in Nevada City, California. Chabot channeled water from a creek into a canvas hose, using the powerful spray to wash away plants and soil and to expose the gold-bearing gravel below. Gold, heavier than soil or rock, collected in a sluice at the bottom of the slope. With substantial modifications, including iron hoses and mercury-filled gold traps, Chabot's innovation became the method called hydraulic mining. Hydraulic mining required vast quantities of water and led to the construction of hundreds of miles of ditches, flumes, and pipelines running through the Sierra Nevada. Hydraulic miners used as much as six hundred thousand acre-feet of water per year, gnawing away entire hillsides with their water cannons.[60]

Hydraulic mining washed down great quantities of soil and rock into the rivers draining the Sierra Nevada. Deep canyons filled up with the "tailings," as miners called the debris. In the winter of 1861 to 1862, the wettest in California history, some of this debris washed down the rivers, spreading over new farms on the valley floor and filling in river channels right down to San Francisco Bay. Farms along the Yuba River near Marysville, California, were buried under as much as seven feet of sand.[61] The debris kept on flowing downstream for decades. By 1905, twenty years after hydraulic mining had been banned in California, the bed of the Yuba River near Marysville was twelve feet higher than it had been fifty years before.[62] Hydraulic miners essentially aggravated existing geological processes, speeding up the delivery of rock, sand, and soil from the top to the bottom of the San Francisco Bay watershed. What made the debris flows so devastating was that they coincided with a tremendous burst of land reclamation in the delta region. Hydraulic mining accelerated sediment delivery just as levee construction narrowed river channels and cut off sloughs that had acted as conduits for flood-waters and water storage areas. Together, the two human activities reduced the available flood-carrying capacity of the river system.[63]

Geologist Grove Karl Gilbert once described hydraulic mining debris as a great slow-motion wave, "analogous to the downstream movement of a great body of storm water."[64] Quite deservedly one of the United States's most famous nineteenth-century natural scientists, Gilbert spent nearly two decades of his life studying the impact of mining on the San Francisco Bay and delta.[65] To demonstrate the volume and impact of sediment washed from the mountains by miners, Gilbert compiled records of the depth of the Sacramento River at the state capital over a period of fifty years. From the first records taken in 1856 up to 1905, the river's bed rose and then began to fall as mud, sand, and gravel entered the stream from mountain tributaries and were slowly carried down to San Francisco Bay by annual high waters. Gilbert pointed out that the wave of debris in the Yuba River, an upstream tributary, peaked a decade or more before arriving in Sacramento. The rivers slowly flushed their burdens of sediment, the grains gradually but inevitably proceeding downstream toward the ocean.[66]

As this wave of debris advanced, experience showed that human laborers alone could not build lasting levees to protect the delta from floods. Chinese men labored on the first serious efforts to drain delta marshlands and protect them from floods, building low walls of peat soil they cut with backbreaking effort from the surrounding floodplain. But solid levees required heavy, inorganic materials. Dredges working within the river channels provided that material. Their great buckets hoisted gravel and sand, deposited from the mountains, from the river bottom up onto the peat, building walls of rock around islands of dry land. The rocky and solid dredged levees were less prone to leakage and offered sturdier defenses against rising rivers.[67] But building stone walls created an unforeseen problem: the heavy rock levees weighed down the under-lying wet peat soils. Crushed by the levees, compacted peat soils sank. Paradoxically, raising a rock levee on peat could increase the danger of flooding.

Another threat to peat soils came from the air. Farmers prepared the reclaimed marshlands by burning the dense stands of rush grasses. After burning, farmers plowed the peat soils to break up plant roots and to permit seeding of crops. But the moment they drained the land and broke the sod, farmers began to lose what they had gained. Burning and plowing greatly accelerated the inexorable soil loss endemic to peat soils. Once exposed to the air, peat begins to oxidize, as carbon is released into the air in gaseous form. The result is much like a slow and invisible fire that burns away the plant material accumulated over millennia. The combined effect of compaction and oxidation rapidly lowered soil surfaces. To compensate, landowners raised levees higher to protect their fields from flooding.[68]

The cycle of constantly rising walls around constantly sinking fields has never stopped. By the 1950s, most delta farmland was eleven feet or more below sea level and disappearing at a rate of one to three inches per year.[69] Landowners had unwittingly accelerated a natural process—oxidation in drained peat soils—and they found that maintaining their grip on this landscape required constant and costly work. Their desire to master the freshwater tidelands made them the servants of their own works. Looking back over irrigation projects on every continent, Karl Wittfogel famously argued that when it comes to managing waterways, human beings have many options. But once a single course of action is chosen—in this case to take land from the water—all options disappear and all energies must go into defending that system against natural forces. Paraphrasing Wittfogel, reclamation can be very productive for humans, but once societies attempt to control the hydrological cycle, they are locked into a hydraulic system with ever-rising demands and costs.[70]

Some nineteenth-century observers recognized these interconnections between the physical elements of the watershed, the ways that mountains, rivers, delta, and bay all responded to the flow of sediment carried by water. Water and sediment made these connections clear, at least to those who worked with them. Grove Karl Gilbert showed that one kind of human activity—hydraulic mining—raised the bed of the Sacramento River, increasing the danger of flooding. Another activity, building levees to contain the river in its banks, helped speed the transport of water and sand downstream and so lowered the danger of flooding.[71] A.D. Foote, in the journal of the American Society of Civil Engineers, described the difficulties these interconnections posed for engineers: "Work done for navigation alone is fatal to flood protection because it contracts the drainage channels in order to give depth at low water, and thus prevents the free passage of the floods. Works for irrigation alone take water needed for navigation. Mining is stopped because the debris fills the drainage channels and spreads over the farmlands. Drainage is blocked by the levee system built for flood protection; and to build levees for flood protection alone is hopeless."[72] Foote recognized the paradox within which reclamationists labored. Engineers sought to improve the productive capacity of marshlands and waterways by controlling rivers. Yet their every effort seemed to throw some other part of the system out of whack.

But once the process had begun, it went forward. New levees encouraged further reclamation in the delta region. So did the delta's abundant freshwater. In a region regularly afflicted by long droughts, delta farmland was nearly drought-proof. It came with irrigation already in place. In 1869, less than 1 percent of California farmland was artificially irrigated. By 1889 about 5 percent was irrigated. Growth in irrigated land was slow in the 1890s and the first decade of the twentieth century but sped up during the 1910s and 1920s. According to economic historian Paul Rhode, "By 1929, irrigated land accounted for nearly 16 percent of the farmland" in California.[73] While no regional statistics are available, it seems reasonable to assume that most of the irrigated land in the state before 1910, and particularly before 1900, was in the Sacramento-San Joaquin delta. Farmers on the delta islands had a special advantage, in that irrigation was a simple matter of installing a floodgate in one of the levees holding out the surrounding freshwater. Tides regularly raised delta water levels above the level of the lower islands and then dropped down below the islands again. Farmers could irrigate on a high tide and drain their fields on the low.[74]

RECLAIMING DELTA ISLANDS

Making marshes into farmland meant hard, unpleasant work. When historians write about "backbreaking labor," we usually have no idea what that really means. We have little sense of the ways people worked. Human hands, backs, and minds have always been central to turning floodplains into farmland, whether in the 1860s or the 1960s. Gradually, machines replaced bodies in doing the heavy lifting required in building walls to keep the rivers out. Reclamation on Staten Island, California, illustrates a trajectory seen throughout the freshwater tidelands of the Sacramento-San Joaquin river delta. An early Staten Island levee builder recalled that the first efforts to build walls against the water relied on modified farm machines and animal labor: "The earliest attempts at reclamation (1864 or 1865) were made by Mr. J.T. Bailey who owned, in partnership with Mr. C.F. Juilard about 1200 acres at the head of [Staten] island. Mr. Bailey constructed a machine similar to a plow, which was moved by horse or ox power, and which cut a ditch two feet wide and two feet deep, the sod from this ditch was turned over, just as a plow turns a furrow, and formed the levee."[75]

Bailey's machine created a soft, low barrier of soil between his fields of wheat and the unpredictable Mokelumne River. Animal and human labor enclosed most of nine-thousand-acre Staten Island with this modified plow, but it was a largely cosmetic effort. Annual winter and spring floods surely broke through or washed away these inadequate levees, though the historical record is silent on Bailey's fortunes.[76]

A second effort at taking land from the waters left a more lasting imprint. Men as interested in land value as in farming bought most of Staten Island in the 1870s. They are best thought of as investors rather than farmers. They treated their property as a short-term investment from which they expected a substantial profit. In 1872, San Francisco land speculators James Ben Ali Haggin and Lloyd Tevis purchased about eight thousand acres on the island. Tevis and Haggin were San Francisco lawyers who had parlayed their earnings and connections into a substantial fortune (railroad magnate Collis P. Huntington called Tevis "the smartest man in California").[77] During the 1870s the partners created a California land empire second only to the vast cattle ranches of Henry Miller and his partner, Charles Lux.[78] In June 1872 the partners hired a more experienced man, L.C. McAfee, to direct a new round of levee construction. In McAfee's words, "Chinamen were employed to build the levee around the head of the island and down the western side about four miles. They were paid 11 cents per cubic yard, measured in the ditch." The partners used two basic methods of levee construction, depending on the location of the barriers relative to the rivers. During floods, rivers laid down deposits of sand on the riverbank. Often, building levees meant simply raising these natural barriers. On the relatively firm riverbanks, horses could be employed to drag a board across the ground. These "scrapers" greatly sped the work of gathering and placing soil. In the wetter peat soils in lower-lying areas of the delta, raising barriers was much more difficult. In the words of the closest student of the practice, "The sod was removed from the ditch with a peat spade, locally a 'tule cutter' or tule knife, and used to face one or both sides of the proposed levee. The material underlying the ditch was tamped into place between the sod block rows on the inside of the single sod wall."[79] Chinese men worked together to dig the peat soil from wide, shallow ditches and then moved it to form a pyramidal earthen structure. The levee they built in 1872 was twelve feet wide and five feet high, with a two-foot-wide crown. Compared to Bailey's pile of plowed dirt, this was a serious structure. By the spring of 1873, the Chinese laborers had raised nine miles of these levees along the sinuous banks of the Mokelumne River.[80]

Writing of these indispensable workers, Herbert Howe Bancroft managed to both praise and dehumanize them: "It may be that our development would have been healthier and happier if we had invented and employed less machinery, but we cannot throw away machines now without serious inconvenience. It is clearly evident that the Chinaman is the least objectionable of any human machine we have amongst us."[81]

While hired Chinese laborers built the first wave of levees in the San Francisco Bay delta, the machines of the U.S. Army Corps of Engineers kept the levees from failing. The privately funded levees of the 1860s and 1870s ultimately came to depend on federal maintenance. American taxpayers took over funding for levee construction, dredging, and channel maintenance in San Francisco Bay's freshwater tidelands. Congress gave the corps responsibility, in the mid-nineteenth century, for protecting "the navigability of waters against various kinds of encroachment. By

the end of the century, the corps was charged with a regulatory responsibility concerning bridges, wharves, piers, channels and harbors, diver-
sions of water, and deposits of refuse and other materials."[82]

The first step came with surveys in 1874, when army corps officers
made plans and received money from Congress to improve navigation
from San Francisco Bay to Stockton. In 1875 Congress appropriated
money for the army corps to deepen river depths (usually by constructing wing dams), close breaks in levees, and remove obstacles; the corps
began dredging the Sacramento River the next year. Beginning in August
1876, corps dredges worked continuously to create and maintain a
30-foot-deep channel, 150 to 300 feet wide, more than forty miles from
Suisun Bay to Stockton.

The problems of mining debris, flood control, and private owners'
desire to reclaim their property in the delta and central valley had
become so intertwined by the end of the nineteenth century that it was
impossible to separate them, so the second step involved work in the
Sierra Nevada. Protecting the delta meant working in the mountains. In
1893, Anthony Caminetti, a U.S. congressman from mining-dependent
but flood-prone Amador County, promoted a federal bill creating a three-
man Army Corps of Engineers commission. The commission would be
charged with building dams in the Sierra Nevada to capture debris.
Commissioners also recommended building wing dams in the rivers to
flush debris downstream. Caminetti acted to help the hydraulic mining
industry resume operations halted by court order since 1884, but he
added, "The people of California do not yet realize what a tremendous
advantage this bill is going to be to them. It is usually spoken of as a
measure for the benefit of miners, but its provisions for the improvement
of the rivers will be found to be still more important." The Caminetti Act
created a California Debris Commission, headed by Colonel C.H.
Mendell of the San Francisco district. The act introduced a federal role in
maintaining delta levees. Up to 1884 the army corps had made a few levees and carried out some localized dredging, but its role was limited.
Now the corps had a federal mandate to manage rivers in every way
necessary to reduce the impact of the mining debris on farms, towns, and
navigation.[83]

In 1907 and again in 1911, administrative reorganization created a "Third San Francisco District" with responsibility for maintaining navigation and flood control in the entire Sacramento and San Joaquin River systems, as well as the ports of Stockton and San Joaquin. This was the third step increasing federal responsibility. In 1910, the California Debris Commission released a comprehensive plan to improve navigation and provide flood control on the Sacramento and San Joaquin Rivers. The plan committed the army corps to maintaining levees and preventing flooding throughout the reclaimed delta lands. It also called for dredging the channel of the Sacramento from Cache Slough to Suisun Bay, leading to massive federal investment in snag boats, dredges, and suction dredges. According to the army corps' historian, "By June 30, 1917, [the suction dredges] had removed more than 24 million cubic yards of mud and debris from the Sacramento River below its junction with Cache Slough." The dredges were working all the way down to salt water in Suisun Bay.[84] It cannot be overstated how closely the army corps had come to know and change this waterscape. A historian of the Sacramento district boasted that by 1935 the army corps engineers had completely remade the delta region, "building miles of levees, dredging millions of cubic yards of material, cutting off sharp bends, snagging, constructing wing dams and removing thousands of obstructions from the natural and manmade channel."[85]

One consequence of the dredging was greatly increased shipping through the delta. In 1931, the State Department of Water Resources reported, "There has been a continuous and fairly steady growth of waterborne tonnage since about 1900 to a present movement of nearly 1,000,000 tons, having a value of $40,000,000 to $50,000,000. Most of this movement is on the lower river below Stockton, where adequate and dependable all-year navigation has been maintained. Over 50 individuals or companies operate freight-carrying vessels below Stockton, comprising sternwheel steamers, motor-screw to boats and freighters, and barges."[86] Dredging increased navigability, which in turn helped commerce. U.S. army corps dredges made the rivers more productive by enhancing the waterways' ability to carry goods.

But as with other efforts to enhance productivity, dredging may have contributed to another crisis in the delta. Seawater from San Francisco

Bay intruded into the delta in 1918, again during the 1920s, and especially in 1931, when salt water made it as far upstream as Stockton. The
salt water threatened industries, destroyed crops, and endangered
municipal water supplies. At the time, contemporaries blamed farmers
in the delta and central valley for the saltwater intrusion. A writer for the
Pacific Marine Review, a publication for ocean shippers, blamed irrigation
by rice growers in the Sacramento valley for drawing down river levels
and allowing seawater to move far upstream. One consequence, said the
author, was an invasion of the wormlike wood-boring mollusks *Teredo
navalis* that wreaked havoc in wooden pilings around San Francisco Bay.
"It is a far cry from rice growing in the upper Sacramento Valley to
worms in the bottom of a ferry boat at Benicia, and the connection
between the two could not possibly have been foreseen six years ago,"
wrote the author. "But the present condition should show irrigation
engineers the advisability of research work to determine just what effect
their reclamation programs will have in upsetting the nice balance of the
ordinary processes of nature."[87] Backing up the shippers in a February
1931 report to Congress, army corps colonel Deakyne blamed farmers for
reducing summer river flows to nearly zero. "In the Sacramento Valley,"
he wrote, "irrigation has expanded to the point where it absorbs almost
the entire low water flow of the river in years of subnormal runoff.
This results in a serious handicap to navigation above Sacramento and
permits the intrusion of salt water into the delta channels."[88] Army
corps staffers blamed farmers for sucking too much river out of the river,
treating rivers like water delivery systems rather than multipurpose
waterways.

It is possible that drought-stricken farmers diverted so much water
from the rivers, and pumped so much groundwater from aquifers, that
they removed the hydraulic pressure previously barring salt water from
migrating up into the delta.[89] But in these same years the army corps
maintained deepwater channels to Stockton and Sacramento. Deeper
channels allowed salt water to penetrate farther upstream, since denser
salt water rides along the bottom. In short, the army corps' own ship
channels may have exacerbated the intrusion of seawater. The corps may
have been working against itself as it fought to keep channels deep and

clear of obstructions, maintain sufficient flows in rivers for navigation, and prevent salt intrusion.[90]

A FINISHED LANDSCAPE

In 1873, the real estate promoter, land speculator, and reclamation visionary J. Ross Browne decried the low population and development of California's freshwater tidelands. He noted that the delta region in particular remained unsettled: "The San Joaquin Valley has been open to settlement for more than twenty years; and yet, with an area of six or seven million acres of land, capable of producing enormous crops, the total population engaged in the cultivation of the soil does not exceed two or three thousand." Browne recommended a mixture of drainage and irrigation. Reclamation would make the delta a place for people: "It attracts population and insures settlement; it builds up towns and villages; it establishes trade and manufactories."[91] For Browne, a flourishing population supported by a healthy economy was the measure of the success or failure of reclamation. He saw reclaimed farmland as a draw to further intensification of population and larger populations overall. Yet the subsequent history of agriculture in the delta has been one of intensive agriculture without intensive settlement. Irrigated agriculture on reclaimed delta wetlands created a landscape without people. It was productive, but it was empty.

The trend toward corporate lands barren of families began early in the delta's agricultural history. Sucheng Chan calculated farm sizes and population figures for two representative California townships, one in Sacramento County, on drier, "mainland soils," and the other in the central delta, where the Tide Land Reclamation Company reclaimed peat lands. In 1860, nearly 30 percent of farms on mainland soils were 80 acres or smaller, and just 17 percent were larger than 320 acres. Twenty years later, small farms continued to dominate this area. In the central delta, by contrast, two-thirds of farms in 1860 were larger than 320 acres, but almost no land was actually cultivable because it remained flooded. Reclamation brought these waterlogged lands into use, and the high cost of developing land led to ever-larger farms. By 1880 most delta farms actually cultivated more than 320 acres.[92] These trends continued into the twentieth century, as speculators and corporate farmers moved to drain and irrigate marginal lands that had once been too difficult or costly to bring into production. With the aid of federal dredging and flood control, and the spur of valuable new crops like asparagus, potatoes, and sugar beets, delta landowners reclaimed far more delta wetlands after 1880 than they had to that point.[93]

In the decades after J. Ross Browne praised reclamation as the key to a productive, happy society, functionally every part of the Sacramento-San Joaquin delta was brought into production. Because of the surrounding, tidally lifted channels, draining delta marshes also simultaneously prepared the land for irrigation. When California's Division of Water Resources mapped the San Joaquin valley in 1931, every acre of the basin lying within the delta was shown as farmland, and every acre of that farmland was shown as irrigated. The delta was, in other words, totally agricultural, entirely irrigated, and completely improved land. Nothing could be done to make it better. It was the perfect agricultural landscape.[94]

But this perfect farmland bore little resemblance to Thomas Jefferson's idealized agricultural landscape, with its harmony of economic production and social reproduction. By 1929 the delta was an entirely corporate agricultural world. Carey McWilliams, one of the region's most acute observers, described an agricultural world run on the scale and principles of modern industry. "Although the fact is still not generally recognized," he wrote, "the distinction between 'industry' and 'agriculture' is rapidly disappearing. More and more, our agricultural activities are being taken over by nonagricultural interests."[95] Reclamation helped create a social landscape that was hard to love. But, like it or not, even critics like Carey McWilliams had to accept the triumph of reclamation. By the second decade of the twentieth century, it was impossible to ignore the wealth made in reclaimed marshland in the Sacramento-San Joaquin delta.

Some of the dreams of men like William B. Hyde had come true: delta farmland efficiently brought together transportation, irrigation, and fertile soil. Abundant capital, machinery, pesticides, and cheap labor combined with exceptionally fertile soils to make delta farms among the most productive per acre of any in the world. Successive specialty crops, including asparagus, potatoes, and sugar beets, were featured in this export-dominated agriculture. Reclamationists' efforts to win land from the marshes had succeeded in the sense that profits were up in the delta region.

By the 1930s, the great freshwater tidelands of California were essentially given over to producing a few commodities for sale. It was barely a place for people. The delta region had few towns, and they possessed few of the things that made for thriving human communities. This was a landscape where people worked but did not stay. The workers were migrants. The land's owners lived far away, often as shareholders in insurance companies or other corporations that owned delta farms purely as investments. This fact was decried by some but baldly embraced by others. Sociologist Paul Taylor quoted an unnamed defender of California's agricultural structure: "The old-fashioned hired man is a thing of the past. . . . There is no place for him, and the farmer who does not wake up to the realization that there is a caste in labor on the farm, is sharing too much of his dollar with labor. . . . We are not husbandmen. We are not farmers. We are producing a product to sell."[96] If the delta was not a place for people, it was no more a place for the native animals and plants that had proved the region's remarkable fecundity. Except for the vast seasonal crops that rotated through the soil, plants and animals were unwanted pests to delta farmers. Where the delta had once been defined as the place where rushes grew, by the 1930s botanists had to hunt for large tule stands.

Prior to human reengineering, the Sacramento-San Joaquin delta was highly dynamic. Seasonally wet or dry, it was dominated by marsh grasses (rushes) that over centuries laid down enormously thick layers of dead vegetation. In the wet, low-oxygen conditions of the delta, these layers of dead grasses slowly built up the acid, organic soil called peat. Another few million years, and this peat would have become coal. But all this stored carbon was sequestered in peat dozens of feet thick. Making farms from wetlands released millions of tons of carbon dioxide into the atmosphere, one of California's great contributions to global climate change. Together with other tidal wetlands of the greater San Francisco

Bay Area, the vast tule marshes buffered the transition from fresh to saltwater habitats. The delta's riches sustained diverse and abundant fish, waterfowl, and mammals.

Simplifying this complex waterscape into a rational agricultural landscape required massive investment and tremendous infusions of human labor and fossil fuels. State and federal governments also subsidized landownership and land monopoly in the delta region through low land prices. Eventually, with subsidies from the U.S. Army Corps of Engineers, reclamationists achieved a working—though tenuous—control over flooding, and delta agriculture became extraordinarily economically productive. This wealth was not equally shared. To some observers, the Sacramento-San Joaquin delta became a kind of capitalist dystopia.[97] New Deal–era reformers described the green and fertile fields of the delta as a social desert. Secretary of the Interior Harold L. Ickes assailed federally subsidized water for large central valley landowners. The struggle between large landowners and advocates of small farms, he said, "is the age-old battle over who is to cash in on the unearned increment in land values created by a public investment."[98] Labor commissioner and activist Carey McWilliams passionately criticized the agricultural delta in the 1930s, describing a depopulated landscape worked by migrant laborers. Delta farms, he said, were "factories in the fields," where workers were replaceable cogs in the machine and profits flowed out to absentee landowners.[99]

Later observers mourned the ecological devastation wrought in the simplified agricultural landscape. When the wetlands went, so did unique species of plants, fish, and animals, including the magnificent tule elk.[100] This social and ecological disaster was made possible only through the concerted efforts of individuals, corporations, and state and federal governments, all of whom sacrificed financially.

Dystopia was never inevitable. The efforts that remade the delta generally were backed by faith in a brighter, not a darker, future. But in practice, controlling where and when water flowed—attempting to manage rivers and tides—remade both nature and society in unanticipated and unwanted ways. Landownership became concentrated, and so did authority to manage the water. Control of water and control of land became inseparable, mutually supporting, and ultimately mutually destructive. There were many possible futures for the delta landscape. But once reclamationists chose one path—the path of for-profit drained farmland—they committed themselves and later generations to an increasingly desperate struggle against tides, floods, and subsidence. Historian Donald Worster points out that all societies that depend on the control of water initially have a choice of whether to pay the inherent terrible social and ecological costs. But once people make that choice, their options suddenly narrow: "In every case there was a critical moment when they might have refused to do so, when they might have rejected large-scale irrigation and its social consequences. Once that moment had passed, however, and a decision to go ahead had been made, they found they had forged for themselves a fate they could not easily undo."[101]

Worster suggests sympathy for the people caught up in "hydraulic societies," trapped in a downward spiral of their own making. Nothing is sadder than the irony of delta reclamation: a dream that was supposed to produce a productive new world instead created wealth for some, but misery for others and an ecologically impoverished landscape for later generations. Reclamationists got to make a choice, but in choosing to drain the freshwater tidelands, they took choices away from their grandchildren.

Reclamationists did not want to remake the natural world of the delta for the mere joy of dominating the earth. They wanted to "finish" an odd and alternately threatening or useless landscape of marshlands into a familiar and productive agricultural landscape. Draining marshes and building levees to stop flooding were fundamentally *constructive* actions. In fact, nineteenth-century reclamationists have much in common with twenty-first-century restorationists. The comparison should be sobering for those who recommend once again remaking the waterscape of the freshwater tidelands.

Reclamationists divided the delta into public and private spaces. As levees claimed land from the wetlands they separated private farmland and privately maintained irrigation works from publicly maintained riverbeds and navigable waterways.[102] But the separation of private and public was never as neat as levees promised. Private profits in fact depended on public maintenance. American taxpayers made reclaimed land profitable by providing the U.S. Army Corps of Engineers' massive California dredges. California and federal laws promoted drainage as a positive good that would reclaim wet wastelands as farmland, making farmers and investors wealthy while providing revenue to local and national governments. Property mattered in pushing nineteenth-century Americans to drain the delta's tidal wetlands to make productive farm- land. But ownership did not mean control, as floods demonstrated repeatedly. Water inescapably tied together the delta landscape, giving life to and destroying public and private land alike.

What seemed like good ideas in the nineteenth century created a cas- cade of consequences in the twentieth century and impossible choices in the twenty-first. Draining and watering the delta ultimately depended on controlling the Sacramento and San Joaquin Rivers upstream. After the state and federal governments dammed the rivers, the delta increas- ingly became an in-between place, a valve in the giant plumbing net- work that sent Sacramento River water south to irrigate cotton and flush toilets in southern California. By the 1960s the delta's islands were less valuable as farmland than as barriers preventing salt water from the bay from contaminating the water supply of millions of people hundreds of miles to the south. The delta's subsiding islands—holes in the water sur- rounded by thin walls of soil and rock—now emerged as the weakest link in the enormously expensive and fragile hydraulic network that sus- tained the nation's largest state and most powerful economy.

This threat to California's water supply only increased in following decades. One of the world's longest continuously operating tide gauges is at Fort Point, near the Golden Gate. Since 1854, the Fort Point gauge has faithfully recorded the two high and two low tides that occur each day. But in addition to marking this daily tidal range, the gauge has mea- sured a rise in the level of the sea itself. Rising sea levels are a threat to all human constructions around San Francisco Bay. But no area is more im- periled than the already fragile delta. As tides rise, they threaten to over- whelm the levees and undo more than a century of labor. The history of the delta, the accreted layers of decisions, leave those in the present with fewer choices now that the tide is rising.[103]

Similar unexpected consequences accrued in other parts of San Francisco Bay. As we will see in the next chapter, nineteenth-century land speculators claimed "swamplands" in the salt marshes of what we now call Silicon Valley. These men grew oysters rather than crops, but some of the same basic issues were at work in both the delta and south bay. Similar questions resonated around the bay and over the centuries: which productive use is best, who benefits, and what is the right and proper use of land?

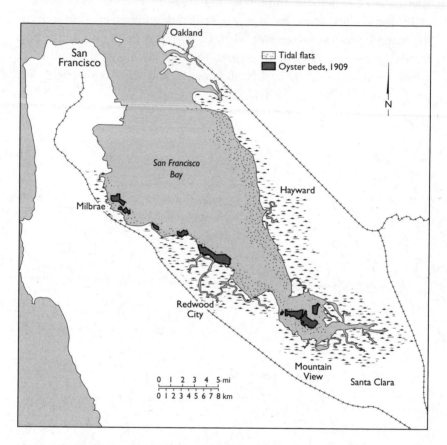

Map 5. Oyster beds and tidal lands of south San Francisco Bay, 1900–1910.

FOUR An Edible Bay

In 1902, twenty-two-year-old Oakland writer Jack London published his first book, an adventure story for boys. In the novel, London's hero runs away from a comfortable middle-class home to test his mettle in the rough world of the San Francisco waterfront. Plucky but naïve, Joe Bronson soon finds himself sailing down San Francisco Bay in a rickety sloop called the *Dazzler*, piloted by hard-drinking French Pete and his tough orphan sidekick, the 'Frisco Kid. The *Dazzler* joins a small fleet of boats congregating in the tidal flats along the eastern shoreline of San Francisco Bay. Keeping a wary eye out for heavy weather, French Pete orders Joe and the Kid to drag a triangular piece of steel, an oyster dredge, over the bay's muddy bottom. Working hard, the *Dazzler*'s crew hauls up mud, slime, and a few oysters with each long tack through the oyster beds. Joe is disappointed at the day's meager take of oysters, but he soon learns that this work is a sham, an alibi. Under cover of darkness, French Pete intends to leave the abandoned oyster beds off Alameda and raid the commercial oyster beds in the Millbrae marshes farther down the bay.[1]

Young Joe Bronson was an unwilling accomplice because he and the 'Frisco Kid stole another man's property. They were pirates—oyster pirates. The muddy bottom off Alameda belonged to a San Francisco corporation. The owners shipped juvenile oysters by train all the way from the Atlantic coast and hired men to spread oysters along plots of bay mud. Oyster growers had purchased these tidelands from the state of California, and their muddy property was as real as, and more valuable than, any farmland. Despite the absence of fences or buildings on the oyster beds, the mudflats were as much private property as lots in downtown San Francisco. In taking oysters from the turbid water, Joe Bronson and his companions broke the eighth commandment and state law.

In his moralistic novel, Jack London saves his fallen hero when Joe and the reformed 'Frisco Kid foil a bank robbery, earning the gratitude of society and the respect of Joe's father. London's young readers learn their lessons: obey your father; stay out of boats with strange men; crime doesn't pay. But in real life, as London well knew from his own experience, oyster piracy was both more rewarding and more dangerous than he described.[2] The happy ending to The Cruise of the Dazzler belies the real tensions between oyster growers and oyster pirates at the turn of the twentieth century in San Francisco Bay.[3] At stake were persistent questions in American history: Who should have access to natural resources? And to whom did the bay belong?[4]

THE ECONOMIC BAY

Those who lived along its shores in the nineteenth and early twentieth centuries made San Francisco Bay a productive economic landscape. People went to the bay to make money and to obtain food. The estuary sustained a range of economic activities, from commercial fishing to grazing cattle in the salt marshes and gathering duck eggs. Commercial fishermen took oysters, salmon, sturgeon, shrimp, crabs, shad, and a number of other valuable fish from the bay. According to the federal census before 1910, every one of California's top fisheries operated in San Francisco Bay and on its shorelines.[5] Although less reliable figures exist for hunting, it is clear that market hunters shot thousands of ducks, geese, and other waterfowl each year for sale in San Francisco's markets.[6] Men hunting for their own tables, or for informal sale, may have taken thousands more.[7]

The bayshore offered other ways to make money as well. From the Spanish era forward, mission and rancho cattle herds traditionally grazed over the entire bay region, unencumbered by fencing. Cattlemen allowed their stock to graze on grasses at the margin of the salt marshes, especially where freshwater streams ran into the bay. These marsh grasses must have been particularly valuable after annual summer drought withered grasses on the surrounding hills.[8] Salt makers used the bayshore in other ways, trapping the salty water of the bay inside shallow pools and allowing sun and wind to evaporate the water away, leaving behind a crop of salt crystals. In 1868 a local business chronicler reported that eighteen salt companies employed 150 workers, producing ten thousand tons of salt worth about $80,000. Salt makers raked in money by selling their product to a variety of industries in the West, from salmon canneries to silver mines.[9] During the nineteenth and early twentieth centuries, then, fishers, hunters, stockmen, and salt makers all participated in a thriving economy based on the estuary and its shoreline.

This estuarine economy converted natural resources, such as grass, fish, and seawater, to cash. But a second group of people made their living from the bayshore. Their economy was based only partly on cash. Following patterns begun by Ohlone peoples centuries before, nineteenth-century women and men gathered duck eggs, trapped fish, hunted animals, collected firewood, and harvested mussels, clams, and oysters from the shoreline. These people used the bay but did so in ways that were only partly mediated by markets. Unknown numbers of people supplemented their household economies by unquantifiable amounts. The lack of data on these informal economies has made both the gatherers and their shoreline less visible to historians, and it has obscured the importance of their activities, which collectively I will call foraging.

For foragers, the world was, literally, their oyster. They took what they wanted for free from a bay brimming with shellfish, fish, waterfowl, and useful marsh plants. In doing so they maintained forms of common-use behavior that were disappearing on solid land. Everywhere in the industrializing nineteenth-century world, poor people lost access to traditional common lands and the products they gathered there. E. P. Thompson famously wrote of the struggles of English country folk forced into wage labor in cities following the enclosure of their common grazing and fishing lands.[10] Historians join anthropologists and legal theorists when they write about struggles to retain common-use rights in industrializing societies. Some of the best U.S. case studies are from Atlantic coastal communities with strong common-access traditions. Anthropologist Bonnie McCay has written about early nineteenth-century battles between traditional users of New Jersey shellfish beds and those who sought exclusive access.[11] When oyster growers gained the legal right to exclusive access to areas long treated as commons, local people resisted by stealing shellfish, kicking off a series of "oyster wars."[12] Historian Louis Warren demonstrated that deer hunters who refused to obey game laws in Pennsylvania saw themselves not as criminals but as defending a tradition of free access to wild meat. Rural people often resisted conservationists in the late nineteenth century. In New York's Adirondack Mountains, in Yellowstone National Park, and in the Grand Canyon country of Arizona, residents fought—sometimes killed and died—to defend their customary hunting and fishing privileges in the face of national efforts to create landscapes without people, wilderness, and national parks. In these examples, private landowners or landless people resisted state and federal agencies' efforts to restrict access to public lands.[13]

Need and tradition compelled local people to cling to their historic rights to hunt and gather in tidal landscapes. European immigrants and Indians alike valued the shoreline as a "zone of abundance," whose shellfish and waterfowl were an important safety net in hard times.[14] Indigenous peoples struggled to retain access to traditional hunting, fishing, and gathering areas on the water's edge. This behavior is one element of a way of life once common in preindustrial North America but increasingly known only indirectly and retrospectively by historians and anthropologists. In the San Francisco Bay Area, foraging today is a remnant of indigenous and preindustrial economies based on diversity rather than intensity.[15]

The strategy of gathering and hunting seasonally abundant foods from nearby landscapes was an outstanding characteristic of central California tribal economies. The San Francisco Bay region has a Mediterranean climate dominated by a dry season and a wet season, both of which are prone to extremes. Drought can last for decades, or a series of wet years may lead to exuberant vegetation. Native peoples responded by basing their economies on complexity and diversity, harvesting widely rather than depending solely on a handful of favored species. Their practices of burning grasslands, pruning shrubs, and sowing grass seeds helped maintain a garden-like edible landscape around San Francisco Bay. Ethnobotanist Kat Anderson calls this strategy "managing the domesticated environment."[16] While not a commons in the European tradition, the tidelands were treated opportunistically by native peoples, as a predictable source of food and other resources.[17]

Yet despite the extensive literature on foraging and common lands, historians have had little to say about these topics in the American West, perhaps because there is no well-known tradition of common use in the West as there is in the eastern United States and Europe. The symbol of the West is more properly the pile of tin cans in front of a shanty or the extravagant imported items on the menu of a gold rush restaurant. Western Americans, as historian Patty Limerick and others have reminded us, often brought everything they needed to conquer the new land.[18] People did, however, eat locally, and eating locally was a simple act with profound consequences.

Commons are distinct from lands improved or created by human agency. Bonnie McCay cites Justinian's *Institutes* as the authority that defined tidelands as commons because they pertain to the ocean, because they are water: "By the law of nature these things are common to mankind—the air, the running water, the sea and consequently the shores of the sea." In English common law, sea and land were exclusive empires of nature. The shore above the tide line was land, and therefore property; below the tide line it was ocean, and therefore commons. In practice, English jurists held that navigation was the key to Justinian's definition. If a river or shallow sea was used for transporting goods, that waterway fell under the category of commons. Nonnavigable waters could be taken up and enclosed by individuals.[19] In Mexican California, Mexican law, following Spanish and Roman law, held that submerged lands were the property of the king, and thus of the nation. This law exempted the tidal wetlands from the land grants that otherwise blanketed the lands around San Francisco Bay. Mexican ranchers and the Americans who followed often grazed their herds in the extensive grasslands of the salt-marsh commons.[20] Grazing was perhaps the least direct means of using the baylands. More common, although less visible to historians (in the sense that so few people bothered to document their own behavior), was collecting goose and duck eggs, spearing fish and frogs, and hunting waterfowl. Residents of the bay region continued to use the bayshore habitats for such productive though not necessarily market-oriented activities in the nineteenth century as others had done for the millennia of native presence in the region.[21]

Foraging therefore embraced a wide range of productive activities in the lands and shallow waters of San Francisco Bay. But clams and oysters were the most accessible and valuable of all tidal resources, as well as some of those most affected by the environmental changes occurring in the nineteenth- and twentieth-century baylands. From a key element in native economies of the region, shellfish became a reliable source of free protein for working-class and poor urban dwellers and a multimillion-dollar industry, the state's most valuable fishery, from the 1870s to the 1910s. San Francisco Bay's shellfish are quintessential tideland products whose story captures the human struggle to control the tidelands' productivity and shows the consequent changing environmental conditions of San Francisco Bay's tidal margin. The story of shellfish insistently raises the question of who should have access to the bay's resources. We begin first by considering the nature of foraging, that most ancient of human economic activities.[22]

PEOPLE OF THE SHELLS

San Francisco Bay's first residents made great use of the bay's plentiful indigenous shellfish species. Indians ate so many oysters, clams, and mussels that the empty shells piled up into bleaching heaps. As recently as 1900, a conchologist noted "the kitchen-middens and aboriginal shell-heaps and mounds that are so numerous on the adjacent shores."[23] As they had been for millennia, shellmounds were a fixture of the nineteenth-century shoreline. Even casual visitors to San Francisco Bay in the nineteenth century knew shellfish were important to human history there because the landscape was quite literally littered with shells. Some of the mounds were enormous: tens of meters across, several meters high, and extending deep into the earth. Josiah Whitney's 1873 *Map of the Region Adjacent to the Bay of San Francisco* showed a few of the largest remaining mounds, including three near what is now the eastern footing of the Dumbarton Bridge.[24] University of California researcher N. C. Nelson, the first person to systematically map the shellmounds, cataloged more than four hundred remaining around the bay in 1909. The mounds ranged from about the size of a dumpster to the width of several football fields. Nelson remarked that his survey no doubt missed many shellmounds that were now invisible, since all around the bay shellmounds were being destroyed every day. Cities filled in around the mounds, contractors excavated the shells to use as a foundation for roads and railroads, and entrepreneurs sold the shells to farmers as lime, a soil conditioner.[25]

In terms of sheer size and antiquity, San Francisco Bay's shellmounds were a match for anything constructed by native peoples on the Pacific coast. In size and composition they bear a striking resemblance to shellmounds left by other coastal peoples around the world. In the nineteenth century, as the discipline of archaeology came into being, European and American amateur enthusiasts began to explore the human past that lay scattered around them. Archaeologists were particularly inspired by the example of Danish researchers, who systematically unearthed shellmounds along the Baltic Sea during the 1860s.[26] One of those inspired was Jeffries Wyman, the first curator of the Peabody Museum at Harvard.

In 1868, Wyman used an analogy from modern life to persuade his readers that going through ancient trash could be intellectually rewarding: "Any one who would take the trouble on going to a strange city, to examine the rubbish in its suburbs and streets, and carefully collect and compare the fragments of pottery, pieces of cloth, of paper, of cordage, the bones of different animals used as food, worked pieces of stone, wood, bone, or metal, might gain some insight into the modes of life of the inhabitants, and form a fair conception of the progress they had made in the arts of civilization."[27]

Wyman's insight that middens, or shell heaps, could be excellent historical sources was taken up with fervor at the University of California. A series of Berkeley archaeologists, including W. Schenk, Max Uhle, John C. Merriam, and N. C. Nelson, explored San Francisco Bay shellmounds.[28] Uhle's 1902 excavations proved something mundane and yet powerful: human beings had stayed in this one spot on the east bay shoreline for many centuries, eating basically the same shellfish species, without great changes in population. (Not until the application of radiocarbon dating would archaeologists understand just how old the shellmounds really were.) Shellmounds were proof that human beings had found that most precious of resources in an unpredictable world: a reliable and nearly inexhaustible source of food.[29]

Uhle, however, didn't see the societies that flourished along the bay shoreline in such positive terms. Instead, Uhle chose to focus, as Jeffries Wyman had long before, on the shellmound people's lack of "progress in the arts of civilization." For Uhle, the fact that Indian peoples ate the same foods for centuries, apparently cooked in the same manner, was not evidence of an admirable capacity to make a sustained living in a place. Eating shellfish was not sustainable development but rather proof of the backwardness and savagery of the primitives who continued to lazily harvest oysters and mussels rather than turning to agriculture. Confronted with a complex manmade structure containing burials, house pits, food waste, cooking areas, and thousands of cultural artifacts, Uhle saw only a pile of garbage: "In the midst of the remnants of food cast aside by him, man clung to his place of abode, raising it more and more above the general level of the ground through the gradual accumulation of these materials. Hence these localities represent, in certain stages of human development, true but nevertheless low types of human dwelling places. The manner of procuring the essentials of life by collecting shells in itself indicates a low form of human existence."[30] Uhle did find some differences in the types of tools and animal remains as his workers burrowed vertically into the mound. The differences were great enough that Uhle described ten distinct strata in the mound. But these strata, he felt, were more alike than different.[31]

Other researchers working on some of the more than four hundred other mounds around the bay echoed Uhle's conclusions. There was so much agreement that it seemed pointless to some to continue studying the mounds. In 1912 the University of California Department of Anthropology directed its attention away from shellmounds and Bay Area archaeology toward ethnographic work with surviving Indian people in California. A later departmental researcher wrote that in 1912 the department had determined that shellmound work "promised so little of positive value that the resources of the department were diverted to rescue ethnographic information from the survivors of the last aboriginal generation of California Indian groups."[32] In the 1910s, California anthropologists shifted their attention to seemingly more fruitful ethnographic work with native peoples far from the urbanizing Bay Area.[33] But foraging, as Uhle acknowledged, existed not just in antiquity but also in modern and urban San Francisco of the nineteenth century.

In nineteenth-century California, foraging was an especially popular activity in the tidelands of San Francisco Bay, where rich shoreline habitats provided abundant, nutritious wild food within easy walking distance of the West's largest urban population. Fresh food was particularly welcome in gold rush–era San Francisco, where men recently arrived from Atlantic shores found little fresh food to buy and yet a familiar smorgasbord of intertidal species available for the taking. In the spring of 1851 the Daily Alta California observed, "The mud flats up in Happy Valley present an interesting view at low tide. About a thousand more or less of the great unwashed tribe of this city are there busily engaged in gathering crabs and clams on which the city epicures may feast. It is an interesting occupation, and the followers of it are usually up to the knees in the delicately scented mud that abounds in the classic vicinity of Rincon Point."[34] One of that "great unwashed tribe," a teenage miner from Plymouth, Massachusetts, wrote his father that packed, muddy Happy Valley "looks much like a muster field, *only more so.*" Seven years later the same man proudly recorded finding "plenty of muscles [*sic*] in the rocks along shore," which he collected in his handkerchief for dinner.[35]

The *Daily Alta California's* mockery notwithstanding, large numbers of newcomers to San Francisco ate what they could gather from the still-abundant salt marsh and tidal mudflats. The gold rush had brought Americans into a new world with one familiar landscape—the area between the tides—but it also led to some of the greatest environmental changes ever to occur in San Francisco Bay.

No human impact on San Francisco Bay has been more extensive or had more dramatic effect than the washing of sediment into the bay by nineteenth-century gold miners.[36] Miners wielding water cannons dumped stupendous quantities of rock and soil into streams as they mined Sierra Nevada heights. Miners found some gold, but for every ounce they captured, tons of soil washed downstream. In the Bear and Yuba Rivers, on the Feather River, and in nearly every one of the streams descending from the Sierra Nevada, hydraulic-mining debris filled up deep pools, collected in the river channels, and overflowed onto the floodplain. Inexorably, these mining "tailings" came down out of the mountains, pouring out onto the Sacramento and San Joaquin valley floors and raising the bed of the Sacramento River thirteen feet at the state capitol.[37] William Brewer, a member of a survey team crisscrossing the state in 1862, struggled for words to describe the scale of the flows in his journal: "The amount of soil removed in hydraulic mining must be seen to be at all appreciated. Single [mining] claims will estimate it by the *millions of tons,* the 'tailings' (refuse from the sluices) fill valleys, while the mud not only muddies the Sacramento River for more than four hundred miles of its course, but also is slowly and surely filling up the Bay of San Francisco."[38]

Brewer correctly predicted that mining debris would have its greatest effect at the bottom of the watershed. The impact was most obvious upstream, where boulders and gravel filled in the riverbeds. But immense

Figure 6. Hydraulic mining in the Sierra Nevada, 1860s. Used by permission of the Society of California Pioneers.

quantities of fine sediments—sand and clayey mud, called "slickens"—flowed onward and into the bays. This fine material remained in suspension longest, settling out as it reached the calm and brackish waters of Suisun and San Pablo Bays. More than a century after the end of hydraulic mining, large portions of San Francisco's bay floor are still paved with former Sierra soil.[39]

The quantities of sediment that gold rush miners liberated were staggering. Geologist Grove Karl Gilbert estimated that one and a half billion cubic yards of sand and mud poured out of the mountains. These numbers are so large as to defy imagination. Gilbert estimated that between

1856 and 1897, hydraulic mining debris directly filled 30 square miles of Suisun Bay to a depth of 3.3 feet. He estimated that mining debris covered 113 square miles of San Pablo Bay to a depth of 2.5 feet, and 272 square miles of San Francisco Bay lost about 8 inches of depth. Another way to conceive of the volume of hydraulic mining debris is that one and a half billion cubic yards is about eight times the amount of earth and stone removed in the decades of construction on the Panama Canal.[40]

The impact of this mud wave on bottom-dwelling species has never been calculated, but it must have been severe. Moving sediments smothered living animals and plants, as the bottoms of the bays were made permanently shallower. Sediments changed both the depth and the consistency of the bay floor. Writing seventy-five years after Gilbert, geologists noted that slickens in San Pablo Bay created a peculiar type of surface. A thin crust of sand covered deep mud deposited by nineteenth-century miners. The sand in effect "armored" the bottom with a sterile, highly abrasive surface, reducing habitat, preventing burrowing animals from penetrating the subsurface, and causing other unknown ecological effects, perhaps including changed current patterns.[41]

This debris wave coincided with one of the greatest climatic events in recorded California history. In 1862, rivers already filled with mining sediments had to absorb the heaviest known rainstorms in California history. So much water fell from the sky from November 1861 to January 1862 that the debris-choked rivers could not carry the flows. Spilling over banks, water flooded large areas of the inland valley, creating an "inland sea."[42] The new state capitol in Sacramento was drowned. So much river water poured into San Francisco Bay that the estuary became nearly entirely freshwater for as much as two weeks. Runoff pouring out of the Golden Gate pushed the mixing zone between fresh and salt water, normally located miles inland in San Pablo Bay, far out to sea. Most estuarine species were probably wiped out in a stroke, given their intolerance of freshwater and the duration of the flooding. The destructive effect of extremely low salinity could only have been magnified by the mud wave that paved the bay floor. One marine ecologist has speculated that the entire estuarine biota of San Francisco Bay may have been wiped out—"reset"—in those two weeks of flooding.[43]

AQUATIC INVASIONS

It is in this context—an estuary in the throes of change, its long-time animal communities devastated by flooding—that we must understand all other environmental change in San Francisco Bay in the late nineteenth century. The timing of the 1862 event was particularly important because in the following decade enormous numbers of new aquatic species were introduced to San Francisco Bay. These species found an estuary recently emptied of its indigenous species and uniquely accessible for colonization. Atlantic oysters and the species that hitchhiked with them would transform the region's eating habits and spark new conflicts between foragers and oyster growers.

All landforms contain a collection of organisms that have arrived from elsewhere or evolved together over time. Some such communities have evolved together for thousands or tens of thousands of years. Individual species can form close relationships over these long time spans, evolving to take advantage of specific opportunities for food or shelter. This concept is intellectually pleasing, connoting stability, order, and predictability. In practice, however, estuaries are not so mentally restful. Formed by a dynamic interplay between constantly down-cutting rivers and advancing seas that drown river valleys, estuaries occupy the active edge of a constantly migrating seashore. They are rich habitats, but they are also unpredictable. Those species that can handle the rapid (geologically speaking) environmental change in estuaries can do very well indeed. No habitat on earth is more conducive to converting minerals and sunlight into chlorophyll, cellulose, cartilage, muscle, and bone. A few square yards of estuarine mudflats or salt marsh can support unequaled densities of animals and plants.[44]

San Francisco Bay is very young even by estuarine standards, no more than ten thousand years old, and its palette of bottom-dwelling species—its "benthic community," in the language of ecologists—likely evolved elsewhere and colonized the estuary over the past few millennia. The bay's species were more or less common to the sheltered and brackish waters of the Pacific coast from present-day Canada to northern Mexico. It was a rich but not particularly diverse fauna.[45] When Europeans and their animal and plant servants arrived in the late eighteenth century, San Francisco Bay's rocky, sandy, and muddy bottom hosted mind-boggling numbers of a single native oyster, *Ostreola conchaphila;* a handful of native clam species, including the bent-nosed clam, *Macoma nasuta;* and just two species of mussels, together with a variety of less meaty mollusks.[46]

This simplicity changed dramatically in just a few decades of the nineteenth century. Human beings were largely responsible for increasing the biological diversity of the bay, but as they did so, they diminished the number and vitality of preexisting species. According to specialists in the field of biological invasion, San Francisco Bay is the most "invaded estuary in the world."[47] Human beings in fact deliberately introduced many of the species that "invaded" the bay. Federal, state, and local authorities worked hard to make California's rivers, lakes, and bays more productive, as they saw it, by adding edible and marketable fish and shellfish. The idea was to add familiar fish and mollusks from Atlantic estuaries that could create new, rich fisheries. This early faith in biodiversity is ironic, since some of the species that U.S. fish commissioners and California fish commissioners labored to introduce to California are now some of the state's least-wanted creatures. Grass carp from China and Germany, for example, which now dominate the sloughs and lakes of California's central valley, have all but extirpated the warm-water fish communities present before 1850.[48]

Importing aquatic species was part of a larger effort to make North American lands more productive. Late nineteenth-century Americans worked hard to "improve" newly colonized Western landscapes, not only by dredging, draining, and irrigating but also by adding familiar plants and animals. This attitude carried over to the water bodies of California. The mania for introductions that eventually brought carp and lobsters to San Francisco was part of a worldwide enthusiasm during the 1870s.[49] On April 2, 1870, California's legislature approved "an Act to provide for the restoration and preservation of fish in the waters of this State." The act created "Commissioners of the Fisheries for the State of California." The commissioners wanted to restore California's potential, not necessarily to bring back the past. They wanted to recreate the limitless abundance that they believed had characterized fisheries in California when Americans arrived, just twenty years earlier. But beyond simply restoring large numbers of fish and game to California's rivers and forests by requiring fish ladders and policing harvest, the commissioners planned to improve California's fisheries by adding new species from the Atlantic.[50]

Armed with a small state appropriation and cooperation from the national fish commission, the state's energetic new fish commissioners dedicated great effort to importing fish and shellfish valued in the east. In the 1870s and 1880s, California's fish commissioners and the national fish commission spent a large portion of their budgets hauling tanks of seawater across the country in a heroic effort to keep sea animals alive long enough to plant them in San Francisco Bay. No trip was more epic than the state's first attempt, in 1879, personally headed by fish enthusiast and hatchery promoter Livingston Stone. Train schedules were inexact in the early years, and Stone and his assistants struggled to keep their fragile cargo alive, adding ice and finally river water, all the while frantically exhorting the train crews. The team of fish managers labored three days without sleep in soaking wet clothing to keep a cargo of lobsters, pout, shad, and striped bass alive. Despite delays, all seemed to be going well until disaster struck. Crossing a rickety Nebraska bridge, a wooden trestle gave way and the aquarium car plunged into the water, bruising Stone and his assistant and dumping thousands of unlucky ocean fish into the Elkhorn River.[51] But Stone and company were not discouraged for long by the disaster. Stone and the fish commissioners went on to bring dozens of species across the country in improved aquarium cars.[52]

Historians have recently begun to revisit the issue of species introduction and the management of artificial fisheries in western North America. Livingston Stone appears often in these stories, which focus on hatchery production and the introduction of game fish such as eastern brook trout, striped bass, and American shad. But it is too often forgotten that the first aquatic species introduced to the Pacific coast were not fish but shellfish. Stone's publicly sponsored expeditions were dwarfed by private oyster growers' imports. In the first years of the gold rush, miners desperate for a taste of home paid high prices for canned oysters shipped around the tip of South America. Archeologists excavating the Hoff Store, a gold rush site in San Francisco's financial district, unearthed abundant evidence of the popularity of both fresh and canned oysters. Among the objects recovered there was a brass tin marked "Isaac Reckhow—Oysters—142 Liberty St—New York." Reckhow is listed in New York City directories as a pickle packer and dealer from 1847 to 1852, meaning that his hand-packed Atlantic oysters made the trip around the Horn of Africa during the first years of the gold rush.[53]

The real thing soon replaced canned oysters. In 1869 one of the first intercontinental trains connecting the Atlantic to the Pacific carried live oysters from New York Harbor to San Francisco Bay. In the following year, entrepreneurs replaced market-size mollusks with barrels full of cheaper spat, baby oysters attached to dime-sized pieces of shell. Local operatives transplanted the tiny oysters onto tidelands at a number of locations around the bay. Washed twice daily in the estuary's nutritious soup, Atlantic oysters rapidly fattened to market size. A staple food of working people, transplanted Atlantic oysters became a multimillion-dollar industry in California as they already were in the east. But San Francisco Bay oyster growers needed a constant supply from the east to maintain their fishery. Probably because of the Pacific's colder year-round temperatures, Atlantic oysters did not successfully spawn in San Francisco Bay or in other western estuaries, necessitating regular shipments from eastern estuaries.[54]

Atlantic oysters are an example of an introduced species that thrived in its new home but depended on the constant intervention of human beings to sustain it. Another, more familiar class of introduced species are known as "invasives." Scientists consider species invasive when they flourish in a new environment to such an extent that they displace native species. The same trains that carried Atlantic oysters as paying passengers also carried hitchhikers, including the eastern oyster's main parasite, the oyster drill. A species of clam that bores holes in oysters and eats them alive, the oyster drill is one of a class of opportunistic animals with a tendency to rapidly take over habitats and push out organisms already present.[55]

Another hitchhiker in the oyster barrels was equally successful and more welcome. Sometime after 1870, soft-shell clams, *Mya arenaria*, arrived in San Francisco Bay, probably in the oyster barrels.[56] Within a decade, medical doctor and shell collector W. Newcomb referred to *Mya* as "the now dominant clam of the fish stalls." Not only did *Mya* become the most important species for San Francisco Bay clammers, by 1881 it had spread from San Francisco to Monterey Bay and elsewhere along the northern California coast. Rather than regretting this rapid spread, University of California regent Robert Stearns encouraged sea captains to further assist the clam. "In the presence of the fact of the rapid increase of this truly excellent edible [in San Francisco Bay]," Stearns urged, "it would be a wise, public spirited act if the captains of our coasting vessels would take the trouble and incur the slight expense attending the planting of this clam at such points as their vessels touch at in the ordinary course of business."[57] In the language of the day, *Mya* improved San Francisco Bay. Fat and tasty, soft-shell clams were a familiar food making good in a new environment. In the flush of their first colonization of San Francisco Bay, soft shells were incredibly abundant, allowing diggers to harvest dozens of the bivalves simply by excavating a single hole in the mudflat at low tide. By 1921 one observer said *Mya* was the *only* clam in San Francisco markets.[58]

   Mya is representative of legions of other introduced species that successfully adapted to conditions in San Francisco Bay. Yet the *Mya* class—the tolerated immigrants, if you will—have become silent or at least unremarked partners in the bay ecosystem. Acceptance of *Mya* is well illustrated in the most impressive summary of recent bay research to date, the San Francisco Bay Area Wetlands Ecosystem Goals Project.[59] The scientists used *Mya* as the indicator of a key habitat as a keystone species ("species strongly influences community structure") in the intertidal zone and, because it is so abundant, as an easily studied indicator of the health of the bay's bottom-dwelling community.[60] In other words, *Mya* has become a fundamental part of San Francisco Bay's intertidal zone. It is a citizen of the biological community. The strange career of this clam, then, throws into question the usual interpretation of "invasive" species. For foragers, *Mya* was no unwanted invasive but rather a useful and valuable member of what would otherwise have been an impoverished ecological community. Like clams, oysters played a special role in working-class life, but where clams were free, oysters were not. Oyster harvest was complicated by property relationships.

Descriptions of waterfront life in nineteenth-century San Francisco are surprisingly rare, given the central role the bay played in the economic and cultural life of the western metropolis. The historian looks in vain for the rich records that other historians have used to reconstruct the social world of New York City's waterfront.[61] In the absence of these sources, it has been all too easy to forget that San Francisco Bay was once a working bay with something akin to the watermen's cultures of Long Island Sound and Chesapeake Bay. We know this vanished world partly through the work of novelist Jack London, a product of the bayshore working-class neighborhoods in West Oakland, Alameda, and San Francisco.

Jack London was born in 1876 to an unmarried couple in San Francisco. London's home life was chaotic, his mother and adoptive father moving frequently to find work. The boy's major source of stability was Virginia Prentiss, a former slave from Tennessee. Prentiss was London's wet nurse and essentially raised the boy through his infancy. Because Virginia Prentiss was married to a very light-skinned man and had light-skinned children, even some fellow members of her Shiloh A.M.E. church believed Jack London was her child.[62] But Jack London was not of the same class as the Prentisses. The Londons were never starvation poor, but the family's constant mobility betrays their poverty. Between the ages of ten and fifteen, Jack London lived in ten different homes in the working-class neighborhoods along the Oakland waterfront. London's African American surrogate mother, on the other hand, offered a stable home with well-defined values and a steadily employed male father figure.[63] It is not surprising, therefore, that so many of London's early fictional stories would feature middle-class boy runaways thirsting for freedom and manly experience, but inevitably end with the boys returning home to loving parents and material comfort. London himself knew well both the excitement of outdoor adventure and the desire for comfort and stability.

Jack London's childhood home, the waterfront neighborhood of West Oakland, was an integrated neighborhood in the 1890s. West Oakland was home to African American sea captains, lawyers, and Pullman car porters, as well as a larger number of working poor from all races. Class, not race, appears to have foiled Jack London's effort to marry Lucy Cauldwell, a childhood playmate whose father was a pillar of the local black community. London was a member of the working poor, far different from the respectable Cauldwells. London's biographer concludes, "Although the Cauldwell cousins may have found Jack's energy and cleverness appealing, he was not really one of them—not when it came to marriage."[64] The teenage Jack London was a waterfront rat and an oyster pirate. He made his income by stealing from the private oyster beds of the central bay.

London embraced oyster piracy after experiencing the grinding labor of industrial work. London's adoptive father worked as a watchman on Oakland's wharves, and the young boy spent much of his time there. The family briefly owned a small sailing skiff, which London learned to sail on San Francisco Bay. He fished for rock cod, explored the wharves, and hunted for ducks with his friend Frank Atherton.[65] As in other working families, every member had to contribute financially. Young Jack London endured hellish conditions as a child laborer in an Oakland cannery. The work was long, the pay poor, and the conditions frightful. London recalled deafening noise and his eyes strained in the near darkness amid the dangerous machinery. Seeking to escape the mill, after graduating from eighth grade, London borrowed money from Virginia Prentiss and bought a boat he called the *Razzle Dazzle*. With his sloop, London joined the gangs of young men who raided the privately owned beds of Atlantic oysters planted along the eastern shoreline of San Francisco Bay.[66]

London based his later writings about San Francisco Bay on his teenage experiences. His activities nearly killed him several times, and they left him an alcoholic, but the young author compiled a full career's worth of experiences to write about. London sailed as a whaling ship's boy to the South Seas, hiked over the Chilkoot Pass during the Klondike gold rush of 1898, joined an army of hobos marching on Washington, and became known as the "Boy Socialist" for his political activities in Oakland and San Francisco. All of these experiences became fodder for later semiautobiographical writings. But London's first book-length work dealt with the freedom and self-confidence he found as a waterman on San Francisco Bay.[67] The bay offered freedom in London's time, though it is indicative of the changes under way that London's recollections are almost the only evidence we have of a bygone era when the bayshore offered a living to those skilled and desperate enough to take it.

Jack London's stories were enormously popular. His ability to communicate his working experience to middle-class readers made London a celebrity. Like Theodore Roosevelt, London celebrated masculine virtues of hard work, outdoor activity, and a life lived courageously.[68] Requested by his editors at Houghton Mifflin to provide a biographical sketch for marketing purposes, London responded with a four-page autobiography. Describing his rough-and-tumble adolescence, he boasted of being a man among men in a thrilling and dangerous environment: "At fifteen [I] left home and went upon a bay life. San Francisco Bay is no mill pond by the way. I was a salmon fisher, an oyster pirate, a schooner sailor, a fish patrolman, a longshoreman, and a general sort of bay-faring adventurer—a boy in years and a man amongst men. Always a book, and always reading when the others were asleep; when they were awake I was one with them, for I was always a good comrade."[69]

London's experience set his stories apart from the typical literature—syrupy sentimental novels and pious morality tales—offered to boys in his era. His descriptions of racing across a foaming white-capped bay in an open boat—the tiller tucked between his legs, one hand on the sheet, and a pistol in the other—were exciting and believable, with details from real working life. In London's fiction, the protagonist was the patrolman who enforced the fish and game laws or the child accomplice, forced to steal oysters, who resists lawlessness. In his own life, however, London appeared equally willing to break the law or to enforce it. In the case of Atlantic oysters, the law was clear: no one might take oysters from lands leased by the state to an individual grower. But when oyster pirates like London stole shellfish from planted beds while pretending to harvest oysters from abandoned beds, they exploited a loophole in the statute. There was no way to tell which oysters had been legally harvested and which were stolen. The

Figure 7.   An oyster bed in Oakland. U.S. Coast and Geodetic Survey, 1857. National
Oceanic and Atmospheric Administration / Department of Commerce.

moral law was even less clear, given that the tidelands leased by the
state were property of the people of California, and that shellfish harvest was a tradition still carried out on the beaches and mudflats of the
bay. For the general public and for popular writers like London, oyster
beds symbolized the monopoly of common resources by privileged
capitalists. Oyster pirates could enjoy community sanction when they
violated this kind of private property. Jack London's choices and the
dilemma faced by hundreds of other oyster pirates were made possible
by the rise of a new industry in San Francisco Bay: private property
located in the former tidal commons.

THE RISE OF SAN FRANCISCO BAY'S OYSTER INDUSTRY

Oysters and clams were astonishingly popular in nineteenth-century America. Oysters in particular were almost omnipresent in the diet of residents of coastal cities. They were also eaten far inland. Oysters and other shellfish are adapted to low-tide conditions. They can create a nearly airtight seal by clamping their shells closed, and if kept in seawater in an insulated space, they will stay alive for several days. Thus, loggers in Idaho, meat packers in Chicago, and miners in Colorado could all enjoy fresh oysters in their diets. Canned oysters had an even more extensive market, reaching consumers all over the world.[70]

It is hard to understand this mania for shellfish today, when Americans are more likely to eat canned tuna than shellfish on a daily basis. But shellfish offer some of the highest food value of any creatures. One authority estimated that six Atlantic oysters served raw provided 100 percent of the recommended daily allowance of iron and copper, 50 percent of iodine, and about 10 percent of an adult's daily need for protein, calcium, phosphorus, vitamin A, and B vitamins. Soft-shell clams, including *Mya arenaria*, are among the best-known natural sources of vitamin B12.[71] Since the 1930s, nutritional scientists have known the tremendous mineral and vitamin content of oysters, prescribing shellfish for persistent iron deficiency, for example. In the age before refrigeration, clams and oysters were veritable vitamin pills, supplying essential nutrients to workers often poorly supplied with fresh fruits and vegetables.[72]

The nutritional value and convenience of shellfish were widely known and appreciated by indigenous people. For several thousand years local people relied on San Francisco Bay's original oyster, *Ostreola conchaphila*; bay mussel, *Mytilus edulis*; and Pacific clams, particularly the prolific surface-dwelling "bent-nosed" clam, *Macoma nasuta*.[73] Not only were shellfish nutritious, they were also abundant. European mariners noticed the molluscan wealth of the Bay Area. Eugene Duflot de Mofras, commanding a French round-the-world expedition, entered San Francisco Bay in 1841. Charting the bayshore and sounding its depths, Duflot de Mofras indicated a vast sweep of the east bay shoreline from near what is now the Port of Oakland all the way down to the mouth of Alameda Creek, saying, "Toute cette partie est entrecoupée de banc de Coquilles d'Huîtres" (All this part is occupied by a bank of Oyster Shells).[74] While it seems likely that Duflot de Mofras referred to dead shells—to past rather than present abundance—his declaration makes clear that the bay had once sustained immense numbers of native oysters.

Native peoples ate a wider variety of shellfish than the less imaginative Americans who followed. Archaeologists excavating a midden site in the foothills lying west of San Francisco Bay were surprised when they unearthed thousands of tiny shells from a diminutive salt marsh snail. Costanoan people had carried baskets of these tiny marine snails miles inland from the bayshore. After drying and weighing live horn snails still found in the remaining nearby salt marshes, the archaeologists nicknamed the species "popcorn snails" because shellmound builders apparently ate them by the handful, extracting a juicy and protein-rich bite from each crunchy shell.[75]

By volume, shellfish such as oysters, bay mussels, and horn snails make up the vast majority of shells in the Jasper Ridge site, as they do in most San Francisco Bay shellmounds. When Stanford researchers calculated the food value represented by so many shells and divided it by the estimated human population at the site, they were astonished at the daily volume of protein-rich shellfish consumed. In terms of daily protein eaten, Indian diets compared favorably to those of the average American and the average English factory worker in 1850.[76] A plate of oysters or a bowl of oyster stew, far from a luxury item, was an everyday meal that could keep a worker going in front of a forge, on the wharf, or in a steam laundry.

Contemporary descriptions make clear that oysters were ubiquitous in nineteenth-century San Francisco. Newspaper correspondent Mark Twain reported on an 1865 theft of oysters from underground storage areas in San Francisco (oysters were commonly stored under wet burlap sacks in basements for days at a time). Twain included stealing oysters on a list with massacre, rape, and firebombing churches.[77] San Francisco novelist Frank Norris, who strove to faithfully reproduce daily life, included oysters in his rendition of a typical turn-of-the-century San Francisco street scene: "There were corner drug stores with huge jars of

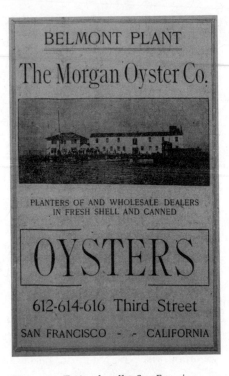

Figure 8. Eating locally. *San Francisco Call,* April 20, 1909. California Digital Newspapers Collection, Center for Bibliographic Studies and Research, University of California, Riverside, http://cdnc.ucr.edu.

red, yellow, and green liquids in their windows, very brave and gay; stationers' stores, where illustrated weeklies were tacked upon bulletin boards; barber shops with cigar stands in their vestibules; sad-looking plumbers' offices; cheap restaurants, in whose windows one saw piles of unopened oysters weighted down by cubes of ice, and china pigs and cows knee deep in layers of white beans."[78] For Norris, oyster sellers were a part of the daily life of San Francisco's working classes, as common and as popular as the espresso stands that now serve a more fastidious class of urban workers on the same city streets.

COMMERCIAL SHELLFISHERIES

At the close of the nineteenth century, oysters were America's greatest fishery. When in 1908 the U.S. Census Bureau conducted a special survey of American fisheries, oysters grown on all three coasts—Atlantic, Gulf, and Pacific—dominated the nation's most profitable harvests. Oystermen sold $15.7 million worth of the shellfish in 1908, almost 30 percent of the total value of all fishery products sold in the United States. Commercial growers raised and sold more than half of these animals. Growers sold $8.3 million worth of market-sized oysters from private beds, almost twice the value of oysters captured by fishermen in public waters. Seed oysters alone brought in nearly $2 million, as much as the annual harvest of lobsters or cod.[79] By volume, the sheer mass of oysters far surpassed every other American fishery except menhaden, a low-value, high-volume baitfish. The greatest oyster producers were on the Atlantic seaboard, serving booming industrial cities from Boston to Baltimore. On the Pacific coast, oysters were also an urban phenomenon. California's market oyster growers, all of whom operated in San Francisco Bay, were the state's biggest fishery earners in 1899 and 1904, falling just behind salmon fishers in 1908.[80]

The oysters making all this money were not the native oysters of San Francisco Bay. California's oyster industry was dependent on imports. The first immigrant oysters were larger and tastier relatives of San Francisco Bay's native *Ostreola conchaphila* brought from the Pacific Northwest. Between 1851 and 1869 a handful of entrepreneurs transported live adult oysters from Shoalwater (now called Willapa) Bay, north of the Columbia River, and stored them on mudflats near the city of San Francisco.[81] A handful of holding beds dotted the Marin shoreline, and others were found at the mouths of tidal inlets along the eastern shore of the bay, notably near present-day Richmond harbor and the mouth of the San Antonio Creek estuary, now the tip of Alameda Island. These sites were favored locales of San Francisco Bay's native peoples, and it is striking how closely the locations of commercial oyster beds correspond to ancient shellmounds.[82]

Such "Olympia" oysters from Washington Territory supplied the California market for a few years after 1850, and there were sporadic efforts to import another Pacific oyster species. Just in time for Christmas dinner in 1865, newspaperman Mark Twain reported that eight tons of shellfish had arrived from oyster beds in Mexico. For Twain, these were tastier than either the native San Francisco Bay oyster or its imported Northwest cousin. In Twain's opinion, Mexican oysters were "far superior to the poor little insipid things we are accustomed to here."[83]

But it was the completion of the transcontinental railroad that introduced a golden age of oysters in California. In October 1869, the following notice appeared in San Francisco's *Daily Alta California:* "The first carload of Baltimore and New York oysters in shells, cans, kegs, all in splendid order, has arrived, packed and shipped by the pioneer oyster house of the west, A. Booth, Chicago, Ill."[84] Booth & Company was an early national fishery concern, operating out of Baltimore and Chicago. The company also owned large salmon-canning operations on the Pacific coast. It appears that Booth & Co. sold mature eastern oysters in the San Francisco market and held some mature oysters in the bay for later sale. In 1871 the company sold its local infrastructure to the Morgan Oyster Company, a firm it may have previously supplied with seed oysters.[85] During the boom period from 1870 to 1920, commercial oyster growers built extensive and elaborate facilities fencing in large areas in the southern part of San Francisco Bay and constructing a series of "oyster houses," or raised platforms amid the fenced beds, in order to both process the oysters and house watchmen to protect the oysters from thieves.[86]

At first, oyster growers parked their newly imported oysters on the shallow mudflats across the bay from the city of San Francisco. These beds were close to markets in San Francisco but were otherwise less than ideal locations for young oysters. Located on some of the shallowest flats in the entire San Francisco Bay system, the oyster beds were exposed and prone to roiling in winter storms. Situated near the mouth of San Pablo Bay, they also endured annual floods of cold, sediment-laden mountain runoff from the Sacramento and San Joaquin Rivers. On several occasions in the 1850s and 1860s, newspapers reported huge losses of oysters from these beds. Despite these dangers, oyster growers did not shift their operations to the more sheltered tidelands of the far south and west bay until after 1870.

Figure 9. Fenced oyster beds, San Francisco Bay, 1889. National Oceanic and Atmospheric Administration / Department of Commerce.

There were both ecological and human reasons why oyster growers stayed put for so long. South of San Francisco, the nineteenth-century bay was shallower and marshier. The edges of marsh faded almost imperceptibly into tidal channels and out toward open water. Miles of marsh might separate solid ground from the open water of the bay. Euro-American settlement patterns reflected the difficulty of accessing the bay. Into the twentieth century, the south bay was largely rural, with towns concentrated at "landings" on tidal sloughs where shallow-draft sailing vessels could sail through the marshes with cargoes of grain, vegetables, and hay for San Francisco markets.[87] The sloughs permitted easy access

Figure 10.   Tonging farmed oysters, 1889. National Oceanic and Atmospheric Administration / Department of Commerce.

to the tidal flats for anyone in a shallow skiff, which may have concerned oyster growers. Jack London's stories suggest that oyster growers were reluctant to move their beds to a better physical location because oyster thieves lurked in the south bay.

Yet commercial growers did move their operations southward in the 1870s. This action helps explain a key paradox of the Atlantic oyster industry in the bay: namely, that the industry's greatest success coincided with the period of greatest disturbance from hydraulic mining. Growers survived the inhospitable conditions by moving their beds as far from the cold, mud-laden rivers as possible, to the extreme south bay. There, the influence of sediment was lessened and salinity levels were more stable. While mining debris filled in fifty feet of river channel in the mountains and several feet of Suisun and San Pablo Bays, it laid down only a few inches of mud in the protected south bay. Growers also adapted by moving their oysters several times between initial seed planting and harvest. This protected oysters from suffocating in sediments and ensured that they would grow.

MONOPOLY AND DECLINE

By the end of the nineteenth century, oysters constituted the most valuable and concentrated fishery in California. In 1888, four companies owned six hundred acres of productive oyster beds in San Francisco Bay, valued at $300,000. Together with approximately four hundred tons of canned oysters brought from the East, local oyster sales in the San Francisco Bay Area reached the staggering annual sum of $1.25 million.[88] At the turn of the twentieth century, oysters were a basic part of the western diet and a key California industry, and no one predicted the oyster's fate in the following decades.

The first decades of the twentieth century saw tremendous changes in the bay's water quality. A boom in population in the Bay Area brought increased sewage flows into the bay. As California fruit and vegetable growers in the Sacramento and San Joaquin valleys shipped their wares to south San Francisco Bay canneries, cannery wastes flowed into what was already the warmest, least-flushed part of the estuary. Industrial production in the region also skyrocketed as slaughterhouses and dairies increased production to keep up with demand. Entirely new industries appeared on the bayshore, including three oil refineries on San Pablo and Suisun Bays and a copper smelter at the Carquinez Strait.[89] Prolonged drought in the 1910s coincided with a great increase in the amount of irrigated farmland in the central valley. In a state still largely without water storage capacity, rivers dwindled to trickles. The influx of freshwater from the Sacramento and San Joaquin Rivers reached an all-time low in 1919. Ocean water pushed so far inland in the absence of downward water pressure from the rivers that the river tasted salty at Sacramento. Salinity levels in the oyster beds of the already salty south bay skyrocketed, with unknown effect on oysters. What is known, from other estuaries such as

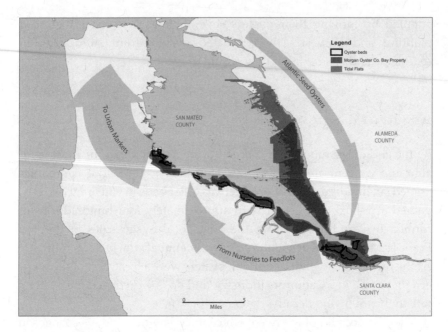

Figure 11.   Morgan Oyster Company property, 1880s–1927. Gabriel Lee, Alec Norton, Andy Robichaud, and Matthew Booker, Spatial History Project, 2009, www.stanford.edu/group/spatialhistory/.

the Chesapeake, is that rapid changes in salinity or temperature can stress oysters and make them vulnerable to disease or other dangers that would otherwise not be fatal. The stresses of the early century were severe.[90]

Perhaps more than any other form of human food culture, shell fishing depends directly on high-quality, healthy habitat. Oyster abundance and size mirror the productivity of the waters oysters live in. Up to World War I, the oystermen of San Francisco Bay reaped a succulent harvest of fat, tasty bivalves. But after a banner year in 1915, oyster harvests unexpectedly dipped to two million pounds in 1916 and then crashed to less than nine hundred thousand pounds in 1917. For the next three years, oyster harvests recovered slightly, but after 1921 San Francisco Bay's oyster production slumped again. By 1933 the industry was finished.[91] San Francisco Bay's collapse paralleled a more gradual decline in oyster production nationwide. From a high of about two hundred million pounds taken annually from 1890 to 1910, U.S. oyster harvests fell to fifty-four million pounds in 1954.[92]

The rise and fall of San Francisco Bay's oyster industry shows the familiar boom and bust of many fisheries. The classic fishery pattern is a sudden rise in landings as fishermen rush to exploit a new fishery, followed by an even swifter decline due to overharvesting. Garrett Hardin described this pattern, in which unregulated access to common property such as fish inevitably serves to destroy the resource, as the "tragedy of the commons."[93] California's oyster industry superficially resembles this model, and ruling out overharvest scholars have looked for a link to pollution as the key factor.[94]

Even before oyster harvests crashed, signs appeared that something was wrong. Around 1905 San Francisco oystermen reported that their bedded Atlantic oysters were thinner and grew more slowly than in years past. Oyster growers described shellfish as "thin" and "watery," in contrast to the fast-growing transplanted oysters they had managed for three decades. The California oyster industry's foremost scholar attributes the change to pollution and says that this was the consensus at the time among oyster growers and scientists.[95] Yet in 1914 growers reported an exceptional growth spurt in oysters on the Burlingame beds, and local oyster growers had always seen peaks and valleys in their production.[96]

Before blaming the oyster's disappearance on contaminated water, we might ask what growers meant by "pollution." In the 1910s and 1920s, scientists suspected that changing water quality was responsible for the sudden failure of eastern oysters to grow, or "fatten." At least three separate University of California studies monitored bay waters in these two decades. The Berkeley scientists were explicitly looking for evidence of pollution, which they defined in contemporary terms as the presence of organic chemicals resulting from biological wastes, particularly sewage and effluents from tanneries and slaughterhouses.[97] The problem with sewage is not that it is toxic to oysters, but rather that it carries diseases that can harm human consumers. Sewage can also excessively fertilize coastal waters. Oysters may benefit from some sewage, as they apparently did in the late nineteenth-century bay. Oysters do, after all, live in nutrient-rich estuarine waters. But too many nutrients can cause problems for both oysters and their human consumers.

Pollution in early twentieth-century San Francisco Bay mostly meant organic pollutants from slaughterhouses, tanneries, and particularly from toilets. These were the classic polluting agents of the early industrial city.[98] Indirectly, sewage and industrial wastes may have greatly influenced oyster and clam populations. Certainly, contemporaries connected rising sewage wastes to declining fisheries. In 1913, commenting on the effect of wastewater on fisheries, Stanford zoologist Harold Heath speculated, "While the wastes discharged from cities and towns may not directly seriously disturb clams or fish, they may destroy the much more delicate organisms on which these larger animals subsist and so vitally affect the fishing industry. Without much doubt this is now an important factor in various localities."[99]

Municipal wastes, laden as they were with chemicals as well as feces, certainly may have played a role in damaging oyster productivity. But biological waste seems less likely to be directly implicated in the destruction of oyster beds because oysters in general have done quite well even in waters heavily fertilized by human waste. Nevertheless, it is not surprising that oystermen would have suspected that sewage was to blame for their oyster's poor performance. Sewage filled the bay as it did coastal waters everywhere. Not until after World War II did a majority of American cities provide even rudimentary sewage treatment (screens), and only in the 1950s did the federal government begin providing the funding that created excellent sewage treatment throughout the nation. The result was that coastal waters were probably at their filthiest—or most fertile—during the first decades of the twentieth century.[100]

Attempting to establish the actual harm from human waste, scientists at the University of California looked for and measured hydrogen sulfide, a foul-smelling gas associated with the breakdown of organic waste. Hydrogen sulfide is prevalent when waste-consuming bacteria use up all the oxygen in water, and it is therefore an indicator of dangerously low oxygen levels in water bodies. Near sewer outfalls in Oakland's industrial waterfront and along the nearby Alameda shoreline, hydrogen sulfide levels were so high that they "caused an inestimable amount of damage to the paint of buildings and marine structures."[101] Nevertheless, three Berkeley scientists concluded in 1928 that despite tremendous waste inputs along every shoreline of San Francisco Bay, hydrogen sulfide levels were high in only a few limited locations and in none of the known oyster beds. Strong tidal currents effectively mixed effluent into the ocean and river waters of the estuary, keeping the whole well oxygenated. Despite the sewage, oysters were not asphyxiating.[102] Yet even where human waste had no harmful effect on oysters themselves, it could have a devastating impact on the oyster industry. Public perceptions of oyster health mattered; no one wanted to eat a potentially dangerous food.

OYSTERS, TYPHOID, AND MARKETS

Oysters are living filters, passing the water around them through their gills and retaining minute bits of plankton, microscopic animals, and anything else small enough to stay in their bodies. As they slurp up the rich estuarine soup, oysters become tiny self-contained reservoirs preserving the contents of tidal flows for a few days. This habit of concentrating the contents of their environment, while an excellent feeding strategy, can make oysters a kind of living refutation to the idea that "dilution is the solution to pollution." Anything in a given body of water will likely pass through the oysters on its bottom and will be concentrated and made available to anyone eating shellfish. Oysters are living archives of their environment.

In the 1890s, oysters were implicated in a disease outbreak striking college students at colleges in Connecticut. Twenty-three students at Wesleyan University developed typhoid fever in late October and early November 1894. Four died in an epidemic made more deadly because it occurred among young people. A Wesleyan biology professor traced all the possible sources of infection and concluded that none of the usual suspects was viable—not open wells on campus located near old privies, not city water, not fresh fruit washed in river water, not milk or ice cream served in dormitories, and not plumbing that might have leaked sewer water into drinking water. All the victims were male, all were students (one professor may have been taken sick), and all had eaten at the initiation dinners for three fraternities on the same night, October 12, 1894. All three dinners featured raw oysters, all purchased from the same local grower, based in Fair Haven, Connecticut. This grower had placed his oysters in the Quinnipiac River, where the oysters "fattened" in freshwater for a few days before sale. Several houses near the oyster beds had private sewer lines draining to the river, including one house whose occupants were ill with typhoid fever on the same date that the oysters were sold to Wesleyan's fraternities. Reporting on his detective work to the Connecticut Board of Health, Professor H. W. Conn underscored that oysters were the disease vectors: "A more typical example of an outbreak of typhoid due to a single source of infection has hardly been found in the history of medicine, and the example furnishes a demonstration of a new source of danger for this disease."[103]

Conn insisted that the link between oysters and typhoid was absolutely certain: oysters had taken in the typhoid microbes with the river water, and students had fallen ill after eating the infected oysters: "If one had planned beforehand a series of experiments designed to prove the possibility of oysters as distributing typhoid, it would hardly have been possible to have devised a more satisfactory series of conditions than those which have attained in this outbreak at Wesleyan."[104] Conn was adamant that the state health board and the public be made aware of the danger: "One thing is sure: The public health is placed in jeopardy when oyster dealers, for the sake of producing plumpness, place oysters in the mouths of fresh water creeks in close proximity to sewers."[105]

Professor Conn did not exaggerate when he warned of the danger from contaminated shellfish. Typhoid fever was one of the deadliest contagious diseases in late nineteenth-century America, accounting for 2,717 deaths in Connecticut alone between 1884 and 1893, an average of about 271 deaths per year.[106] The Wesleyan example, however, suggested that typhoid could be easily avoided; consumers simply had to avoid eating raw shellfish.

The Wesleyan case received immediate and widespread attention as one of numerous turn-of-the-century revelations of dangerously unsanitary conditions among the country's food processors. Upton Sinclair's

The Jungle (1906) startled the reading public with a grim description of some of the country's largest meatpacking operations. Commenting on the success of his shocking novel—the best-selling book in the United States during the spring of 1906—Sinclair wryly commented: "I wished to frighten the country by a picture of what its industrial masters were doing to their victims; entirely by chance I had stumbled on another discovery—what they were doing to the meat-supply of the civilized world. In other words, I aimed at the public's heart, and by accident I hit it in the stomach."[107]

Oyster and meatpacking scandals spurred federal investigations of meatpacking facilities and demands for greater regulation of food processing. In 1906, the Pure Food and Drug Act and companion legislation authorized federal inspection of meatpacking establishments. State and federal agencies acted to reduce the danger of contagion by quarantining suspect foods or regulating their consumption. Scandals like the Wesleyan case and Sinclair's exposé contributed to a growing sense of outrage at the abuses of industrial capitalism and a rising distrust in the safety of food. As the public grew alarmed, consumers bought less meat, poultry, and oysters. As a result of pollution, environmental changes, fill of shoreline areas, and fears of food poisoning, San Franciscans turned away from shellfish at the same time that San Francisco Bay became a less beneficial habitat for oysters.[108]

When oyster growers could no longer profitably plant and harvest their eastern seed, and when experiments with Pacific oysters also failed, large expanses of near-shore tide flats were opened to other uses. Oyster beds near Brisbane, resting on leased state tidelands, reverted to state ownership in the 1930s. Within a few years, the Port of San Francisco claimed the tidelands as the site of a new San Francisco airport. The abandoned oyster beds, filled with soil and sand, are now the runways of one of the nation's busiest airports.

During the decades the San Francisco Bay oyster industry existed, its success prevented other uses of those habitats. In retrospect, Atlantic oyster beds were fairly benign. Commercial growers raked and fenced the mudflats, and they organized massacres of oyster-eating native bay rays, but their shellfish thrived in the fertile waters of the bay without radically altering the habitats they occupied. Some ecologists "grade" agricultural crop systems on the basis of their capacity to support native plant and animal communities. Shade coffee plantations in highland Central America, for instance, make use of an overstory of African jacaranda trees, a second story of orange and grapefruits, and an understory of coffee bushes. The complex structure of the coffee-citrus-shade tree agricultural ecosystem, although consisting entirely of imported plants, mimics the cool rain forest it replaced, and biologists observe that shade coffee plantations support approximately 80 percent of the bird species found in the native forest. No such study exists for Atlantic oyster beds, but based on surviving descriptions of these aquacultural systems, it appears that commercial oyster beds supported at least some of the plant and animal species once found in San Francisco Bay. There were, of course, important differences: unlike native oysters, their Atlantic counterparts provided no larval spat for consumption by fish; oyster growers staked their beds to prevent large fish or mammals from accessing beds; and finally, as we have seen, growers accidentally imported a number of unwanted invasive species. Yet all these impacts pale next to the destruction wrought by fill or the later diking and dredging by the cement and salt industries that took over the former oyster beds. As oyster beds became airport runways and salt ponds, the dead shells were dredged to yield lime for chemical industries, poultry growers, and cement producers.

DEAD SHELLS AND A DEAD BAY

Max Uhle dismissed foragers both in his own time and in antiquity as primitives. Uhle's narrow-minded dismissal reflected the legal and social environment of his day. As the bayshore became a place for private industry and private property, the status of those who used the shoreline as a commons—never exactly honorable—declined further. Harvesting food from the bay was simply not as normal in the twentieth century as it had been in the nineteenth. Few would have guessed at the turn of the century that just twenty years later most of those who lived around San

Francisco Bay would turn their backs on it. But then, few in 1900 recognized the ecological impact and psychological power that pollution would wield later in the century. As late as 1913, fisheries scientist Harold Heath worried that the excessive popularity of clam digging was the greatest danger to clams in San Francisco Bay. Heath noted that soft-shell or mud clams *(Mya arenaria)* in San Francisco Bay's mudflats reached maturity and marketable size after only one full year of growth. Digging or raking destroyed young clams before they could reproduce. Arguing for greater state control over clammers, Heath charged that "wholesale, irresponsible digging is probably largely accountable for the depleted condition noted in the case of many of the clam beds of the State." Looking ahead, Heath foresaw greater pressure by commercial clammers and foragers alike, warning that as populations grew, so would demand for accessible marine resources like bay clams. In an ideal world, state-owned tidelands would be "owned by or leased to responsible parties who consider the future as well as the present." Private ownership would ensure long-term productivity, Heath believed. But since the beds were the property of the state, Heath grudgingly admitted that "the general public is entitled to the benefits." Heath never mentioned a threat from pollution.[109] And private oysters, not public clams, disappeared.

California officials had always turned to restrictions on harvest to address real or imagined crises in fish populations. The state's first reaction was to limit how and when fishermen could pursue their quarry. Often these restrictions baldly enforced the social prejudices of the day. The state's first fishing license bill applied only to "Mongolian"—that is, Chinese—fishermen. Asian men, but not their white competitors, were required to purchase state licenses to fish. Years later, urging an expanded closed season in 1914 for Dungeness crab (a species found both in the bay and in the ocean beyond the estuary), Frank Weymouth reminded the state fishery commission and the state legislature that "we are still in the position of conserving a natural resource, a task of comparative ease when contrasted with that of restoring it after it has been exhausted. Let us maintain our favorable position."[110] Weymouth's warning was followed by closed seasons, size limits, restrictions on harvesting gear, and licensing requirements for commercial and even sport fishers. All of these requirements were onerous for foragers, who could not afford to pay for licenses.

Fear of disease, lost habitat, reduced shoreline access, and increased state regulation all played a role in reducing the number of people seeking wild food and in changing public perceptions of foraging. The transformation of attitudes from the gleeful mayhem of the gold rush era is strikingly visible in one of the first environmentalist books about San Francisco Bay. Harold Gilliam, writing in 1957, noted that a few people in the Bay Area still dug clams and pried oysters from the rocky areas south of San Francisco and along the Marin shoreline. But he warned that danger lurked for the shellfish forager: "Properly cooked, they are palatable and safe, but inexperienced chefs run the risk of typhoid."[111] This statement from a writer known as an advocate for the bay illustrates how far attitudes had shifted since the previous century. What had once been a source of food for everyone was now seen as providing only risky food for marginal people. The middle-class way to enjoy the baylands was to look at birds rather than to hunt them, and to ride the waves in a pleasure craft rather than in a work skiff.[112]

The decline of San Francisco Bay's Atlantic oyster industry in the early twentieth century has been traced in part to lack of oxygen and excessive nutrients in bay waters due to overloading the bay with wastes. An expanding industrial economy also left its mark, poisoning shellfish in the vicinity of outfalls. Mostly, however, the shellfish industry seems to have declined because people stopped buying clams and oysters. This was partly thanks to new scientific understandings of disease and the connections between shellfish grown in water polluted with raw sewage and outbreaks of typhoid. The famous outbreak at Wesleyan linked oysters directly to disease. State health commissions followed Connecticut's lead in carefully monitoring shellfish for contamination, often very publicly. In the early twentieth century, California health officials also undertook a high-profile campaign to prevent paralytic shellfish poisoning, instituting annual bans on harvesting wild mussels. Disease episodes and public warnings about danger from shellfish played an unquantifiable but likely important role in reducing demand for commercial shellfish.

Losing the oyster industry hurt many beyond the growers themselves. Harvesting local foods from the bay shallows helped maintain a direct relationship with that place. It was an expression of trust: nature provides, and people eat. Losing that trust led to a fundamental shift in use and in perception. In the twentieth century, far fewer people relied on San Francisco Bay for food than in previous generations. In part this was due to changes in ownership and property law, changes that denied large portions of the bay to common use. The bay also provided less to eat after decades of pollution, colonization by aggressive species, and fill of crucial shoreline habitats. Finally, many residents of the Bay Area turned away from the bay. They no longer saw the bay as nature's smorgasbord but rather as a potential trip to the hospital.

Californians were not the only Americans to turn their backs on the idea and practice of eating locally. Nationwide, Americans stopped buying shellfish from urban harbors during the early twentieth century. Food production was increasingly centralized, and all kinds of foods were grown and processed far from consumers and packaged and distributed on a national scale. Food historian Harvey Levenstein reminds us that these fearful decades gave us the fruit cocktail, processed cheese, and evaporated milk.[113] Unable to make a profit growing oysters, the Morgan Oyster Company, last of San Francisco Bay's growers, sold most of its oyster beds in 1923 to Pacific Portland Cement Company. For nearly fifty years thereafter, cement companies dredged the Atlantic oyster shells and the ancient native oyster reefs that lay beneath, converting oyster shells to cement to build the highways and cities that now ring the bay. The ancient oysters of the bay are now embedded in the bridges, roads, and structures that make modern life possible in the region.[114]

Yet even with the total destruction of the Atlantic oyster in San Francisco Bay, foraging did not cease. Other species, including the resilient *Mya arenaria*, were still available to those willing to climb over fences and to risk illness. In the mid-twentieth century, foraging became an illegal activity, an underground behavior, ever more closely associated with society's marginal members—recent immigrants, the poor, social outcasts. And partly because of this association, eating out of the bay became more dangerous. State officials responded to pollution by simply declaring that wild foods

Figure 12.   Ideal Cement factory, Redwood City, California, ca. 1920s. California State Lands Commission and San Francisco Estuary Institute.

should not be eaten. Public access to San Francisco Bay's wild foods shifted from collecting tideland species to sport fishing from boats, an activity that costs more money and that targets different species. Later, when striped bass, halibut, and salmon catches also declined, the State Department of Fish and Game imposed lower daily catch limits and encouraged catch-and-release fishing. As the state and environmentalists increasingly warned the public that wild foods were dangerous, people changed their relationship to the bayshore. This had consequences. Rather than addressing the problem of increasing pollution and disappearing habitat, Americans around San Francisco Bay slowly came to accept that they could not eat out of the bay. Lost uses led to lost interest. By the middle decades of the twentieth century it seemed natural that San Francisco Bay would be a refuge for birds but not for people.

No one has sold or stolen a San Francisco Bay oyster since 1956. However, one unexpected shellfish is flourishing in the bay. In recent decades, researchers monitoring local water quality began noticing an unfamiliar species clustering around the outfall pipes of one of the worst polluters in the region, the Chevron oil refinery at Richmond. This odd little mollusk is *Ostreola conchaphila,* the native oyster of the bay, seldom seen since the nineteenth century. Apparently, the little native oyster hung on through the hard years of mining debris and low oxygen in one of the most unlikely places in the bay, the refinery outfall pipes. Exactly how this happened remains a mystery. These oysters are loaded with toxic heavy metals and industrial chemicals. They cannot be eaten, but they are flourishing. The native oyster's success has inspired a handful of dedicated scientists and conservationists to seek to restore the native oyster and its once massive reefs to other parts of San Francisco Bay. *Ostreola conchaphila*'s continued presence is a reminder of just how complicated this hybrid landscape can be.[115]

Like the bay they live in, these surviving oysters are a living record of a century and a half of mining, urban effluent, and industrial wastes. They are only a partial success, because they cannot be safely eaten. No one can use them, either commercially or as foraged food. Only when it is once again safe to eat from San Francisco Bay can we call restoration a success.

The story of shellfish in San Francisco Bay is surprising in several ways. It indicates, first of all, the complexity of environmental change and the ways in which such change is often caught up in the complexities of human social change. What was bad for native oysters could be good for eastern oysters; the mud and pollution that was bad for the bay's ecology as a whole actually benefited introduced oysters. The success of Atlantic oysters depended upon being made property, but that property was unstable because the remnant oysters in abandoned beds were indistinguishable from cultivated oysters.

These kinds of lessons are staples of environmental history. But this story goes beyond those traditional lessons. Oyster farming was merely one episode in the search for productivity that has typified not only San Francisco Bay but also tidelands and wetlands in general over the last hundred years. That each landscape seems so fleeting, and such a failure in hindsight, should give us pause. Maximum productivity for a single use has not given much of a guide to using the bay in the long run. The fate of San Francisco Bay's oysters reminds us that environmental change always takes place within human frameworks that are unable to contain it. Garrett Hardin's so-called tragedy of the commons makes little sense within the complexity of actual social and cultural relations and the complexity of environmental change. Making oysters private also created pirates. Both growers and pirates could use the law as a shield. The ability of oysters to survive in the muddy bay was not the result of the virtues of private property, and private property could not protect oysters against further changes in the bay.

A bay lost to oyster growing was not, however, lost to other forms of production. In the early decades of the twentieth century, oyster growers gave way to a different industry that also relied on the bay's shallow waters. Salt makers produced an essential raw material for a wide range of Western industries, and their product was pollution-proof. The shift from oyster growing to salt making reflects a larger shift from food production to industrial production around San Francisco Bay. The bay became more valuable and useful as a repository of waste than as a place to grow food. Yet salt makers too would be challenged, beginning in the 1950s, by demand for real estate in the tidelands. These demands focused attention on the bayshore and led to popular movements and state efforts to wrest control of the shoreline away from private owners. Behind these efforts were newer ideas about the productivity of the tidal wetlands, ideas inspired by increasing demand for recreational use of nearby nature and the newly popular science of ecology.

FIVE From Real Estate to Refuge

Fly into any Bay Area airport, and a singular view dominates the landing approach. Planes come in low over pools of still, shallow water. The pools placidly reflect nearby hills and the sky above. Still water stretches for miles along both shores of southern San Francisco Bay, walled off from the bay by thin mud levees. Passengers with window seats can see that the ponds are not brown, like the adjacent muddy bay shallows roiled by wind and tides, nor blue, like the deep central bay channels. The ponds instead are a series of shocking colors: lime green, orange, rusty red. The water looks artificially dyed or, more likely, polluted by some industry. These placid pools are in fact the production facilities of one of San Francisco Bay's oldest industries, salt making. The color comes from bacteria that thrive in the saline environment. Evaporated, or solar, salt has been produced in the

Figure 13.   South San Francisco Bay salt ponds, photographed by the crew of the Space Shuttle *Endeavor,* June 2002. NASA STS111–376–3.

shallow waters of San Francisco Bay's tidal wetlands, without interruption, for nearly 150 years.

Side by side with and nearly indistinguishable from the commercial salt ponds are other diked pools. These ponds are managed as bird habitat rather than for salt production. They are kept at a specific salinity for brine shrimp, which reach extraordinary densities in this managed environment. The shrimp are an ideal food for migrating shorebirds. On a fall or winter day the ponds are covered with birds, many of them migrants en route from Canada to Mexico or even further. These ponds constitute the San Francisco Bay National Wildlife Refuge, the nation's first and most extensive urban wildlife refuge. Since the 1960s, the federal government has been buying the salt ponds and converting them to bird habitat. What in the 1960s was a vast salt mine is now largely a refuge, and recent events suggest that the remaining commercial salt ponds will also leave private ownership.

The vanishing salt ponds and the rise of the refuge suggest a circular story: from industrial to wild, from private to public. This is one way to tell the story of the bay's tidal wetlands, a trajectory that seems to neatly close the circle begun in the nineteenth century when the tidelands were first converted to privately owned real estate and stripped of much of their wild character. Biologists, managers, and environmentalists talk about the ongoing process as "restoration," as bringing back the essential qualities of the tidelands before they were transformed into economically productive landscapes. But this simple story is misleading. There are other landscapes to be considered. Residential and recreational developments looked in the 1950s and 1960s to be the future of the bayshore. Before the refuge there was Redwood Shores, a planned city of sixty thousand built on four thousand acres of filled salt ponds in San Mateo County. Redwood Shores offered suburban housing for an expanding population, carved from the last buildable space in the area, the bay itself. Across the bay, the Berkeley Marina—home to a hotel, restaurants, and hundreds of boat slips—likewise occupies former tidal wetlands. Berkeley's marina was once just one of many intensive recreational developments planned for the bayshore.[1]

The marinas and shoreline residential areas are circumscribed landscapes now, but that was not how the future looked after the Second World War. Any history of the bay has to explain not only why the salt ponds are still present, and why a wildlife refuge has appeared, but also why Redwood Shores and the marinas did not spread further. This is the story of the remaking and reimagining of the bayshore as a place that produced birds rather than minerals, and open space rather than development.

SALT FROM THE MARSHES

San Francisco Bay is ideally suited to producing salt from seawater. Annual rainfall is less than twenty-two inches, and winds blow steadily across the bay in every month of the year. Net annual evaporation is between thirty-four and forty-three inches, meaning that between three and four feet of water evaporate from the salt ponds each year, leaving behind an ever-saltier concentrate.[2] Ohlones harvested a substantial crop of salt crystals from shallow shoreline basins that filled with salty bay water at high tides and then slowly evaporated over the course of the year. Ohlones directly consumed this salt or traded it to neighboring peoples.[3] During the period of Spanish and Mexican colonization, friars at Mission San Jose oversaw the native salt harvest. Itinerant American trapper Jedediah Smith described the scene in December 1827: "From the S. E. extremity of the bay extends a considerable salt marsh from which great quantities of salt are annually collected and the quantity might perhaps be much increased. It belongs to the Mission of San Jose."[4]

In his calculating way, Smith both described the salt harvest and looked ahead to an era in which Americans would dominate the bay's salt industry. Up to 1848, Americans in California followed the Californio method of "salt-gathering," collecting an annual supply for personal use. But the gold rush provided huge new markets for salt and, as a consequence, extended the American tradition of squatting on others' land. An early chronicler of the region's salt industry recalled: "About the year 1852, a few Americans, owing to the high price of salt in the San Francisco market . . . resorted to the Mexican salt-grounds, and, with little or no show of right to do so, established themselves in the business of salt-making. They worked leisurely; earned money, but not very rapidly; made few improvements, and these of minor importance, and were in reality salt-gatherers, instead of salt-makers."[5]

By 1857, a permanent salt industry had developed in the natural salt pannes among the marshes near what is now the eastern footing of the San Mateo Bridge. In that year, a salt maker first enclosed his salt ponds with a levee to regularize production.[6] A few years later, the discovery of the Comstock lode silver mines in Nevada generated great demand for salt. The "patio process" learned from Mexican miners required great volumes of salt to refine pure silver from raw ore.[7] Producing largely for ore refining and local food processing, San Francisco Bay salt makers harvested thirty thousand tons of salt in 1886 and forty-one thousand tons in 1893.[8]

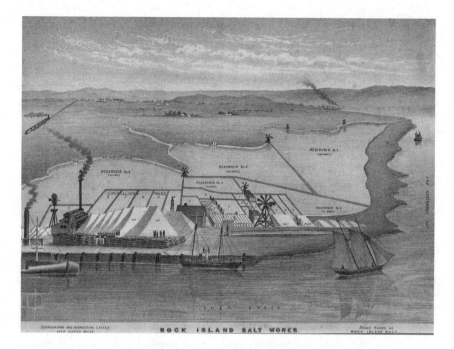

Figure 14. Salt works near Hayward, California, 1878. *Official and Historical Atlas Map of Alameda County, California.* David Rumsey Map Collection, www.davidrumsey.com.

As salt was transformed from a necessity for personal consumption into a key ingredient in the industrial development of California, the scale and process of its production also changed. Initially, harvesting salt was not very different from other foraging activities in the baylands. Gathering could be eased by placing wooden stakes or bundles of reeds in the salt pannes to offer a surface for the salt to crystallize on, or horse-drawn scrapers might enhance a single person's labor. But even aided by simple tools, salt harvesting took advantage of a fundamentally natural process.[9] This era passed when salt makers began producing in earnest for the silver mines.

Making salt an industrial-scale product first required owning the means of production. Like all other tidelands, the salt ponds have a convoluted legal history. It was one thing for salt companies to start using underwater lands and quite another to establish legal title. Tidelands moved into private hands through three basic avenues: state sale of tide-lands, private theft of state lands, and swampland claims. As we saw in chapter 2, beginning in 1869 the state sold its interest in large areas of San Francisco Bay's tidal margin through the Board of Tide Land Commissioners. The biggest purchasers in the three south bay counties of San Mateo, Alameda, and Santa Clara were oyster growers, as dis-cussed in chapter 4. These purchases granted control over areas between high tide and mean low tide. Consolidated by the Morgan Oyster Company in the 1890s, a huge block of property passed intact to the Ideal Cement Company. From the 1930s Leslie Salt Company dominated the shoreline above the legal high tide. This monopoly control had impor-tant consequences.

Leslie, which incorporated to monopolize salt production in the bay, also inherited huge areas of salt-producing tidal wetlands from a hand-ful of smaller producers. These areas, while possibly legal tidelands, were not sold as such. Many of these areas fell into private hands through corruption. Mexican-era land grants, which legally ended at the edge of high tide, in practice often included watery areas as well. It fell to survey-ors in the U.S. General Land Office in San Francisco to mark the line be-tween upland and tidelands. This office was plagued with corruption scandals throughout the late nineteenth century. Given that determining the boundary between tidelands and swamp and overflowed land was never simple, and that legal title to tidelands—and therefore access to the open bay—was so valuable, it is little wonder that corrupt surveyors might have occasionally mapped salt marshes or even open water as up-lands.[10] Finally, tidal wetlands moved into private hands through a third medium, purchases of swamp and overflowed land.

Federal swamplands were explicitly defined as those lands lying above the reach of the tide. The federal law that granted California its swamp and overflowed lands was modeled on Arkansas's freshwater swamps. But in California, where salt marshes and creeks merged nearly seamlessly, it was easy for claimants to include tidal wetlands in their swampland grants. This practice appears to have been widespread in the south bay.[11] Historian Alan Brown has identified at least one pioneer salt

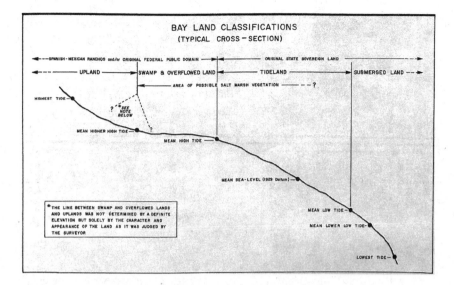

Figure 15. Ownership in the tidelands. San Francisco Bay Conservation and Development Commission, *Ownership.*

producer near the present site of the San Mateo Bridge as a beneficiary of a swampland claim: "John Johnson, who is said to have been the first to enclose his salt pond with a levee (about 1857), took up 73 acres here under a swamp-land survey in 1856; Christian F. F. Beck claimed much of the rest at the same time."[12] Johnson and Beck purchased their land from California for $1.25 per acre as *swampland,* occasionally flooded by rivers or streams. What they gained, however, was actually *tideland,* washed by the salty bay, as their property's use for salt making indicates. The product they made on this property was both prosaic and essential.

MINING THE WATER'S EDGE

Salt—sodium chloride—is an omnipresent household mineral, noted for its crystalline purity and its essential role in cooking. Salt is among humanity's oldest and most effective means to preserve foods. Salting makes possible such familiar products as olives, butter, pickles, and the full gamut of cured meats, from fish to bacon to ham and salami.[13] California's nineteenth-century food industries, including salmon and tuna canning, relied on cheap, abundant salt.[14] Twentieth-century fruit and vegetable canneries at the south end of San Francisco Bay also relied on salt to protect their products from fermentation and the dangerous bacterial by-products of uncontrolled rot: botulism and salmonella. Salt allowed entrepreneurs to transform California's natural resources into commodities. Through salt, local foods could become products for sale into international markets.

Preserving food was just one of the ways that salt infiltrated modern life. Salt also became the key raw material in a spectrum of industrial processes ranging from bleaching paper to refining gasoline. "Salt," one scholar wrote, "is to industrial chemistry as copper is to electricity."[15] Without copper, electrical circuitry would be impossible; without salt, bleaching and caustic industries would fail. The benefits from this humble mineral are immense. Salt undergirds the twentieth-century revolution in water treatment that together with vaccinations lengthened the average American life span by twenty years. It is the single most essential mineral in modern industrial society.

Salt can be mined from underground deposits left by ancient seas, but the world's largest mineral reservoir is the oceans. Solar salt making is the process of concentrating elements found in seawater. In seawater, these elements are so diffuse that they are valueless. After months of evaporation by sun and steady bayshore winds, San Francisco bay water becomes bittern, a blood-colored mineral slurry. Sodium chloride (table salt) is just one of the compounds found in bittern. Bittern also yields compounds of magnesium and potassium. Magnesium is used in corrosion-proofing steel, in explosives, and in a wide range of chemical products.[16] Explosives factories like Giant Powder once occupied the remoter parts of San Francisco Bay's shoreline. California's first oil refineries were located on San Francisco Bay at Richmond, Oleum, and Rodeo. All used large quantities of salt in refining gasoline.

These associated uses of salt eventually made San Francisco Bay the hub of a significant regional chemical industry. In 1890, Dow Chemical applied electricity to salt brine and produced both caustic soda and hydrochloric acid. "Brine electrolysis" became the basis for the modern chemical industry, providing an enormous number of useful industrial chemicals. Chief among these were chlorine gas and sodium carbonate (soda ash).[17] Dow opened a chemical plant in 1917 in Pittsburg, California, on San Pablo Bay, producing the raw materials for modern industry from Leslie Salt Company's bittern.[18] Other chemical companies also relied on San Francisco Bay salt. California Chemical Corporation (later Westvaco Chemical) first built a plant in the central bay at San Mateo in 1926 and later another plant immediately adjacent to the Leslie Salt Company salt piles in the southern arm of the bay, at Newark.[19] In 1957, a local journalist described how bittern from Leslie's plant in Newark moved by pipeline directly to the Westvaco Chemical plant, "a ten-acre maze of pipe lines, boilers, tanks, and chemical aromas." Westvaco converted the bittern into "chemicals sold for a hundred uses, from insecticides to soil conditioners." Magnesium liquids from the plant went next door to Lavino Company, where they were used in making firebrick, the lining for furnaces, stoves, and chimneys.[20]

Many of Westvaco's products began as chlorine. No salt by-product was more versatile. Chlorine made from San Francisco Bay salt bleached toilet paper white in Pacific Northwest paper mills, purified Los Angeles's drinking water, and treated San Diego's sewage. Chlorine was used in making cleaning fluids, chloroform, insecticides like DDT, and a host of other compounds.[21] Chlorine was also an essential ingredient in polychlorinated biphenyls (PCBs), used by Bay Area manufacturers to keep electrical transformers from overheating and exploding. Polyvinyl chloride (PVC) plastics made from San Francisco Bay salt showed up in everything from lawn furniture to plastic-wrapped meat trays at the supermarket.

As plastic, bleach, antacid tablet, or insecticide, salt took on chemical forms that were, on the one hand, extraordinarily valuable to human beings and, on the other hand, exceedingly toxic. Chlorine, which is associated with so many useful products, is also implicated in many of the modern world's most potent toxins. PCBs were useful in preventing transformer fires, but they turned out to be both wickedly poisonous to living creatures and astonishingly persistent in the environment. PCBs flushed into the bay now infest bay muds around San Francisco Bay, accumulating and growing more deadly as they work their way up the food chain. When burned, chlorinated compounds produce one of the most toxic substances known to humanity, dioxin. Dioxin is present in San Francisco Bay's water and in the flesh of creatures that live nearby, including human beings. Salt makers, by helping make possible better living through chemistry, also opened the Pandora's box of chemical contamination.

In addition to these indirect consequences, making salt diminished the tidelands' biological productivity. Salt ponds were taken from the bayshore. Salt makers built low dams around their property, blocking out the tides. The only time bay water circulated in the ponds was when salt makers allowed new water in once a year or when they flushed impurities out into the bay. Dikes converted mile after mile of dynamic tidal wetlands—salt marsh, mudflat, bay shallows—into stagnant pools. When salt makers blocked out the tides, they robbed the estuarine system of its fertile margin.

Hearing this litany of industrial uses, it is easy to forget that salt remained a natural product of San Francisco Bay's tidal wetlands. Leslie Salt Company came to control this productivity. First incorporated in 1901, following decades of mergers among the small, often family-owned salt operators of San Francisco Bay, Leslie in 1924 began consolidating the production facilities and marshland holdings of the remaining salt producers. By 1936, Leslie controlled some forty-four thousand acres of tidal wetlands on both shores of the southern arm of San Francisco Bay. Leslie continued to produce salt on these properties, replacing anti-quated equipment and unifying the various systems into a single unit connected by a gigantic cross-bay plumbing system.[22] By 1947 Leslie's San Francisco Bay salt ponds produced five hundred thousand tons of salt, worth $3 million. In 1952, U.S. salt miners produced about twenty million tons of salt, worth $71 million. Only iron ore and clays were pro-duced in larger quantities. California produced one million tons of salt that year, with a value of $6 million, just 6 percent of the U.S. total. But California's salt had far greater regional importance than its small national role suggests, for Leslie supplied the industrial needs of caustic and bleaching industries from California to Oregon, Washington, Arizona, Nevada, and Idaho, shipping by water when possible.[23]

Like other products of the bayshore, salt was produced in a limited space. As population climbed in the aftermath of the Second World War, space on the shoreline became ever more valuable, until the land gradually became worth far more than the salt it produced.[24] Leslie's owners and managers understood early that their greatest treasure was not the perennial harvest of "white gold" from salt ponds but rather the potential real estate value of the shoreline property itself. As the largest private owner of tidelands in California, the directors of Leslie Salt Company began to think of other, more profitable uses early on. They first thought to develop their tidelands as farmland.[25] This was not as unlikely at the time as it seems today. Many areas outside city limits reverted to farmland during the 1920s and 1930s; developers in Puget Sound, in southern California, and in the city of East Palo Alto (just uphill from the salt marshes) planned suburban homes with large lots for animals, gardens, or small farms.[26]

By the 1950s, however, Leslie's directors were planning other uses for their salt ponds. The company's directors saw that booming population had driven up land prices and that Leslie's thousands of acres of tidal flats were some of the last remaining unbuilt flat spaces in the region. The company implemented a shift in policy by filling several thousand acres of salt ponds near Redwood City in San Mateo County. The company planned a "high value real estate development" on the filled land, grandly titled Redwood Shores.[27] Engineering problems and objections from neighbors kept the project from reaching its full size, but it was apparent that Leslie would try to develop other parts of its vast domain.

Even as Leslie's visions for the bayshore were changing, some Bay Area residents and planning officials began to view the bayshore as the region's most valuable parkland. Whether developed or undeveloped, the bay itself was the largest remaining stretch of open space in the area, if hardly pristine. Pollution crusaders and parks advocates shared a common interest in expanding public authority over the shoreline. Many activists also believed that baylands were a public resource being treated

Figure 16. Newly filled bay for Redwood Shores development, early 1960s. U.S. Geological Survey Photo Library, Denver, Colorado.

as private property. By the 1950s, the future of the bayshore still seemed likely to include far more residential development than marsh. But events would change that.

In the fall of 1959, as shorebirds flew up the Pacific flyway to the marshes and salt ponds along the bayshore, a key event helped galvanize public opinion in favor of protecting San Francisco Bay's remaining undeveloped shoreline as open space. Since C. E. Grunsky first proposed the idea in the 1880s, a series of agricultural visionaries, industrial promoters, land speculators, and urban boosters had urged construction of dams across San Francisco Bay. Variously sited at the Carquinez Strait, between Richmond and San Rafael, and in the south bay, these dams were supposed to convert San Francisco Bay into a series of freshwater reservoirs and make the region drought-proof. They would also halt salt-water from intruding into the delta and permit the drainage of most of San Francisco Bay for new housing and industrial sites.[28] In 1959, prodded by local members of Congress, the San Francisco office of the U.S. Army Corps of Engineers published a plan and maps showing "areas susceptible of reclamation in San Francisco Bay area." The plan blandly reported that 78 square miles of marshland were ready for filling, with an additional 248 square miles of submerged land available. In total, the army corps reported, 325 square miles of San Francisco Bay's 487 square miles of remaining tidal wetlands were ready for development.[29]

The army corps recommended massive fill around the edges of the bay to meet projected demand for housing, industrial locations, and transportation facilities. Filling the bay would mean replacing large areas of marsh and open water with houses and roads. Opponents protested that fill would also destroy a significant public resource: the aesthetic and recreational use of the open marshes. The corps, a public agency, was advocating changes that would have largely benefited private real estate developers. San Francisco journalist Harold Gilliam passionately voiced an alternative: "For most of the bay to be replaced by mile after mile of solidly built-up suburbs would be to eliminate the area's greatest natural advantage. . . . It is in effect a huge untrodden park, offering space, perspective, and beauty—items which are not usually visible on a balance sheet and which will inevitably become increasingly rare as California's population increases to three or four times its present size. In the metropolitan regions such areas of natural space as still remain—and this includes the bay—should be jealously husbanded."[30]

Gilliam conceived of San Francisco Bay as an enormous park. The bay was valuable, he argued, beyond its capacity to produce salt or fish, its utility in transporting goods, or its potential as residential and commercial space. That value, as open space, would only increase over time as the land surrounding the bay filled with people and their works.[31]

A 1963 map of ownership of San Francisco Bay tidelands illustrates what was at stake. The map shows that most of the bay floor still remained property of the state of California, managed by the State Lands Commission. Cities around the bay claimed portions of the shoreline and nearby waters for harbor districts at Oakland, Richmond, Berkeley, and Martinez. The federal government controlled a few shoal areas around military bases, the federal penitentiary at Alcatraz Island, and the former immigration quarantine station on Angel Island. Some bay shoreline was also in private hands, particularly in Marin County, the San Francisco and Oakland waterfronts, and south of San Francisco. On both sides of the south bay, a handful of garbage companies continued to dispose of solid waste in marshes they had bought for the purpose. Private holdings dated from the nineteenth century, when the state of California had sold or granted tidelands to individuals or corporations.[32]

The heaviest concentrations of privately owned tidelands were the Santa Fe Railroad's already partially developed properties between Berkeley and Richmond and, especially, the salt ponds and former oyster lands that wrapped the entire south bay from San Mateo south to San Jose and back up the eastern shore to Hayward. By 1968 three corporations controlled the great majority of privately owned tidelands in San Francisco Bay. Ideal Cement Company had purchased several thousand acres of former oyster beds from the last San Francisco Bay oyster company and continued to mine the bay floor for calcium-rich shells. Westbay Associates, a development corporation holding ten thousand acres of Ideal Cement property, included among its partners the Crocker Land Company and David Rockefeller, the millionaire developer and scion of the famous eastern family. The largest private owner of baylands, however, was Leslie Salt Company. Leslie controlled significant marshland in the south bay and thousands of acres of tidelands closer to the delta, some forty-four thousand acres in all. These private lands, long dedicated to such low-value enterprises as shell mining or salt production, now became the focus of development proposals in the postwar era.[33]

Coleman C. Johnson, president of Leslie Salt Company, spoke out publicly and vociferously against restricting the company's ability to develop its salt ponds. The company's development plans were at stake. Addressing the city council of Fremont in 1969, Johnson complained that a proposed wildlife refuge in the south bay was only the "latest and largest" effort to shift Leslie's property into public hands. Further takeaways would cripple the company's operations, and "Leslie could be forced to discontinue salt production entirely in the San Francisco Bay area." A large local employer, he implied, would be forced to lay off workers and stop paying substantial property taxes. Johnson objected to all future public uses of Leslie company property, but he particularly feared the impact recreational users might have on Leslie company operations. Criticizing local government support for a wildlife refuge, which might permit fishing, hunting, boating, and camping, Johnson warned, "It seems evident to us that this amount of traffic and activity, together with the construction of roads and other facilities to accommodate them, probably would prevent continued salt production in the area."[34]

Leslie's plans to develop its salt ponds into real estate conflicted with public officials' plans for the salt ponds. Cities and counties coveted Leslie's salt ponds for a number of purposes, most commonly to increase the number and kind of recreational opportunities for bayside residents. In the 1960s residents of the Bay Area increasingly saw their baylands as open space, islands of green off-limits to residential and industrial development.[35] Parks, of course, connoted *recreation*, and recreation was the word of the day in leisure-obsessed postwar California. Californians were supposed to live outside, in patios and on decks. *Sunset* magazine, headquartered in Menlo Park, south of San Francisco, promoted "Western Living," illustrated by glossy photos of backyard barbecues and poolside cocktail parties. Recreation, too, moved outdoors. Californians were expected to quit bowling and start fishing, hiking, and camping. Leisure activities changed with the times. The postwar years were the golden age of motorized recreation. Boating became power boating. Swimming became waterskiing. These new forms of powered outdoor recreation demanded both more space and more infrastructure to support them than the foraging and beachcombing typical of earlier generations.

But in the postwar years, recreational spaces—particularly open waters suitable for the water sports so popular in California—were extremely limited in the San Francisco Bay region. In a major review published in 1963, influential bay observer Mel Scott decried the lack of recreational access to San Francisco Bay. The bay itself might be a vast open sheet of water, but how would people get into the water? Of

276 miles of shoreline, Scott revealed that just four miles were open to the public. "Is San Francisco Bay," he asked, "one of the most neglected recreational resources in this metropolitan region?" Scott supported conservationists' desire to protect the bay while approving cities' plans to develop water-based recreation. "San Francisco Bay needs to be protected as a scenic asset; it also needs to be further developed as a recreational resource."[36] Scott's words were echoed in subsequent governmental reports. In 1968, the Bay Conservation and Development Commission reported on the existing state of recreational facilities along the shores of San Francisco Bay. "Although there are large quantities of open space and water surface still remaining in the Bay Area," the commissioners wrote, "much of it is inaccessible or unavailable for public use. Free public access to the Bay for recreation, when compared to the recreational demand, is remarkably limited." The public could access the water at just twenty-five points along the entire bayshore. A paltry thirty-two hundred acres of public shoreline parkland served millions of people in one of the nation's largest urban centers.[37]

Early in 1968, bay commission staff gathered data from cities and counties around San Francisco Bay and calculated the extent and use of public beaches on San Francisco Bay. They found just a handful of public beaches and intense demand. Nearly 1.85 million people visited San Francisco's small (one-third mile long) Aquatic Park beach in 1966. Perhaps only stadiums hosted more recreational users per square foot.[38] Access for fishermen was equally limited. Citizens could fish at just twenty-one public access sites along the 276 miles of bay shoreline. Fishermen heavily used the few existing piers: over a thousand people fished from Berkeley's municipal pier each day.[39]

Limited access and high demand troubled planning officials all around the bay, but the planners were most concerned about the future. Projecting recent economic trends forward, they were convinced that Bay Area residents would need far more recreational spaces. "With the expansion of automation and improvement of other production processes," they forecast, "the work week will be reduced and leisure time will increase." Some scholars were even predicting that by the year 2000, some Americans would likely work for just one hour per week, and "this one working hour may consist of nothing more than pushing a series of buttons." Less time at work would mean more time to play. That play would be outside. The public would demand more and different kinds of recreational spaces around San Francisco Bay. "Recreation regarded only as games, sports, and play is an obsolescent concept," they wrote. Land must be set aside for the greater demand, and this land "must allow sufficient space for new, as well as current, forms of recreation." Where parks had once been places to rest on days off, they argued, in the future, "leisure time will be used not so much to restore energies exhausted in work as to use energies untouched by work." A more energetic, well-paid, and invigorated population would want to spend more time outdoors, being active. "Recreation," they prophesied, "may come to be no longer regarded as opposed to work; the park will no longer be considered as simply a sanctuary in the heart of the city." Modern recreation would be outdoor recreation, and planners warned that suitable land would grow ever more scarce. "The expansion of facilities for recreation will certainly be required and land for this expansion must be bought before it becomes prohibitively expensive."[40]

Bay commission staff in 1968 knew that the cities and counties around San Francisco Bay were actively planning new outdoor recreation developments. Today those plans seem startlingly ambitious, even laughable. The tiny town of Alviso in the marshes of the far south bay expected a $200,000 grant from the state to build a yacht harbor holding eight hundred motorboats. Berkeley's city council pondered a developer's $30-million proposal to build a fifteen-story hotel and a five-hundred-slip marina near the city's old waterfront dump. An alternative plan called for an eighteen-hole golf course on a part of Berkeley's waterfront that in 1962 was still open bay.

Parks and development might seem contradictory land uses. But in the early 1960s, development pressures in the rapidly growing Bay Area were partially driven by the perceived need for recreational areas. In 1964, Californians passed a massive statewide park bond act, providing state funds for shoreline recreation. Noting that the state owned just two public beaches in all of San Francisco Bay, California's State Resources Agency offered $2.3 million of these park bond funds to local jurisdictions to develop "water-related parks" along the entire urban and suburban east bay shoreline, from Richmond to Fremont.[41] The most dramatic of these plans was a combined flood-control project and recreational development envisioned for marshlands at the mouth of Alameda Creek and the isolated Coyote Hills, near the eastern entrance to the Dumbarton Bridge. Planning officials from Alameda County and the cities of Fremont, Newark, Union City, and Hayward created a joint commission, the Regional Small Craft Harbor Study Committee, to plan for recreation in the area. Committee members hoped to construct a series of freshwater lakes in the marsh, the largest three times bigger than Oakland's Lake Merritt. Water sports and power boating would be featured, with support facilities including boat launches, berths, fueling docks, a boat repair shop, a marine stadium for speedboat racing, swimming ponds, parking lots, and a unique motel for boaters called a "Boatel."[42]

For the Regional Small Craft Harbor Study Committee, the sky was the limit. With funding available from the deep pockets of California's Department of Parks and Recreation, a small-craft harbor in the Dumbarton-area marshes seemed imminent. The committee members dreamed of a San Francisco Bay equivalent to the massive marine playgrounds of southern California. They wrote, "The hills and the flood control project make this general area most desirable as an aquatic park of the same magnitude as the Mission Bay project in San Diego or the Marina Del Rey project in Los Angeles."[43] These were big dreams for a shoreline that in 1962 consisted largely of marsh grasses and diked salt ponds.

In general, such plans emphasized types of recreation that required extensive infrastructure and a remaking of the shoreline. Santa Clara County's plan boasted a full-color foldout map of shoreline recreation possibilities in the salt ponds and remnant marshes of the southernmost bay: "Now a neglected, inaccessible area of salt ponds, marsh land, and garbage dumps, the waterfront could be the attractive marine playground indicated in the sketch. There is water for boats and boatmen of all kinds: two large yacht harbors, protected basins for small sail boats, winding inland waterways for outboard and power launch exploration, a wide expanse of bay and a strong breeze for full rigged sailing."[44]

Santa Clara County planners reimagined the same features that made the bayshore difficult for nineteenth-century navigators—strong breezes, winding sloughs, shallow water—as advantages for twentieth-century recreational users. In their rendering, the bayshore could become the focus of a new, upwardly mobile kind of recreation. Alameda County—together with the cities of Hayward, Union City, Fremont, and Newark—planned for motorized sports in the marshes and salt ponds near the eastern approach to the Dumbarton Bridge.[45]

RECREATION AND REFUGE

What seemed like a choice between two options—residential fill or developed recreation—in fact went in another direction. The people doing the choosing were changing, and they moved in a new direction that was different from what had come before. Instead of filling the bay to create land or dredging the shallows for water sports, newly powerful environmentalists sought to preserve open land and open water as environmental amenities. These activists used familiar means to accomplish new ends: state regulation to prohibit further fill and a wildlife refuge that would place ownership of the salt ponds in the hands of federal government.

A federal wildlife refuge seems an unlikely victor over recreation in postwar California. Why a refuge and not space for leisure? How did bird habitat trump other uses of San Francisco Bay? To understand this history we need to acknowledge the power of wildlife discourse for an increasingly affluent, suburban American public in the decades after 1945.[46]

In the 1950s and 1960s, Americans broke with the privations of economic depression and war and greatly increased their consumption. Consumers bought more cars, ate more steak, and lived in newer, bigger houses. Historian Samuel Hays argues that this consumption extended to "environmental amenities." That new car was best enjoyed while driving on a scenic highway, with the windows down to let in fresh air. A bigger, better house also included views of a lake, a mountain, or a river. Outdoor recreation became a popular means of consuming nature. Many recreational activities that surged in the postwar era—camping, fishing, boating, hiking—incorporated natural places. Nature itself became a new kind of commodity. Nature had always provided commodities in the traditional sense of raw material—lumber, mining ore—but now, nature served as an amenity that increased value. A "water view," for example, could be worth more to the sale price of a house than an extra bathroom or a remodeled kitchen. Hays carried this observation further, arguing that consumers confronted a political system long dominated by disputes between three kinds of producers: labor, agriculture, and business. Postwar consumers thus gave a political boost to nascent efforts to protect open space, expand parks, and prevent further development of undeveloped spaces such as shorelines. According to Hays, "By providing new focal points of organized activity in common leisure and recreational interest groups, and by emphasizing community organization to protect community environmental values against threats from external developmental pressures, consumer impulses went through a degree of mobilization and activity that they had not previously enjoyed. . . . Environmental action reflects the emergence in American politics of a new effectiveness for consumer action not known in the years before the war."[47]

Hays maintained that consumerism, the desire for a better quality of life, drove environmental activism. This consumerism had a specific focus, in the San Francisco Bay Area, on the region's primary natural feature: the bay itself. The bay, and its accessible shoreline, were among the most treasured places in the region, but also among its most threatened. Runaway suburban growth in the south bay—the very area where Leslie's salt ponds were located—meant that the public was increasingly walled off from the water by new developments like Redwood Shores, while the bay itself was shrinking as developers filled it in to make land.

If modern environmentalism reacted to suburban sprawl, it also drew much of its energy from the popular concept of the ecosystem, which saw the environment as a "'web of life' rather than just a storehouse of commodities to be extracted or a physical or chemical machine to be manipulated."[48] Environmentalists saw increasingly scarce open spaces as more valuable in their undisturbed state than as developed land. This prioritization of open space dovetailed perfectly with increasing public awareness of the concepts of ecological science. Ecologists argued that San Francisco Bay was a system in which changes made to any part of the bayshore could negatively influence other parts of the bay. Thanks to environmentalism's embrace of popular ecology, many in the region came to see San Francisco Bay as a whole. But as local people increased the scale of their view of the bay, they also changed perspectives on how to manage the bay because some basic issues extended far beyond local jurisdictions. As the cities around San Francisco Bay grew larger and suburbs sprawled into previously unbuilt spaces and outlying areas, the human footprint on the region grew ever heavier. Confronted with the problems of growth, locals increasingly turned to the federal government for help.[49]

Residents of the Bay Area were not alone, of course, in demanding protection for their water, land, and air during the 1950s and 1960s. Events in California mirrored national developments. Congress changed the rules by which federal land management agencies operated by passing a series of acts between 1964 and 1972: the Wilderness Act, Land and Water Act, National Estuarine Protection Act, National Environmental Policy Act, Clean Water Act, and Endangered Species Act. These acts required federal agencies to consider their potential impact on water and air quality and to calculate the effects of logging, mining, road building, and other actions on animal and plant habitat. Other federal legislation of the era directed federal agencies to preserve land from development. The Department of Housing and Urban Development provided matching funds to cities and counties to buy parks. Federal funding for sewage treatment had even more impact than regulatory legislation, leading to dramatic improvements in water quality nationwide.[50]

Pollution control was a key feature of this new federal role in managing the environment. Since the 1899 Refuse Act, the U.S. Army Corps of Engineers had required a permit before dumping solid waste into waterways. After the Second World War, faced with increasing pressures from rapid urban and suburban growth, Congress authorized money to support local water pollution control. A 1956 amendment appropriated $3 million for state water pollution efforts and $50 million per year for grants to help local construction, with the federal government paying up to 30 percent of the cost. Congress appropriated $100 million in 1961, and again raised the federal contribution in 1965 and 1966.[51] By the late 1960s water quality had appreciably improved in San Francisco Bay.

The national government's success in reducing pollution inspired environmentalists to look to the federal government to address other elements of their agenda. Activists found common cause with federal agencies when they realized that the federal government could become the means for achieving some of their ends. Sprawling suburbs sparked responses nationwide, but they were particularly visible on the Pacific coast, where regional identity prized natural beauty. In Western cities such as Seattle and San Francisco, air and water pollution, and the disappearance of undeveloped spaces around cities, preoccupied a generation of postwar political leaders.[52]

Like reformers of the early twentieth century, these postwar activists shared a faith in the power of government to resolve crises. Typically white, middle-class professionals comfortable with authority, they relied on organization, education, and research to identify problems and their solutions. Postwar urban conservationists, whether in Seattle or San Francisco, had great faith in comprehensive planning as the means to resolve all sorts of urban problems. Campaigns followed a familiar pattern: identify an urban problem, form a committee to research its causes and consequences, reach consensus on the best possible solution, build a coalition to press for governmental action, and resolve the issue through cooperative local, state, or federal actions. These civic activists organized in nonpartisan groups such as the League of Women Voters, where they argued that better planning and informed decision making would resolve many of the problems of urban growth.[53]

In the San Francisco Bay Area, many of the symptoms of runaway suburban growth, including pollution, rampant conversion of wildlife habitat to housing, and loss of public spaces, were manifested in the bay itself. The bay reflected many of the issues worrying midcentury Americans but at the same time possessed the region's largest reservoir of undeveloped open space in the salt ponds. A group of civic activists sought to use the bay to bridge the desire to protect environmental amenities and the need to better plan growth.

RECLAIMING THE BAYSHORE

A comedian working a San Francisco beatnik club in 1965 played on local sensitivities when he mocked both the city's foul namesake bay and the pretensions of the region's sprawling south bay suburbs. With a calypso beat that slyly reversed the advice to Americans traveling overseas, Tom Lehrer warned foreign visitors to San Francisco, "If you visit American city/You will find it very pretty/Just two things of which you must beware: Don't drink the water and don't breathe the air." Playing on the daily flow of the tides past San Francisco toward the south bay, Lehrer teased, "The breakfast garbage that you throw in to the Bay/They drink at lunch in San Jose."[54] Lehrer's barbs hit home because they showed up the sad condition of the region's most striking physical feature. Would you really leave your heart in San Francisco if you knew it would be awash in sewage?

By the late 1960s some kind of large-scale conversion of San Francisco Bay's remaining undeveloped tidelands—whether private real estate development, public recreational development, or the army corps plan—seemed inevitable.[55] Local activists responded by pushing state legislators to create a new bay commission. As its name suggested, the San Francisco Bay Conservation and Development Commission projected a moderate stance open to development as well as preservation. But in practice, commission staff sought new state powers over both state land and privately held baylands. Bay commission publications attacked the legal title of all privately held submerged lands and some tidelands and swamplands around San Francisco Bay. Bay commission staff argued that the people of the state retained a legal right, a public interest, in San Francisco Bay's bottomlands, and therefore the public retained the right to determine whether lands, even privately held areas, should be filled.[56] Previously, California's agencies rarely tested their power over tidelands. The State Lands Commission had preferred to swap parcels of land quietly to clear disputed titles rather than to challenge the murky titles held by many private owners.

Now the new state agency acted more aggressively. The bay commission's founding legislation opened with a preface that read like a manifesto for public ownership of the bayshore:

The Legislature hereby finds and declares that the public interest in the San Francisco Bay is in its beneficial use for a variety of purposes; that the public has an interest in the Bay as the most valuable single natural resource of an entire region, a resource that gives special character to the Bay Area; that the Bay is a single body of water that can be used for many purposes, from conservation to planned development; and that the Bay operates as a delicate physical mechanism in which changes that affect one part of the Bay may also affect all other parts.[57]

The bill passed in 1965 ensured that San Francisco Bay would be "analyzed, planned, and regulated as a unit," by creating a temporary commission whose sole purpose was to produce a plan for the proper use of San Francisco Bay. The language in the bill—planning, beneficial use, natural resource, conservation, and public interest—was conservative. But in 1969 California's legislature expanded the agency's jurisdiction and powers by making the San Francisco Bay Conservation and Development Commission a permanent state agency with regulatory power over all fill of San Francisco Bay tidelands and within one hundred feet from the water's edge. The bay commission was also given the power to require landowners to grant public access to the shoreline.

These new powers were challenged, and the bay commission validated its new authority over San Francisco Bay's tidelands by winning a series of lawsuits filed by disgruntled private investors and local governments.[58] The most serious challenge was filed by a collection of private investors hoping to develop thousands of acres of submerged land in San Mateo County putatively belonging to Ideal Cement Company. The so-called Westbay Associates brought suit to clarify their legal title and to develop their claimed properties. The lawsuit was not resolved until 1980, when the state and the investors negotiated a settlement that destroyed Westbay's hope to create a ten-thousand-acre industrial and commercial park on filled tidelands.[59]

The bay commission's eventual legal victories were much less certain in the 1960s, and locals turned to a second institution to settle the lingering question of how to protect undeveloped wildlife habitat in Leslie Salt Company's privately owned salt ponds. Preserving wildlife and creating recreational opportunities both required new ownership and new management of the salt ponds. This meant enlisting the expertise and the financial power of the federal government.

Federal agency personnel had their own long-standing interest in San Francisco Bay tidelands. In a 1954 national inventory of wetlands, fish and wildlife researchers had insisted that further loss of wetlands to development threatened both wildlife and sportsmen everywhere across the nation: "Never before in the Nation's history has been it so necessary to plan for the setting aside of land and water areas to serve the future needs of fish and wildlife, as well as to provide for the recreational needs of people who depend on these resources."[60]

Agency personnel recognized both the outstanding habitat value of wetlands to fish and waterfowl and their economic value to the hunters and fishermen who pursued game animals. The two were not necessarily opposed. So long as recreation meant observing, pursuing, or killing fish and migratory birds, preserving wildlife habitat could be perfectly consonant with developing outdoor recreation.[61] Both habitat and recreational demand were concentrated on the thin strip of ocean and bay shoreline, an area also undergoing intense pressure from urban and suburban growth.[62] An influential 1956 report, *Vanishing Shoreline*, reported that just 640 miles of U.S. coastline remained available for public purchase, and this land was going fast. Congress quickly acted to address these needs. The 1961 Housing Act included money to buy open space and parkland, and during the 1960s Congress greatly increased funding to buy private land to protect it from development.[63] By the mid-1960s, federal authorities in California possessed both more expertise and more money to protect undeveloped recreational open space and wildlife habitat than any state or local agency.

As federal officials decided that ownership was the only long-term solution to protecting wildlife habitat in San Francisco Bay, a group of local planning officials in the south bay were coming to the same conclusion, but for different reasons. As a member of the Santa Clara Planning Department, Arthur Ogilvie had been involved in the county's ambitious 1959 recreation plan, which envisioned highly developed water sports recreation areas in the south bay salt ponds. But by the late 1960s, Ogilvie determined that massively modifying the shoreline for recreation was both ecologically unwise and unlikely to win approval from local, state, and federal authorities. Like many others, he had come to see open space as the primary value of the salt ponds: not what they could become but what they seemed to represent already. And like many others in the region, Ogilvie grew concerned that the San Francisco Bay Conservation and Development Commission, stuck in legal battles, could not stop private landowners from filling their tidelands. Regulation could only do so much to protect open space. Ogilvie came to believe that only federal ownership would resolve the intractable problem of what to do with Leslie Salt Company's salt ponds.

Ogilvie helped organize a group of like-minded south bay citizens into the ponderously titled South San Francisco Bay Lands Planning Conservation and National Wildlife Refuge Committee. It was as recording secretary for that group that Ogilvie spoke to a congressional subcommittee in 1969. Ogilvie began by noting the complications facing any form of land development in the salt ponds. Subsidence and deep mud soils meant that any use of the salt ponds for building structures would require "extremely expensive development work." Ogilvie asserted that the cost of fill was so high that "we can ill afford to do much else than recreation, open space, and national wildlife refuge in the area because it is not suitable for conventional development." With the other members of his organization, he told Congress, "We see the wildlife refuge as one of the best land uses possible at this stage."[64]

In 1970, public pressure to preserve open space, such as Ogilvie's congressional testimony, linked with the long-standing agency interests to protect wildlife habitat and provide for recreation. In that year the secretary of the interior directed the Bureau of Outdoor Recreation, in conjunction with the Bureau of Sport Fisheries and Wildlife, "to study the wildlife and recreation values of the South San Francisco Bay and to determine the actions necessary for protection and use of the area." In their 1971 report, the two agencies endorsed a San Francisco Bay National Wildlife Refuge on twenty-two thousand acres of salt ponds in the south bay. The proposed refuge would achieve three goals: it would preserve "baylands natural resources" in the form of habitat for migratory birds, ducks, seals, and three endangered salt marsh animals; it would maintain open space;

and it would "provide for wildlife oriented recreation," including "environmental education," in the south bay's tidal wetlands.[65]

In six brief chapters, the 1971 report bluntly spelled out the need to permanently protect south San Francisco Bay's salt ponds and offered ecological, recreational, educational, and economic justification for creating a refuge. By 1970, the south bay retained much of the remaining undeveloped shoreline in the region, but these areas were threatened by urban development, new highways and airports, and consequent water pollution. Existing legal and regulatory protections were inadequate. While the newly created San Francisco Bay Conservation and Development Commission could legally protect state-owned submerged lands under the open bay, Bureau of Outdoor Recreation staff indicated that "the situation relative to salt ponds is less certain." Local and state authorities currently restricted development in the salt ponds through zoning regulations. However, bureau staff continued, "the best guess is that the salt ponds could be restricted to salt production as long as it is economically feasible, but, after that point, total prohibition of development would be difficult."[66] So long as salt ponds produced wealth, they also paid taxes. But if salt no longer paid, local governments might be tempted to permit development in the baylands to produce new revenues. Local regulation was "politically vulnerable," the report concluded. "Local zoning has historically been subject to intensive pressure, leaving it at the mercy of special interests." Outright federal purchase, bureau staff wrote, could resolve this insecurity and permanently protect the salt ponds. "A Federal partnership in land regulation," the report continued, "may add strength and permanence to [local] land use controls." A federal wildlife refuge on part of the south bay's salt ponds might help protect baylands beyond the refuge's boundaries.[67]

Eventually, the federal government did buy the salt ponds. In 1972, San Francisco Bay Area congressmen successfully sponsored a bill appropriating money to acquire some twelve thousand acres of salt ponds from Leslie Salt Company, using funds from the Land and Water Conservation Fund and waterfowl hunters' license fees paid into the Migratory Bird Conservation Fund. State and local governments contributed the money for another twelve hundred acres.[68] These purchases were supported by

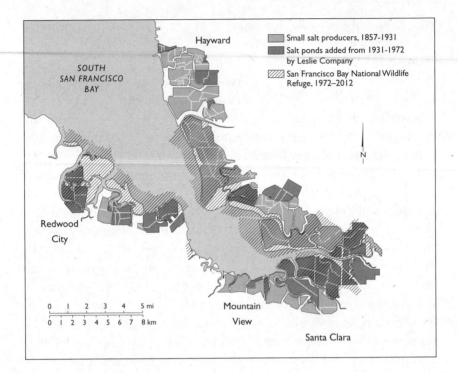

Map 6.   Salt ponds to national wildlife refuge.

new controls on the remaining salt ponds of the bay. Federal personnel explicitly designed the San Francisco Bay Wildlife Refuge to work in tandem with state regulations. "Establishment of the National Wildlife Refuge would be contingent on appropriate actions by the State of California to strengthen its regulatory powers as they apply to salt pond areas," wrote the Bureau of Outdoor Recreation's director.[69]

The refuge grew slowly from its initial basis in 1977. Congress appropriated money repeatedly between 1977 and 2003 to purchase salt ponds from Leslie Salt Company and its successor, Cargill. By 2003 the San Francisco Bay National Wildlife Refuge controlled most of the salt ponds and most of the bayfront in south San Francisco Bay. The conversion of bay wetlands into salt mines had evolved to a further step, a wildlife refuge made of former salt ponds.

FROM REAL ESTATE TO REFUGE

The establishment of the San Francisco Bay Conservation and Development Commission in 1965, its permanent renewal in 1969, and the funding of the San Francisco Bay National Wildlife Refuge in 1972 were revolutionary events in baylands history. The bay commission, on the one hand, restricted what landowners could do to their property, largely ending the long-standing practice of maximizing the economic potential of tidelands by filling them in. The wildlife refuge, on the other hand, abruptly transferred the bulk of San Francisco Bay's remaining privately held salt ponds into federal ownership. The long history of shifting public tidelands into private hands now reversed itself, with a federal agency suddenly the manager of the region's largest body of tidal wetlands.

The shift was also a return to earlier conditions resurrected in a new form. The bay commission reasserted a public interest in the tidelands that had been mostly dormant for a century since California's 1879 constitution banned further sales of tidal lands to individuals. And the national wildlife refuge eventually became the largest manager of salt marsh and shallow water habitats in San Francisco Bay, encompassing twenty-six thousand acres of former privately owned salt ponds.

These two institutions, the bay commission and the national wildlife refuge, reflected changing attitudes toward the bayshore, but more had changed than attitudes. The shift from seeing the bay as potential real estate to seeing it as valuable open space cannot be understood apart from the developmental process that was changing the bay. The bay commission and refuge exhibit two kinds of public purpose that crystallized in opposition to development plans in the San Francisco Bay Area. Together they represented a fundamental shift in the way Californians valued the tidal wetlands of San Francisco Bay and in their expectations for what tidelands ought to produce.

While the San Francisco Bay Conservation and Development Commission sought to restructure the basis for land use in the bay and its charter sought to work within existing structures, the San Francisco Bay National Wildlife Refuge used private property norms to claim private land for a subset of the public. The refuge was conventional in relying on the norms of real estate transfer. Unlike the commission, the refuge did not create new regulatory powers or reinterpret the meaning of ownership in the tidelands. The refuge bought land and development rights from private owners, acting in many respects like any other large landowner.

Yet the national wildlife refuge was radical in a different way. It was the fullest expression of a viewpoint that the tidelands were a precious ecological space best left empty of people. With a refuge in place, only transitory users could now pass through the tidelands—duck hunters, canoeists, and hikers. A refuge was not necessarily devoid of productive uses. Recreational hunters harvested a product in the refuge when they shot ducks and geese. But hunting depended on maintaining the biological productivity of the tidal wetlands. The annual harvest of ducks and geese was a by-product of wetlands, not a substitution for wetlands. When the refuge was carved out of private lands in 1972 its lands been mined for salt or shells, or exploited by oyster growers, for a century. The refuge properties had been among the most economically productive baylands in San Francisco Bay before they were purchased and redefined as waterfowl habitat. Now this productivity of the refuge's tidal wetlands benefited waterfowl.[70]

Between 1959 and 1985, nearly two million people moved into the San Francisco Bay Area, as the region's population rose to about five and a half million people. Looking back on this tremendous growth, longtime local observer Mel Scott noted general disagreement between "groups with widely divergent ideas of 'progress.'" But one thing had united these disparate residents of the region. Even the most divergent groups had agreed on the great value of San Francisco Bay to the area's landscape, climate, and historic past. Thanks in part to highly organized and vocal citizen groups, the San Francisco Bay Area, said Scott, more than any other metropolitan area in the United States, still retained its natural advantages. Citizens and political leaders collaborated to reduce pollution, preserve open space and parks, and hold on to "scenic and economic assets," such as farmland and, in particular, the bay itself.[71] Mel Scott was right to celebrate how much had been saved. Citizens were fortunate that the refuge had protected a large section of the bay's tidal shoreline from being paved over like so much of the surrounding flatlands. Yet much had changed, too. By the 1960s it was no longer safe to eat from San Francisco Bay. Much of the bayshore remained off-limits to the public, despite massive transfer of private salt ponds to nominally public ownership by the U.S. Fish and Wildlife Service. Organizers for a walking trail to ring the bay faced major obstacles. Pockets of entrenched industrial developments, public ports including two of the region's three commercial airfields, and a number of military bases blocked public access. The bay remained too often a mirage in the distance, seen but not touched.

It is critical here to remember how much had changed in the south bay from the 1840s to the 1970s. What had once been a landscape largely devoid of human beings, a place where European sailors got lost in a maze of winding, vegetation-lined tidal sloughs, was by the mid-1960s a vast expanse of identical, mud-walled evaporation ponds where corporate managers, not the tides, dictated the flow of water. These salt ponds were the latest in a series of economic uses of the tidal wetlands that had ultimately stripped the marshes of their very identity as tidal habitats. Environmental changes brought on by those economic uses helped dictate the future possibilities for the tidelands. Some uses, such as recreation and wildlife refuge, seemed in the 1960s to be more natural than others—more compatible with an ecological view of the bay. But wildlife habitat and recreation were also favored because they were among the few available choices after 150 years of manipulating the bayshore. It might still have been possible to breach holes in the dikes, drain the salt ponds, and raise oysters in the south bay mudflats, for example, but no agency would have permitted growers to sell them. Too many persistent toxins from bayside industries now tainted the bay's water and its mud bottom. Nor was the bay capable of supporting the abundance or diversity of species once present. By the 1960s, the ancient native oyster reefs that the Atlantic oyster beds rested on had been dredged up for cement and chicken feed. A century of building levees for salt ponds had narrowed the bay itself to essentially a deep shipping channel bracketed by hypersaline salt ponds. This bay was no longer a place to grow shellfish or to net shrimp. Subsidence due to overdrafting of freshwater aquifers under the bay, toxins in bay water and sediments, the absence of aquatic plants, and depleted fish populations all narrowed the possible productive uses of the baylands.

By the 1960s among the few remaining choices was further transformation of the baylands through fill into real estate. This was ruled out by a fierce public reaction based on the perception that San Francisco Bay was a public resource. The San Francisco Bay Conservation and Development Commission, validated by state legislation and court rulings, prevented the wholesale fill of the bay shoreline that might have covered the edge of the bay with privately sponsored industrial parks, housing developments, and landfills. Bay commissioners also made it clear that publicly funded recreational developments would have to meet the same standards. Instead of a series of marinas and luxury waterfront hotels such as the development at Berkeley, most local jurisdictions ended up with pocket-sized marshes or relatively undeveloped shoreline parks. Still, these were productive uses of the shoreline because they permitted public access for recreation—they made use of the baylands for human purposes.

San Francisco National Wildlife Refuge therefore reflected the limited possibilities of the twentieth-century tidal wetlands. In the refuge, productivity was redefined in ecological terms, as the maximum production of waterfowl. The salt ponds were modified slightly by allowing more water to circulate. They were enhanced, turning accidental bird habitat into permanent, high-quality waterfowl feeding areas. Both commission and refuge spoke to the productivity of the tidal wetlands, but the landscapes they watched over were very different kinds of productive landscape than the Ohlone Indians had known or than the ghost marshes underlying San Francisco. The refuge was a compromise, a place indelibly marked by industrial society yet serving as a precious island of waterfowl habitat in the midst of one of the world's great urban areas.

CONCLUSION **Rising Tides?**

Before modern chemical industries, estuaries' remarkable ability to con-
serve, recycle, and concentrate nutrients made these among the best
places on earth for people to find something to eat. Such concentrations
of energy are hard to find in nature. Understandably, people wanted to
live near estuaries and tidal margins. Nineteenth-century Americans
captured this richness in their saying, "When the tide is out, the table is
set." In an industrial world, the nature of tidal wetlands takes a perverse
twist. The wetlands' natural function of trapping particulate matter
means that the marshes and mudflats filter and concentrate industrial
wastes as well as organic nutrients. And in the wastes are chemicals and
compounds deadly to animals, including human beings. Industrial
activities like metal smelting, paper making, and petroleum refining
produce highly toxic by-products such as mercury, lead, chromium, and

a host of chlorinated compounds. Among the best known are polychlorinated biphenyls, or PCBs, and dioxin. These industrial by-products
attach to soil particles and settle in marshes and mudflats, where they
retain their toxicity for many years.[1]

Unfortunately, the dictum "dilution is the solution to pollution" does
not apply to these poisons. Indeed, the reverse may be true, thanks to the
food chain. Dispersed throughout the water and mud of San Francisco
Bay, a small quantity of mercury can still unerringly find its way into
human bodies through the process of bioaccumulation. Filter feeders,
like clams and oysters, sieve out some of the toxin as it circulates in the
bay's muddy water. Filter feeders accumulate mercury in their fatty tis-
sues, and their entire load passes up the food chain to fish or birds that
eat shellfish. These animals eat many clams and therefore concentrate
many small doses of poison in their own flesh. The clam eaters are in
turn eaten by other, larger predators and pass on their odorless, tasteless,
but diabolical gift. Eventually, a human being eats a bay fish or duck, and
the accumulated toxins pass into the human body.[2]

These persistent toxins present current inhabitants of the San
Francisco Bay region with a series of difficult choices. They are the
legacy of another time, the inheritance of previous generations' quest
for productivity. Mercury and PCBs represent the by-products of the
economies of the past two centuries. Nineteenth-century miners used
mercury to strip gold and silver out of the Sierra Nevada, and speculators converted this capital into real estate and reclaimed farmland in
the delta and beyond. In the twentieth century, shipyards and factories
used PCBs to cool the motors and insulate the power transformers that
together brought power and electricity to the region and sparked an
economic boom from the 1930s to 1970s. This wealth supports the
present generation. But unlike the Ohlone Indians, whose mounds of
waste collected for centuries with little impact, the economies of the
nineteenth and twentieth centuries have left a toxic legacy. That legacy
is with us in the bay. A bioassay of bay mud is like a catalog of the industrial sins of past generations. Now we find that our choices are
limited by the remnants of vanished industries, by past generations'
ways of using the bay.

The toxic accretion of the past is not an academic point. It is a pressing issue. Hundreds or possibly thousands of people—no one seems to know how many and no one is counting—eat fish and shellfish from San Francisco Bay each day. They and their families are imperiled by mercury in fish and PCBs in clams. Meanwhile, a broad coalition of bay residents hopes to restore tidal marshes in the Bay Area and perhaps stave off the extinction of a number of bay plants and animals.[3] Restoration would mean opening up salt ponds and diked farmlands to the tides once again. The tides would stir bay mud that has not seen currents in decades. Buried within the layers of mud are tons of mercury that washed down with hydraulic mining debris. Opening up the ponds to circulation once again could liberate the mercury and, by exposing it to oxygen, create a chemical reaction that makes relatively harmless elemental mercury into toxic methyl mercury. "This could be a prescription for disaster," one scientist said about restoration efforts. "We could end in 10 years with a suite of marshes that have dramatically increased methyl mercury levels in fish around the estuary." Even restoring the wetlands, it turns out, is complicated by past efforts to improve them.[4]

More than the past's toxic legacy bedevils restoration. Whether to restore and to what condition are old questions that connect to persistent disagreement about the purpose of the tidelands. When different people look at the salt ponds (or the bay margin before the salt ponds were built) they see different landscapes and different futures. If the goal is waterfowl production, it may be best to leave the salt ponds alone, as was done in the past at the Don Edwards San Francisco Bay National Wildlife Refuge. Salt ponds, with minimal tinkering, turned out to be ideal feeding grounds for ducks. If the goal was to grow ducks, maintaining salt ponds was enough. If, on the other hand, the concern is with endangered salt marsh mice, or the burrowing owls that eat them, then grassy marshes are the ticket, and not just any grass but the native salt grasses.[5] Because those marshes were destroyed a century ago, having marshes means making new ones. Because restoration privileges the past—it is supposed to be, after all, a return to some previous condition—how salt ponds are defined is crucial to their future use. Is this a salt pond or a former marsh? Or was it a saline pan? Perhaps neither, but rather former bay shallows now filled in by stream deposits? These scientific questions, which seem to be matters of fact, have political consequences. Beneath everything else lie the questions that have shrouded the tidelands since the nineteenth century: How will the tidal margin be used? And who gets to use the tidelands?[6]

These debates, already contentious, are only made more urgent by the recognition that world sea levels are rising. Marshes are the first line of defense against the damage caused by storms and flooding. Restoring marshes is now not just a matter of defending animal habitat but of defending the built environment that makes the Bay Area's economy work. Roads, airports, and harbor facilities around the bay are all near sea level. Surrounding these spaces with restored marsh might protect them and reduce the huge cost of walling in this essential social infrastructure.[7]

The salt mines of San Francisco Bay are now the focus of one of the world's most ambitious and most expensive ecological restoration projects. Armed with historical ecology studies, the latest management techniques, and hundreds of millions of federal dollars, the South Bay Salt Pond Restoration Project has begun breaching levees on fifteen thousand acres of salt ponds to create tidal marshes, mudflats, and other wetland habitats. The project shares some similarities with past efforts to remake the bay. Restorationists use some of the same tools (dredgers, dikes, and levees) as the land speculators and farmers who drained the delta. Like the oyster growers and salt miners, restorationists hope to make the bay more productive. And like the environmentalists who created wildlife refuges, restorationists justify transforming the bay as better for both human beings and for nature. But there are some significant differences that make this effort both urgent and hopeful. This time, history matters. The restoration project attempts to use the past as a guide, creating marshes where marshes once existed rather than randomly across the landscape. And this project is more cautious and more deliberate than past efforts. Using the principles of adaptive management, restorationists are flexible in their planning. If, for example, they discover that breaching the levees causes a spike in methyl mercury, they can slow or reverse their decisions. Most of all, the salt pond restoration project is much more democratic than past changes. Public meetings and publicly accessible reports mark a sea change in the way the bayshore is managed.[8] This at least is the goal.

The salt pond restoration project aims to bring back some of the bay's lost wetlands, but it cannot restore the lost connections between the bay and its people. Of all the remarkable changes in San Francisco Bay's shoreline over the past two hundred years, none is more dramatic than its abandonment as a place of work. In 1750, the bay's edge still concentrated one of the densest human populations in native North America. The people lived off the animals and plants provided by the rich mud and fecund marshes. A hundred and fifty years later, many people still fished and gathered in the tidelands—oyster growers, shrimp fishers, salt harvesters—and many more valued the rich fertility of drained and cultivated tidal soils. Today the Bay Area is home to seven million residents. These people live next to, over, and on the very edge of the land. If San Francisco, Oakland, and Redwood City got any closer to the water they would fall in. The same is true for San Diego, Los Angeles, Seattle, and Juneau, and that is only the West Coast of the United States. Yet today a walker on the tidelands anywhere along the bay is unlikely to see a single person working. The only people on the bayshore—excepting of course the million commuters who cross the bay daily by car and train—are other walkers, out for a stroll. Ecologists and environmentalists who want to restore the bay—people genuinely concerned for the heritage of future generations—should remember that among the greatest losses in the past century has been human knowledge of the tidal edge, knowledge gained through working in those places. If history tells us anything about the bay, it is that people have always known the bay as a resource for food. That fading sense of connection is a radical change, even more radical than the past century and a half of chemical poisoning, filling, draining, and diverting rivers. The greatest danger for the human relationship to San Francisco Bay is to ignore it. Removing people and their work from the tidal margin would be a terrible loss.[9]

There is some hope that Californians have begun to understand the bayshore rather than just to imagine it. People have begun to see the bay as their front yard, not their back yard. People dump things and bury things in their back yard. They store unwanted junk for later, they hide stuff, and they work in the back yard. Front yards, at least for more affluent Americans, are places to pass through but not to remain. Their owners keep them pretty by mowing the lawn and appreciate them as viewscapes. It is less easy to hide something in the front yard. This metaphor indicates the dangers as well as opportunities in the present vision of the bay. It is this tension between using the bay (and embracing it) and preserving the bay (but ignoring it) that typifies the American relationship to San Francisco Bay, its land, its water, and its shore.[10]

As we have seen, people in the past thought they were improving the bay's margin for their own and future generations. They acted as they saw best. Just as their actions had unintended and unexpected consequences, we can only guess what the consequences of our own actions will be. We cannot be sure what shadows our actions will cast, or if future generations will condemn or praise us. We can only hope that future generations around San Francisco Bay see the complexity of our own decisions and the limits we operated within.

In the minds of many people, San Francisco Bay is sterile. It serves in the media eye as a picturesque backdrop to the Golden Gate Bridge, a glossy postcard. But this vision leaves out people. The shore, even in its most flourishing marshes, is too often seen as a place to drive past and fly over.[11] Lack of imagination may not rank high on the list of ecological sins. But for more than a century, the people of the Bay Area were in danger of forgetting their greatest treasure. Right there, in front of them, sat the bay. Thanks to four decades of public purchases, improved sewage treatment, declining industrial effluents, and environmental regulations, the bay is more accessible and cleaner than it has been for nearly a century. A coalition of public-minded and ecologically savvy San Francisco Bay residents is currently attempting to shape new uses of the shore that will enhance its biological productivity and open it to all members of society. Will the bay be the front yard or the back yard of future generations?[12]

Notes

INTRODUCTION

1. These numbers fluctuate somewhat with the fortunes of the local economy, but downtown San Francisco has been the region's central workplace since the nineteenth century. Population data is from the U.S. Census, 2007 estimate, http://quickfacts.census.gov/qfd/states/06/06075.html (accessed February 23, 2009). Commuter data is from the San Francisco Bay Area Metropolitan Transportation Commission, "San Francisco County-to-County Commuting," www.calmis.ca.gov/file/commute-maps/sanfrcommute.pdf (accessed February 23, 2009).

2. Other scholars have used the concept of hybrid landscapes to refer to heavily modified wetlands. Richard White identifies this concept as part of a "cultural turn" among environmental historians. See White, "From Wilderness to Hybrid Landscapes." I am most influenced by White, *Organic Machine*. Other important works include deBuys and Myers, *Salt Dreams*; Fiege, *Irrigated Eden*; Langston, *Where Land and Water Meet*; and Wilson, *Seeking Refuge*.

3. John Steinbeck, unpublished preface for a handbook on common marine invertebrates of the California coast from Tomales Bay to Half Moon Bay, [1940], Letters to Gwendolyn C. Steinbeck and Other Papers, MSS 71/40c,

Bancroft Library, University of California, Berkeley. Ricketts first described the book in a 1939 letter to his friend, mythologist Joseph Campbell. E. F. Ricketts to Joseph Campbell, October 7, 1939, Edward F. Ricketts Papers, M0291, Special Collections, Stanford University Libraries. See also Edward F. Ricketts, "S.F. Bay area book," "S. F. Bay-area book," and "EFR Essay No. 2," Box 11, Folder 31, Edward F. Ricketts Papers, M0291, Special Collections, Stanford University Libraries. For more about this never-finished book, see Hedgpeth, *Outer Shores*, 31–41.

4.   Ted Steinberg has used the same metaphor in another way, comparing a river's deposits of sediment to the legal history of property. See Steinberg, *Slide Mountain*.

CHAPTER 1

1.   One of the defining characteristics of technological modernity is that we can, in fact, now experience each of these views. For a brilliant visual survey of bay habitats both human and natural, see Center for Land Use Interpretation, *Back to the Bay*. For a nighttime view from space showing the density of human settlement in the San Francisco Bay Area, see NASA, "Earth's City Lights," http://visibleearth.nasa.gov/view.php?id=55167 (accessed December 3, 2012). For a variety of images of bay landscapes, see the David Rumsey map collections online at http://davidrumsey.com (accessed November 9, 2012). For a map view of tidal bay habitats, see San Francisco Estuary Institute, *EcoAtlas*, www.ecoatlas.org (accessed May 25, 2004).

2.   This description of San Francisco Bay's natural history and ecology derives from Goals Project, *Baylands Ecosystem Habitat Goals*; Goals Project, *Baylands Ecosystem Species and Community Profiles*; and Whipple et al., *Delta Historical Ecology*.

3.   Atwater, "Ancient Processes," 39–40.

4.   Excess nutrients also create problems. Too much phosphorus and nitrogen overstimulate aquatic plants, which as they rot exhaust oxygen in the water and kill marine animals. This process of overfertilization, called eutrophication, is most common in bodies of water with poor circulation, but it can become a localized problem even in well-flushed estuaries, as we will see in the case of San Francisco Bay's twentieth-century shellfisheries. On eutrophication generally, see the textbook by two San Francisco Bay Area scientists, Horne and Goldman, *Limnology*, 464–473. For a famous case study of human-caused eutrophication, that of Lake Washington in Seattle, see Edmondson, *Uses of Ecology*, 285–287. For a discussion of eutrophication in estuaries, see Barlow, Lorenzen, and Myren, "Eutrophication of a Tidal Estuary."

5.   For accessible descriptions of life at the bottom of the watershed generally, and at the bottom of San Francisco Bay in particular, see Cooper, "Salt Marshes"; and the essays collected in Conomos, *San Francisco Bay.*

6.   Shaler, "Beaches and Tidal Marshes of the Atlantic Coast."

7.   A basic source is Skinner, *Historical Review of Fish and Wildlife Resources.* As San Francisco Bay fisheries declined, fishermen moved into offshore and southern California fisheries such as tuna and sardines. For this shift, see McEvoy, *Fisherman's Problem,* 65–92.

8.   On the remarkable currents of estuaries, and of San Francisco Bay in particular, see the essays in Conomos, *San Francisco Bay;* and Chin, Wong, and Carlson, *Shifting Sands and Shattered Rocks,* a recent publication by the U.S. Geological Survey.

9.   Even this spectacular quantity, thanks to widespread destruction of the wetlands, represents a ten- to twenty-fold reduction in carbon supply since the 1850s. See Atwater et al., "History, Landforms, and Vegetation of the Estuary's Tidal Marshes," 375–376.

10.   Vancouver's and Menzies's journals have long been basic sources in California history. See Eastwood, "Menzies' California Journal"; and Eyer, *Vancouver in California,* 2:236–237.

11.   Eastwood, "Menzies' California Journal," 265–340.

12.   Literature on Ohlone management of Bay Area ecosystems is flourishing. See especially Lightfoot and Parrish, *California Indians and their Environment;* Blackburn and Anderson, *Before the Wilderness;* Bean, *Ohlone Past and Present;* and Striplen and DeWeerdt, "Old Science, New Science."

13.   Brown, "Salt for the Scraping." See also Heizer, "Salt in California Indian Culture." The term "a landscape of shellmounds" is from Fagan, *Before California.*

14.   Striplen and DeWeerdt, "Old Science, New Science."

15.   Rick and Erlandson, *Human Impacts on Ancient Marine Ecosystems,* 1–19.

16.   "Troy and Jericho" is from Eaton, "Still Waiting for the Book." For numbers and dimensions of shellmounds, see Nelson, "Shell Mounds of the San Francisco Bay Region." For burials and description of uses, see, among others, Schenk, "Emeryville Shellmound"; Uhle, "Emeryville Shell Mound"; Nelson, "Ellis Landing Shellmound"; and Gifford, "Composition of Californian Shell Mounds." For an approachable overview of the shellmounds and a discussion of their fate as exemplified by the Emeryville mound, see the two-part article by Sandra Sher, "Native Legacy of Emeryville." Australian scholar Betty Meehan argues that the San Francisco Bay shellmounds were critically important in shaping the discipline of archeology, making possible the influential "Berkeley School" of material culture. See Meehan, *Shell Bed to Shell Midden,* 4.

17.   On Ohlone economies and daily life, see Milliken, *Time of Little Choice.* Malcolm Margolin provides a highly imaginative account in *Ohlone Way.* Barbara

Bocek quantified Ohlone food consumption using shellmounds in the south bay; see her dissertation, "Hunter-Gatherer Ecology and Settlement Mobility." I thank Stanford campus archaeologist Laura Jones for her comments and for providing unpublished data.

18.   Nelson, "Shell Mounds of the San Francisco Bay Region." Archaeologist Barbara Bocek notes that Nelson missed several known shellmounds in the south bay, a sign that the four-hundred-odd mounds he did map merely scratch the surface of native peoples' dependence on shellfish.

19.   Everywhere in California, Indians suffered during the process of removal and incorporation into the Spanish missions. For an overview, see the essays in Heizer, *Smithsonian Handbook of the North American Indian*; see also Rawls, *Indians of California*, 13–21. For a harrowing description of the mission and American periods, see Hurtado, *Indian Survival on the California Frontier*.

20.   Rawls, *Indians of California*, 18.

21.   Randall Milliken describes plots to attack Bay Area missions and at least one conspiracy to rise up against Franciscans at Mission San Jose in 1804. Milliken, *Time of Little Choice*, 126–127, 155–156, 182–183, 281–285.

22.   Von Langsdorff, *Voyages and Travels*, 171.

23.   For examples of Spanish military expeditions against runaways and valley peoples, see Milliken, *Time of Little Choice*, 184–185, 189–191, 210–211, and 215–218. For a chronological sense of the expanding radius of Spanish control and disappearance of native villages, see ibid., 165–167, 179, 191, 193.

24.   Jackson and Castillo, *Indians, Franciscans, and Spanish Colonization*, 79, 127–128.

25.   California's horse-raiding nomads are reminiscent of Plains Indian peoples such as Comanches and Cheyenne, though the latters' histories are much better known. See West, *Contested Plains*; DeLay, *War of a Thousand Deserts*; Hamalainen, *Comanche Empire*. "Indians' New World" is from Merrell, *Indians' New World*.

26.   Duhaut-Cilly, *Voyage autour du monde*. Robert Jackson and Richard Castillo, using mission archival records, estimate that Mission Santa Clara held 14,500 cattle, 15,500 sheep, and 850 horses in 1828. Jackson and Castillo, *Indians, Franciscans, and Spanish Colonization*, 127–128.

27.   Randall Milliken describes Indian complaints about mission livestock destroying food crops in *Time of Little Choice*, 72–74, 98–99, 148, 221.

28.   Testimony of Harry G. Wade, March 21, 1860, in Proceedings of Francisco Berreyessa et al., Heirs of Guadalupe Berreyessa v. United States, for the Place Named "Rincon de los Esteros," Land Grant Case No. 239 (U.S. District Court for California Northern District 1863), 123–128, Bancroft Library, University of California, Berkeley.

29.   Historian Albert Hurtado describes the gold rush period as a time of genocide for California's native peoples. See Hurtado, *Indian Survival on the*

California Frontier. For the fate of California Indians in the gold rush era, see Heizer, *They Were Only Diggers;* and Heizer, *Destruction of California Indians.*

30. Halleck (1815–1872), from Oneida County, New York, was an officer in the Army Corps of Engineers. He later served as inspector of lighthouses on the Pacific coast, helped write California's first state constitution, directed a mercury mining operation, and gained fame as general-in-chief of the United States and chief of staff during the U.S. Civil War. "Henry Wager Halleck," *American National Biography Online,* www.anb.org/articles/04/04-00455.html (accessed August 9, 2011).

31. Hurtado, *Indian Survival on the California Frontier,* 92–96. For a comprehensive discussion of Indian labor and legalized slavery in American California, see Rawls, *Indians of California,* 81–108.

32. The later American experiment with "allotment" and its failures suggests that division of communal Indian lands generally ended badly, whether in 1830s Mexican California or 1880s U.S. Oklahoma. On allotment, see White, *"It's Your Misfortune,"* 114–116.

33. We know Iñigo's story thanks to the historical detective work of anthropologist Randall Milliken and historian Lawrence Shoup, who carried out contract investigative work on the site of a proposed Santa Clara County commuter rail station. See Shoup and Milliken, *Inigo of Posolmi.* For a description of the grant, see Beller, Salomon, and Grossinger, *Historical Ecology of Western Santa Clara Valley,* 27–31, 40.

34. In southern California, Californios (as Spanish-speaking Californians called themselves) continued fighting for several more months. For Battle of the Mustard Stalks, see Edwin Wilson Fowler, "Biographical Sketch of William Squire Clark Planned for Chronicles of the Kings," [1888], William Squire Clark Collection, MSS C-D 245:4, Bancroft Library, University of California, Berkeley.

35. After the end of fighting, American military officials struggled to understand, let alone enforce, Mexican laws. An American official in California doubted that a single copy of the Mexican laws governing California existed anywhere in the province. In this situation, great authority necessarily devolved to local officials, who often carried out functions of the legislative, judicial, and executive branches of government. See King, "Report of T. Butler King," 333.

36. This brief narrative draws from W.W. Robinson, *Land in California;* Grivas, *Military Governments in California;* Uzes, *Chaining the Land;* and G. Nash, *State Government and Economic Development.* On the U.S. land system generally, see Gates, *History of Public Land Law Development;* and Rohrbough, *Land Office Business.*

37. Lowell Bean argues that mission Indians used, and therefore "owned," the mission lands they worked. Their dispossession after secularization made Ohlones into landless peasants, a shift that must have been almost as wrenching

as leaving their native villages for the missions. Bean, *Ohlone Past and Present*, xxi. For an attempt to graphically represent land grants and Indian resistance, see De Groot and Booker, "Struggle for Ownership."

38.   This sketch of northern California in the 1840s is based on Weber, *Spanish Frontier in North America*, and essays in Heizer, *Smithsonian Handbook of the North American Indian*.

39.   On diseños, see Perez, *Land Grants in California*. An excellent graphic illustration of the relationship between mission and rancho boundaries is found in Morrison and Greger, *Mission and Rancho Lands of Mission San Jose*.

40.   This notion was republican in that it saw the basis of society as land, but it was a partial republicanism that depended on unfree laborers who themselves were denied land. The most lucid discussion of Mexican land grants is still Lounsbury, "Records of Mexican Land Claims in California." For a summary of Mexican laws in place in 1846, see Jones, *Report on Land Titles*.

41.   On Hispanic ideas of property and common access, see Montoya, *Translating Property*.

CHAPTER 2

1.   California Board of Tide Land Commissioners, *Report of the Board of Tide Land Commissioners*, 109, 134–140. For map, see Allardt, *Map No. 1 of Tidelands*.

2.   The starting point is Horwitz, *Transformation of American Law*. More recently, see Alexander, *Commodity and Propriety*. See also Rose, "Comedy of the Commons." Environmental historian Theodore Steinberg raised similar issues in his *Nature Incorporated* and expanded on the topic of landownership in *Slide Mountain*. Matt Klingle examined some of the same questions about Seattle's tidelands in his *Emerald City*.

3.   Williams, *Keywords*, 204–205.

4.   Ellickson, *Order without Law*, 52–62.

5.   On the commons, see the discussion in chapter 4 of this book.

6.   Soulé, Gihon, and Nisbet, *Annals of San Francisco*, 162–163.

7.   See Goals Project, *Baylands Ecosystem Habitat Goals*, 118–119.

8.   Michael N. Pearson and David Igler have developed this concept of a littoral society in the Pacific. See Pearson, "Case for the Coast"; Pearson, "Concept and Problems"; and Igler, "Diseased Goods." See also Igler, "Longitudes and Latitudes."

9.   Dana, *Two Years Before the Mast*.

10.   Longtime San Francisco printer and city supervisor C. A. Murdock made the claim for Richardson's house and supplied the 1844 figures in *Backward Glance at Eighty*, 101.

11.   Hittell, *History of San Francisco*, 120–128.

12.   Vance, *Geography and Urban Evolution*, 9–14.

13.   Lounsbury, "Record of Mexican Land Claims"; and Fritzsche, "San Francisco, 1846–1848."

14.   Goodwin, *Establishment of State Government*, 13–15.

15.   Ibid., 13–17; for Polk quotation, see Polk, *Diary*, 496–497.

16.   Hittell, *History of the City of San Francisco*, 106, 111, quotation page 18.

17.   Goodwin, *Establishment of State Government*, 281.

18.   King, "Report of T. Butler King," 333.

19.   Ibid., 333–334.

20.   Thomas Oliver Larkin, Eliab Grimes, and William Heath Davis to Robert Field Stockton, October 8, 1846, Larkin Papers Copy IV: 303, Bancroft Library, University of California, Berkeley.

21.   William Tecumseh Sherman, March 1847, as described in chapter 2 of his *Memoirs*. Italics added.

22.   On the grant, see Bryant, *What I Saw in California*. See also Goodwin, *Establishment of State Government*, 25–27, 29, and 41; Delgado, *To California by Sea*, 81; and Fritzsche, "San Francisco, 1846–1848," 17–34, quotation page 20.

23.   New York City's water lots are a focus of the foundational study of American municipal property law by Hendrik Hartog, *Public Property and Private Power*. It is clear from Hartog's work and that of Nancy S. Seasholes on Boston that the tradition of transforming the tidal margin to make urban real estate dates to the earliest period of American city building.

24.   For this technique, see the fine study of the historical development of Boston's shoreline by Nancy S. Seasholes, *History of Landmaking in Boston*. See also Seasholes, "Boston's Topographical Development in Maps."

25.   Pollard's Lessee v. Hagan, 44 U.S. (3 How.) 212 (1845).

26.   For the story of Sutter and Marshall's effort to get title to the gold country on the American River, see Bancroft, *History of California*, 6:40–44; for proclamation invalidating Mexican mining law, see Grivas, *Military Governments in California*, 119.

27.   Grivas, *Military Governments in California*, 32–37.

28.   For 1849 map, see Eddy, *Official Map of San Francisco*. For 1850 survey and sale, see Delgado, *To California by Sea*, 82. Two works provide a useful introduction to the legal culture of American California and the evolving judicial treatment of property claims: Bakken, *Practicing Law in Frontier California*; and Fritz, *Federal Justice in California*.

29.   One wonderfully insightful work on the deep roots of American land speculation is Charles Royster's study of efforts by leading Virginians, including the nation's first president, to profit from speculation in a swamp-draining scheme. See Royster, *Fabulous History of the Great Dismal Swamp*, esp. 49–104.

30.   Wheeler, *Land Titles in San Francisco.*

31.   Fritzsche, "San Francisco, 1846–1848," 20. City officials renamed Yerba Buena "San Francisco" in March 1847. See Soulé, Gihon, and Nisbet, *Annals of San Francisco,* 178–180. But as late as 1868 many locals still called their city "mud flat," which, of course, it was. See "Returned."

32.   Fritzsche, "San Francisco, 1846–1848," 20–25.

33.   On the "Colton grants" generally, see Soulé, Gihon, and Nisbet, *Annals of San Francisco,* 269. San Francisco lawyer and sometime state official Paul Hubbs reported on the legal uncertainty of water lot title in a series of letters to John Wilson, another lawyer and speculator. See Hubbs to Wilson, May 2, May 6, and July 1, 1854, John Wilson Correspondence and Papers, C-B 420:1, Bancroft Library, University of California, Berkeley.

34.   Soulé, Gihon, and Nisbet, *Annals of San Francisco,* 358–370.

35.   Delgado, *To California by Sea,* 82–84. I am indebted to Mr. Delgado, the director of Maritime Heritage at NOAA and former chief underwater archaeologist for the U.S. National Park Service, for his advice on this section.

36.   Sherman, *Memoirs,* 1:100–101.

37.   Ibid., 1:105–107, 132–133, 138.

38.   Quoted in Royster, *Destructive War,* 133–134.

39.   Bancroft, *History of California,* 6:178.

40.   Ibid., 6:173–175, 178.

41.   Ibid., 6:168.

42.   Eddy's map is reprinted in Kemble, *San Francisco Bay,* 9.

43.   This danger continued until at least the eve of the Civil War. Arriving in San Francisco in 1864, newspaperman C.A. Murdock recalled that pedestrians still "skirt gaping holes in the planked wharf, exposing the dark water lapping the supporting piles, and are assailed by bilge-like odors that escape." Murdock, *Backward Glance at Eighty,* 107. The continuing danger from poor drainage in downtown San Francisco is evident in letters from property manager George W. Merritt to real estate magnate Adolph Sutro. See George W. Merritt to Adolph Sutro, February 22 to July 11, 1889, Box 1:2, Adolph Sutro Papers, 1861–1899, JL 004, Special Collections, Stanford University Libraries.

44.   Bates, *Incidents on Land and Water,* 101–102.

45.   Ibid., 106.

46.   On fill, see Dow, "Bay Fill in San Francisco"; and Olmstead and Olmstead, *San Francisco Waterfront.*

47.   For editor's prediction, see "The Fire of Yesterday," *Daily Alta California,* May 5, 1851.

48.   It is not clear which species of wood-burrowing animals caused the destruction in the 1850s. According to the exhaustive study by the San Francisco Bay Marine Piling Committee, the culprit was most likely a species from the

genus *Bankia,* native to western North America. This animal bores into the wooden piling below the water line and then tunnels actively within the piling. Damage is therefore invisible until the piling suddenly fails, sometimes spectacularly. Hill and Kofoid, *Marine Borers,* 15–16, 190, 205.

49. Purkitt, *Letter on the Water Front Improvement;* see also Hill and Kofoid, *Marine Borers,* 13–16.

50. "Terrible Conflagration! San Francisco Again in Ruins! Several Squares Destroyed! Loss about $5,000,000. Several Lives Lost!" *Daily Alta California,* May 4, 1851. For wind, see "Reflection After the Event," *Daily Alta California,* May 6, 1851. For visibility in Monterey, see "Reflection of the Fire," *Daily Alta California,* May 6, 1851.

51. "The Fire of Yesterday," *Daily Alta California,* May 5, 1851. For fragment of Long Wharf, see *California Courier,* June 19, 1851, cited in Waldorf, "Gentleman from Vermont," 113.

52. Dow, "Bay Fill in San Francisco."

53. *Daily Alta California,* April 12, 1851.

54. Bonnett, *San Francisco by Land and Sea.*

55. Murdock, *Backward Glance at Eighty,* 108.

56. Royce, *California,* 169. Cites *Daily Alta California,* July 19 and July 31, 1851.

57. See "Pamphlets on San Francisco Lands," 4:1–4, Bancroft Library, University of California, Berkeley. For wharves trapping sediment, see testimony of Captain James Alden, U.S. Navy, in California Legislature, Assembly Committee on the Bulkhead, *Testimony against a Bulkhead or Seawall,* 3–4. Pro-bulkhead publications include Purkitt, *Letter on the Water Front Improvement;* and J.P. Robinson, *Report upon Condition and Requirements.* Testimony both for and against a bulkhead is collected in Special Committee of the California State Assembly, *Testimony and Report of the Committee.* For bulkhead and seawall in San Francisco politics, see G. Nash, *State Government and Economic Development,* 106–123.

58. Enos, "Condition of Laborers," 19–20. For Sansome Street between Filbert and Green Streets, see ibid., 52, 54. For English statement, see ibid., 61. At times it seemed that the seawall was driving the city's excavation and regrading efforts. A city supervisor up for reelection in 1884 found that he had incurred the wrath of the city's powerful seawall contractor, the San Francisco Bridge Company. City supervisor John T. Sullivan charged that foreman Thomas Barry had threatened to use the Bridge Company's influence to have Sullivan defeated. Ibid., 113–114.

59. Hittell, *History of San Francisco.*

60. The seawall effectively destroyed San Francisco's remaining tidal habitats by replacing beach or shore with a stone wall. But pilings and rock walls became intertidal habitats in their own right, as ecologists Edward Ricketts and

Jack Calvin recognized with a chapter in their book on the intertidal habitats of the Pacific coast. Ricketts and Calvin, *Between Pacific Tides*.

61. Shumate, *Rincon Hill and South Park*.

62. Population figure from Commonwealth Club of San Francisco, *Population of California*, 7. See also Johnson, *Founding the Far West*, 238.

63. California Board of State Harbor Commissioners, *Biennial Report for the Two Fiscal Years Commencing July 1, 1896, and Ending June 30, 1898*.

64. For nine hundred acres, see State Harbor Commissioners, *Biennial Report, 1906–1908*, 15.

65. The Ewing seismograph at the University of California in Berkeley recorded that the earthquake began at 5:12 A.M. and lasted two minutes. San Francisco *Mining and Scientific Press*, vol. 92, April 21, 1906, 1.

66. Soulé, "Earthquake and Fire Effects," 136.

67. Captain Charles J. Cullen, "Report," in Frederick J. Bowlen, *Materials Relating to the San Francisco Fire Department*, Vol. 7, Copies of Reports of Fire Officers in the 1906 Fire, Microfilm 983:3, Bancroft Library, University of California, Berkeley.

68. Earthquakes shook Mission Dolores and the Presidio in 1808 and 1818. For dates, see Hittell, *History of San Francisco*, 66, 354, 370. On the earthquake of 1865, see Sharpsteen, "Vanished Waters of Southeastern San Francisco."

69. Hansen and Condon, *Denial of Disaster*, 20.

70. Darleth, "Destructive Extent of the California Earthquake of 1906."

71. Watkins, "San Francisco Earthquake." Watkins wrote the letter on April 24, 1906, and it was first published seventy-five years later.

72. Ibid., 262.

73. For a description of the fire, see Gilbert et al., *San Francisco Earthquake and Fire of April 18, 1906*; and California State Earthquake Investigation Commission, *California Earthquake of April 18, 1906*.

74. Hansen and Condon, *Denial of Disaster*, 62. See also "Vast Army Has Left the City," San Francisco *Chronicle*, April 25, 1906. Thanks to the Southern Pacific Company's saltwater-pumping machinery, the company's depot and tracks downtown did not burn, freeing them to carry passengers out of the city. For Southern Pacific ferries and trains, see the Southern Pacific publicity brochure, "San Francisco Imperishable," available online at the Museum of the City of San Francisco primary source collection website, www.sfmuseum.org/conflag/imperish.html (accessed June 15, 2005).

75. See California State Earthquake Investigation Commission, *Map Showing 1906 Apparent Earthquake Intensity*.

76. The links between 1906 and 1989 are explored in "The 1989 Loma Prieta, CA, Earthquake and Its Effects," a special issue of the *Bulletin of the Seismological Society of America* 81, no. 5 (October 1991).

77.   Bill Cronon has also used the phrase "ghost landscapes" to describe the cutover lands deforested by Chicago's nineteenth-century lumber industry. Cronon, *Nature's Metropolis*, 168–169. San Francisco Bay's ghost tidelands have much in common with other landscapes transformed by industrial economies. But an important difference from other such transformed landscapes, as will become clear in chapter 5, is that tidelands by their nature are more resilient than most other landscapes. They are both harder to permanently eradicate—as the 1906 earthquake showed—and easier to superficially transform.

78.   The primacy of property also informs a long-standing question in San Francisco historiography: why was the looting and stealing that was blamed on Sidney convicts in 1849, and again in 1851, the occasion of so much concern and such organized and violent reprisals? Law and order—meaning the protection of property—were the overriding concern of established San Franciscans, including the city's merchant elite. See Soulé, Gihon, and Nisbet, *Annals of San Francisco*, 553–587.

CHAPTER 3

1.   Goals Project, *Baylands Ecosystem Habitat Goals*, 26–30.

2.   Galloway and Riley, "San Joaquin Valley, California."

3.   On the natural history of the freshwater tidelands region, see Bay Institute, *From the Sierra to the Sea*, 2.54–2.76; Minick and Bohn, *Delta West*, 13–23, especially map of the region by Patricia Booker, 17; Bakker, *Island Called California*.

4.   For pines, larches, and larkspur, see Brown, *Description of Distant Roads*, 62.

5.   For Crespi, Font, and *pielago*, see ibid., 103. Brown notes that the term "delta properly belongs to alluvial fans where great rivers spread and shallow as they debouche into oceans or lakes, rather than tidal confluences such as this one." For Anza, see Bolton, *Anza's California Expeditions*, 145–147.

6.   Ecological historian Alan K. Brown suggests that "epimarine" is the most appropriate term. Brown, *Description of Distant Roads*, 100.

7.   Richard White notes that the delta's vast wet grasslands were similar in some respects to Hudson's Bay, Canada, and that European visitors were similarly perturbed by the difficulty both of navigating and of using these watery grasslands. Pers. comm., May 5, 2004.

8.   Sullivan, *Travels of Jedediah Smith*.

9.   Taxonomists have repeatedly revisited the bulrush family, *Scirpus*, in the past century. The San Francisco Bay delta's common tule bulrush was once called *Scirpus lacustris*. Other related forms include *S. americanus* and *S. californicus*. See the discussion in Faber, *Common Wetland Plants*, 43, 52–55. Botanist Peter Baye

notes that several languages refer to bulrushes and cattail reeds as a single unit, based on their utility—in Greek, *Typha* is interchangeable with "marsh," suggesting the interdependence of this species with standing water. Peter Baye, pers. comm., May 15, 2003.

10. For the habitat and life history of Pacific coastal forms of *Typha* and *Scirpus*, see Guard, *Wetland Plants of Oregon and Washington*, 68, 88–89; see also Baye, "Tidal Marsh Plants."

11. Such dreams can turn to tragedy when they lead to stories without conclusions, without happy endings. This definition of tragedy as stories without conclusions derives from Aristotle's *Poetics*. I am grateful to David Kennedy for the concept and citation. Pers. comm., March 15, 2000.

12. On the delta mounds, see Cook and Heizer, "Physical Analysis of Nine Indian Mounds"; for mound contents, see Cook and Treganza, "Quantitative Investigation of Indian Mounds."

13. Muir, "The Bee Pastures."

14. Fremont, *Report of the Exploring Expedition*, 248–249.

15. Buffum, *Six Months in the Gold Mines*, 29.

16. Bancroft, *History of California*, 7:1. Linda Nash discusses finishing in her study of health and California's Central Valley, "Finishing Nature." See also L. Nash, "Transforming the Central Valley." Another fine recent study is Valencius, *Health of the Country*.

17. Bidwell, "Life in California Before the Gold Discovery."

18. Gates, *Farmer's Age*, 18–19.

19. Historians could much improve our understanding of California history, from the Spanish era forward, by placing its development in the context of other states established on the margins of the Spanish empire. For an example of the utility of this approach, see Weber, *Spanish Frontier in North America*. Paul Wallace Gates deserves credit for placing Western land policy in the context of southern and midwestern history; see his *History of Public Land Law Development*.

20. King, "Report of T. Butler King," 348.

21. *U.S. Statutes at Large* 9 (Act of September 28, 1850), 519. Benjamin Hibbard traces the history of this act to Louisiana's state-funded flood prevention effort. Hibbard, *History of Public Land Policies*, 269.

22. From the early days of the new republic, federal land policy was designed to raise revenue through the sale of public lands; passing land to the states was supposed to permit the same arrangement at the state level. Hibbard, *History of Public Land Policies*, 1–3, 33, 64. See also Prince, *Wetlands of the American Midwest*, 140–148; and Rohrbaugh, *Land Office Business*, 34. Despite this policy, approximately 40 percent of California remains federal land to this day.

23. For the story of the 1850 swampland act, see Gates, *History of Public Land Law Development*, 321–330; Hibbard, *History of Public Land Policies*, 269–274; and Robbins, *Our Landed Heritage*, 154–156.

24. For a narrative history of California swampland legislation to 1868, see Kelley, *Battling the Inland Sea*, 35–36, 41–62; and J. Thompson, "Reclamation and Abandonment." See also Peterson, "Failure to Reclaim," 45–60. For 790,000 acres and two hundred persons, see California State Joint Committee on Public and State Lands, *Report Upon the Condition of the Public and State Lands*.

25. Haight, "Governor's Message," 41.

26. George, *Our Land and Land Policy*, 36–37.

27. George, "What the Railroad Will Bring Us," 305.

28. Ibid., 302.

29. Ibid., 306.

30. Greeley, cited in California State Joint Committee on Public and State Lands, *Report Upon the Condition of the Public and State Lands*, 10–11.

31. Gates, *History of Public Land Law Development*, 321–325. See also Pisani, "Beyond the Hundredth Meridian," 476.

32. For a more sympathetic view of Green and his role in drainage politics, see Kelley, *Battling the Inland Sea*, 35–62.

33. California State Land Commission, *Report of the State Land Commission*, 43.

34. Ibid., 42.

35. Ibid., 44.

36. Ibid., 44.

37. California State Joint Committee on Public and State Lands, *Report Upon the Condition of the Public and State Lands*, 61–64, 208.

38. Tide Land Reclamation Company, *Fresh Water Tide Lands of California*, 1; and "Incorporations," *Sacramento Daily Union*, June 16, 1869. Of these men, Lloyd Tevis is the central figure and the least known. Tevis came to California in 1849 and established a law practice with his brother-in-law, James Ben Ali Haggin. Tevis was president of Wells Fargo and owner of or investor in Pacific Express Co., Spring Valley Water, the Sutro Tunnel, and Bank of California. Tevis was also a major landowner in his own right (with Haggin, his partner) in delta swamplands on Staten Island, California. No papers survive, and the man is shrouded in mystery. What we know of Tevis is through letters written by his friends and business acquaintances, men like William C. Ralston and C. P. Huntington. The 1880 federal census does record a woman who might be Tevis's wife living in San Rafael, California, north across the bay from San Francisco. Martha E. Tevis, single white woman, aged fifty years, born in Kentucky in 1830 and a homemaker. National Archives Film T9–0068, p. 112B.

39. The company prospectus, first printed in 1869, claimed ownership of 120,000 acres and a capitalization of $12 million. Tide Land Reclamation Company, *Fresh Water Tide Lands*, 5.

40. As described in Tide Land Reclamation Company, *Fresh Water Tide Lands*, 5.

41. William Bierlie Hyde, "FIRST DRAFT Preliminary private prospectus Incorporation of the California Steam Cultivation Company Capital Stock $1000 000," Box 1, Letterbook 2: 96–99, William Bierlie Hyde Papers, MS 267, Special Collections, Stanford University Libraries.

42. Ibid.; Hyde, "Preliminary private prospectus of the Incorporation of the California Steam Cultivator Company," Box 1, Letterbook 2: 100–106, William Bierlie Hyde Papers, MS 267, Special Collections, Stanford University Libraries.

43. Hyde to Henry D. Bacon, November 24, 1871; Hyde to Bacon, January 11, 1872, William Bierlie Hyde Papers, MS 267, Special Collections, Stanford University Libraries.

44. Hyde increasingly focused on his steam plow to the exclusion of all other elements. See Hyde to I. Friedlander, "Statement relating to the Steam Plow property owned by Wm. B. Hyde and O. Hyde," June 1872; and Hyde to Friedlander, September 2, 1872, William Bierlie Hyde Papers, MS 267, Special Collections, Stanford University Libraries. Roberts sold much of his delta properties to Thomas H. Williams just four years later. "Real Estate Transfers," *Sacramento Daily Union*, March 25, 1876, 5.

45. For Roberts's levee, see W. H. Parks to George D. Roberts, December 30, 1871, George D. Roberts Correspondence, MSS C-B 466:3, Bancroft Library, University of California, Berkeley. See also William Bierlie Hyde to H. D. Bacon, January 11, 1872, Box 2, Folder 10, William Bierlie Hyde Papers, MS 267, Special Collections, Stanford University Libraries.

46. Steinberg, *Nature Incorporated*, discusses nuisance abatement.

47. On labor conflict in late nineteenth-century California agriculture, see Street, *Beasts of the Field*, particularly 205–231. On labor strife in the late nineteenth-century United States generally, see Painter, *Standing at Armageddon*.

48. U.S. Congress, *Report of the Joint Special Committee to Investigate Chinese Immigration*, 441.

49. Labor historian Richard Street describes illness and death among Chinese men reclaiming the Tide Land Company's property on Twitchell Island in 1870. Street, *Beasts of the Field*, 263.

50. The work regime is described in ibid., 262.

51. U.S. Congress, *Report of the Joint Special Committee to Investigate Chinese Immigration*, 440, 442.

52. J. P. Thompson, "Settlement Geography," 223. Flooding helped drive recurrent efforts to plant rice in California. See "Rice Growing in California."

53. Chan, *This Bittersweet Soil*, 185.

54. In 1876, Roberts and his brother Joseph sold 8,798 reclaimed acres on Grand Island to Thomas Williams for $300,000. This was big money in the nineteenth century. "Real Estate Transfers," *Sacramento Daily Union*, March 25, 1876, 5.

55. For risks, see J. P. Thompson, "Settlement Geography," 223; and Chan, *This Bittersweet Soil*, 181, 185.

56. Assistant state engineers interviewed landowners and carefully surveyed irrigation projects in the San Joaquin valley in 1878, and their notes describe both methods of building levees and the problems plaguing reclamation. For peat soils and cracks, see E . E. Tucker, "Swamp Land District No. 118," Field Note Book #91, Box 23: State Engineering Department; and "Mandeville Island Swamp Land District No. 59 Mr. J. Beedy Authority," Field Note Book #93, William Hammond Hall Papers, AC 91–07–04, California State Archives, Sacramento.

57. Bray, Bates, and Land, *Dredging*, 1–7.

58. The outstanding book on dredging in California is Thompson and Dutra, *Tule Breakers*.

59. McPhee, *Assembling California*, 455–457.

60. Hagwood, *Commitment to Excellence*, 7.

61. Kelley, *Battling the Inland Sea*, 73.

62. Hagwood, *Commitment to Excellence*, 17.

63. Consulting engineer James Eads asserted that levee construction worsened the effect of flooding in the valley, in part by narrowing the area over which water could spread and also because improperly constructed levees regularly broke. These impacts were further aggravated by hydraulic mining debris. "The evil effects of these disturbances of the regimen of the river have been greatly aggravated by the detritus carried into its bed from the hydraulic mines located near the canons tributary to it." Eads, *Report of James B. Eads*, 5.

64. Gilbert, *Hydraulic Mining Debris in the Sierra Nevada*, 29–30.

65. Stephen Pyne underplays Gilbert's contribution to the study of eustasy and river dynamics in his otherwise fine biography. Pyne, *Grove Karl Gilbert*.

66. Gilbert assumed that debris moved downstream at about the same rate that it entered the river in the first place, so that once debris stopped entering the Sacramento River system, it would predictably move through the river and into the delta, bay, and ocean. Later scholars modified Gilbert's conclusions by pointing out that as floods move debris out of tributaries like the Bear River, they also mobilize more debris stored in smaller and smaller creeks. In sum, some hydraulic mining debris is still moving out of the Sierra. James, "Storage and Transport of Hydraulic Gold Mining Sediment."

67. For Chinese workers, see Street, *Beasts of the Field*, 260–266; and Chan, *This Bittersweet Soil*, 181–186; for description of problems with cut-peat levee

walls, see Browne, "Agricultural Capacity," 303. For specific cases, see L. E. McAfee, "Swamp Land District No. 148," January 1, 1876, Box 23: Book 91, William Hammond Hall Papers, California State Archives, Sacramento.

68.   On seepage under rock levees on peat soils, see Browne, "Agricultural Capacity," 303. On the process of oxidation in peat soils, see Ingebritsen and Ikehara, "Sacramento-San Joaquin Delta."

69.   Roberts, "Reclamation of California Delta Lands," 95.

70.   Donald Worster summarizes Karl Wittfogel's argument in *Rivers of Empire*, 22–60.

71.   Gilbert, *Hydraulic Mining Debris in the Sierra Nevada*, 31, 65–67.

72.   Foote, "Redemption of the Great Valley of California."

73.   Rhode, "Learning, Capital Accumulation, and Transformation."

74.   For advantage, see Tide Land Reclamation Company, *Fresh Water Tide Lands*, 6; for tide gates, see Browne, "Agricultural Capacity," 302.

75.   E. E. Tucker, "Staten Island," Box 23: State Engineering Department Field Book No. 89, William Hammond Hall Field Books, California State Archives, Sacramento.

76.   Ibid.

77.   Reference from Richard White, pers. comm., March 15, 2004.

78.   On the Miller and Lux land empire in California, see Igler, *Industrial Cowboys*; on Miller and Lux management of wetlands in Oregon, see Langston, *Where Land and Water Meet*.

79.   J. P. Thompson, "Settlement Geography," 240–241.

80.   S. E. D. Field Notebooks, pp. 9–10, Book 8, Box 1978, Hall Papers, California State Archives, Sacramento.

81.   Bancroft, *Works*, 279.

82.   Holmes, *History of Federal Water Resources Programs*, 4. For quotation, see President's Water Resources Commission, *Report of the Commission*, 112–121.

83.   Hagwood, *Commitment to Excellence*, 9.

84.   Ibid., 19.

85.   Ibid., 36.

86.   California Department of Public Works, Division of Water Resources, *San Joaquin River Basin*, 504–506.

87.   "Sowing Rice—Reaping Shipworms."

88.   Cited in Hagwood, *Commitment to Excellence*, 31.

89.   Galloway, Jones, and Ingebritsen, *Land Subsidence in the United States*, 82.

90.   On salinity, see Hill and Kofoid, *Marine Borers*; see also California Department of Public Works, Division of Water Resources, *Variation and Control of Salinity*.

91.   Browne, "Reclamation and Irrigation," 381–382.

92.   Chan, *This Bittersweet Soil*, 168–169.

93.   J. P. Thompson, "Settlement Geography," 219.

94.   California Department of Public Works, Division of Water Resources, *San Joaquin River Basin*, 122–123.

95.   McWilliams, *Small Farm and Big Farm*, 7.

96.   Taylor and Lange, *American Exodus*, 147.

97.   The *Oxford English Dictionary* defines *dystopia* as "an imaginary place or condition in which everything is as bad as possible."

98.   Ickes referred to landowners' efforts to overturn the 160-acre limitation in the 1902 Reclamation Act. Ickes to Frank Clarvoe, editor of the *San Francisco News*, October 31, 1945. Cited in P. Taylor, "Statement to House Government Operations Committee," 533.

99.   McWilliams, *Factories in the Field.*

100.   For descriptions of lost abundance, see Dasmann, *Destruction of California*; and Moyle, "Introductions in California."

101.   Worster, *Rivers of Empire*, 47.

102.   Ari Kelman describes levees playing a similar role in marking off private from public in New Orleans in *A River and Its City*. See also Barry, *Great Mississippi Flood of 1927.*

103.   On the Fort Point gauge, see Theberge, *150 Years of Tides on the Western Coast.*

CHAPTER 4

1.   London, *Cruise of the Dazzler*, 149–169.

2.   Indeed, London told another version of this story from the perspective of a state officer. In "On the Oyster Beds," London wrote of another boy-becoming-a-man who daringly captures a gang of oyster pirates in these very same waters. See *Tales of the Fish Patrol*. London wrote about his career as an oyster pirate and fish patrolman in his powerful and partly fictional autobiography, *John Barleycorn.*

3.   Among London's first book-length works were *Cruise of the Dazzler* (1902) and *Tales of the Fish Patrol* (1905). Both tell substantially the same stories, from the perspective of the oyster pirate in *Cruise of the Dazzler* and from the perspective of a state patrol agent in *Tales of the Fish Patrol*. London had been a published author for only a little over two years when *Cruise of the Dazzler* appeared. For dates of writing and publication, see Jack London, Magazine Sales Notebooks, Huntington Library, cited in James Williams, "Jack London's Works by Date of Composition," http://london.sonoma.edu/Essays/comp_date.html (accessed November 5, 2012).

4.   American historians have long investigated land tenure, access to natural resources, and public versus private property. For scholars from Frederick

Jackson Turner to Paul Wallace Gates, Peter Onuf, and Donald Pisani, the public lands have been a central theme in both national and regional historiographies. Environmental historians have also contributed to this discussion. Half a century ago, in *Conservation and the Gospel of Efficiency,* Samuel Hays demonstrated that access to natural resources was a critical element in the growth of the American state. A number of recent studies have examined changing access to natural resources found on Western public lands and traced the transformation of relations between local communities and the American state. This book contributes to those discussions, but rather than a confrontation between local communities and an emerging state, I see a triangular relationship between state authorities, nonmarket or semimarket local producers, and corporate commercial users—in this case, oyster growers. For other examples of this relationship, see Spence, *Dispossessing the Wilderness*; Montoya, *Translating Property*; Catton, *Inhabited Wilderness*; Jacoby, *Crimes against Nature*; and Warren, *Hunter's Game.*

5. Bureau of the Census, U.S. Department of Commerce and Labor, *Fisheries of the United States.*

6. For figures on market hunting of waterfowl, see the reports of the California Board of Fish Commissioners during the 1870s and 1880s.

7. For pot hunting and sport hunting in San Francisco Bay marshes, see A. Arnold, *Suisun Marsh History*; and Neasham, *Wild Legacy.*

8. For grazing in the marshes, see testimonies in Proceedings of Francisco Berreyessa et al., Heirs of Guadalupe Berreyessa v. United States, for the Place Named "Rincon de los Esteros," Land Grant Case No. 239 (U.S. District Court for California Northern District 1853), 123–128, Bancroft Library, University of California, Berkeley.

9. For 1868, see Cronise, *Natural Wealth of California,* 152–153. For industrial users, see Ver Planck, *Salt in California,* 107–115.

10. E. P. Thompson, *Making of the English Working Class.*

11. McCay, *Oyster Wars and the Public Trust*; and McCay, "Pirates of Piscary." For a fine study of the link between privatization of watery commons and industrial growth in nineteenth-century America, see Steinberg, *Nature Incorporated.* Another New England study is Judd, *Common Lands, Common People.* On the nineteenth-century United States, see the essays in Hahn and Prude, *Countryside in the Age of Capitalist Transformation*; see also Merrill, "Cash is Good to Eat." Legal historian Carol Rose has written perceptively on the definition and meaning of property. See Rose, *Property and Persuasion.* Eleanor Ostrom demonstrated that, far from leading inevitably to tragedy, common ownership of natural resources can both be more effective than private ownership and accrue social benefits to the community doing the managing. See, for example, Ostrom, *Governing the Commons.*

12.   See Wennersten, *Oyster Wars of Chesapeake Bay.*

13.   Warren, *Hunter's Game.* For Adirondacks, Yellowstone, and Grand Canyon, see Jacoby, *Crimes against Nature.*

14.   "Zone of abundance" is Bill Cronon's phrase. Cronon, *Changes in the Land,* 30. On the key role of foraged shellfish in native economies of the Northwest coast and their special value in seasons of scarcity, see Moss, "Shellfish, Gender, and Status."

15.   Pacific Northwest tribes' decades-long attempts to retain access to traditional fishing and hunting lands provide an interesting and complicated alternative. See, for example, United States v. Washington 384 F. Supp. 312 (W. D. Wash. 1974).

16.   Blackburn and Anderson, "Managing the Domesticated Environment"; for coppicing, sowing, and burning, see M. Anderson, "Native Californians as Ancient and Contemporary Cultivators."

17.   On native economies of the San Francisco Bay region, see the discussion in chapter 1 of this book.

18.   Limerick, *Legacy of Conquest,* 17–18. See also White, *"It's Your Misfortune,"* 181–211.

19.   McCay, *Oyster Wars,* xix–xx.

20.   For Mexican-era grazing in the salt marshes, see chapter 1 of this book. See particularly the testimony of Harry G. Wade, cowboy on the Rincon de los Esteros land grant, March 21, 1860, in Proceedings of Francisco Berreyessa et al., Heirs of Guadalupe Berreyessa v. United States, for the Place Named "Rincon de los Esteros," Land Grant Case No. 239 (U.S. District Court for California Northern District 1853), 123–128, Bancroft Library, University of California, Berkeley. For U.S.-era cattle grazing, see journal of Alfred Doten, November 18 to 20, 1856, in Clark, *Journals of Alfred Doten,* 315–317.

21.   For firsthand descriptions of living on the bayshore and eating a surprising variety of wetland creatures, see Alfred Doten's diary entries from October 1856 to May 1857. Clark, *Journals of Alfred Doten,* 311–358.

22.   On human beings as tidal foragers, see Meehan, *Shell Bed to Shell Midden.*

23.   Stearns, "Exotic Mollusca in California."

24.   Whitney, *Map of the Region Adjacent to the Bay of San Francisco.*

25.   Nelson, "Shell Mounds of the San Francisco Bay Region." And see Roberts and Booker, *Shell Mounds in the San Francisco Bay Area.*

26.   On the history of shellmound archaeology and the Danish example, see Meehan, *Shell Bed to Shell Midden.*

27.   Wyman, "Account of Some Kjoekkenmoeddings."

28.   Betty Meehan pays tribute to the "Berkeley School" of archaeology of material culture, which she says was founded as a result of these excavations. See Meehan, *Shell Bed to Shell Midden,* 4. See also Schenk, "Emeryville Shellmound";

Uhle, "Emeryville Shell Mound"; Nelson, "Ellis Landing Shellmound"; Nelson, "Shell Mounds of the San Francisco Bay Region"; and Gifford, "Composition of Californian Shell Mounds."

29. Shellmounds provided exciting clues about the way people had lived in the region. Uhle found obsidian, a volcanic rock, when digging into a shellmound near the mouth of Temescal Creek in present-day Emeryville. Obsidian does not naturally occur in central California, so Uhle realized that the stone must have come to the shores of San Francisco Bay as a trade item from people near Mount Shasta or east of the Sierra Nevada.

30. Uhle, "Emeryville Shell Mound," 17, 31.

31. Whatever his biases against San Francisco Bay peoples, Uhle cannot be dismissed as a hack: long after his death, he remains a towering figure in the prehistory of South America. His pioneering work on ancient Peruvian civilizations established his place in archaeology. See Menzel, *Peru and Max Uhle*.

32. Beardsley, *Temporal and Areal Relationships*, 4. A later researcher, William Egbert Schenck, was present when the shellmound was leveled by steam shovel for industrial construction in 1924 and 1925. Schenck noted 651 burials unearthed by the steam shovel in the main part of the shellmound and found another forty-one bodies in three trenches that he and his assistants dug. Together with the bodies unearthed in Uhle's study and by haphazard work on the site, Schenck's discoveries raised the total of burials in this single mound to at least seven hundred.

33. The sensational "discovery" of Ishi, an aboriginal man from the Sierra foothills of northern California, and his relationship with his captors at Berkeley, cemented this shift, which directed attention away from the peoples of the Bay Area for many decades. On Ishi and California anthropology, see Heizer and Kroeber, *Ishi, the Last Yahi*; and Sackman, *Wild Men*.

34. "Crabbing," *Daily Alta California*, April 13, 1851.

35. For "muster field," see Alfred Doten to Captain Samuel Doten, October 6, 1849, in Clark, *Journals of Alfred Doten*, 52. For "muscles," see Alfred Doten journal entry for February 6, 1856, in ibid., 259.

36. Mining debris outdid even later anthropomorphic filling. Fill was more localized, affecting mostly marshes and intertidal mudflats near the cities of the central bay. For the extent and consequence of hydraulic debris, see Gilbert, Chin, and Krone in following footnotes.

37. Gilbert, *Hydraulic Mining Debris in the Sierra Nevada*, 29.

38. Brewer, *Up and Down California*, 328.

39. See Chin, Wong, and Carlson, *Shifting Sands and Shattered Rocks*; for Suisun and San Pablo Bays, see Krone, "Sedimentation in the San Francisco Bay System."

40. Gilbert, *Hydraulic Mining Debris in the Sierra Nevada*, viii; for narrative, see Bay Institute, *From the Sierra to the Sea*, 3:23.

41. Krone, "Sedimentation in San Francisco Bay," 90–92.

42. The term is from Kelley, *Battling the Inland Sea*.

43. Hedgpeth, "San Francisco Bay," 11–12. For a suggestive article on the impact of freshwater floods on Pacific coast estuarine communities, see MacGinitie, "Some Effects of Fresh Water."

44. On energy in estuaries, see the work of H. T. Odum, especially Odum, Copeland, and McMahan, *Coastal Ecological Systems of the United States*. For natural history and ecology of San Francisco Bay, begin with Josselyn, *Ecology of San Francisco Tidal Marshes*. See also the essays in Conomos, *San Francisco Bay*.

45. This shared biota is described in Edward F. Ricketts and Jack Calvin's classic account of Pacific coast intertidal habitats, *Between Pacific Tides*, and subsequent editions.

46. This paucity of intertidal fauna is markedly different from the diverse ecological communities that dominated Atlantic estuaries. For comparable species listings in eastern estuaries, see Carson, *Edge of the Sea*; Crowder, *Between the Tides*; and Pollock, *Practical Guide to Marine Animals*.

47. This phrase is taken from Cohen and Carlton, "Accelerating Invasion Rate in a Highly Invaded Estuary." On invasive species in San Francisco Bay, see also Cohen and Carlton, "Nonindigenous Aquatic Species in a United States Estuary"; and Carlton, "Biological Invasions and Cryptogenic Species."

48. For the story of aquatic introductions to California during this period, see California Board of Fish Commissioners, *Report of the Commissioners of Fisheries*; see also Towle, "Authored Ecosystems"; and Dill and Cordone, *History and Status of Introduced Fishes*. On introduced species' devastating impact on California native fish communities, see Moyle, "Introductions in California."

49. On the larger context of "improving nature" in California and English-speaking colonies worldwide, see Tyrrell, *True Gardens of the Gods*. For a broad view of species introductions, part of what Alfred Crosby calls a "portmanteau biota" that permitted European "ecological imperialism" worldwide, see Crosby, *Ecological Imperialism*; and Crosby, *Columbian Exchange*. But, for a critique of Crosby's claim that European species dominated transoceanic transfers, see also Tyrrell, "Beyond the View from Euro-America."

50. Skinner, *Historical Review of Fish and Wildlife Resources*, 11.

51. California Board of Fish Commissioners, *Biennial Report, 1879–1880*, 18; for the train wreck, see Towle, "Authored Ecosystems," 64. On Livingston Stone's pioneering work in Pacific salmon hatcheries, see J. Taylor, *Making Salmon*. For U.S. fish commissioner Spencer F. Baird and his role in fish introductions, see B. Anderson, "Biographical Portrait"; and Jordan, "Baird and the Fish Commission."

52.   See Kinsey, "Fish Car Era in Nebraska"; and Leonard, *Fish Car Era of the National Hatchery System.*

53.   Hattori and Kosta, "Packed Pork and Other Foodstuffs." Food historian Joseph Conlin reprints a gold rush–era menu from San Francisco's What Cheer restaurant, which advertised "oysters fried in crumbs" for fifteen cents, fried clams for ten, and clam chowder for a nickel. Conlin, *Bacon, Beans and Galantines,* 118–123, 141.

54.   Skinner, *Historical Review of Fish and Wildlife Resources,* 32; see also Scofield, *California Fishing Ports.*

55.   *Crassostrea virginica* translates roughly as "rough-shelled Virginia oyster," reflecting the European origin of its namers and the location of its first identification in the New World. On invasives, see A. Miller, "Assessing the Importance of Biological Attributes for Invasion Success."

56.   San Francisco physician Dr. W. Newcomb reported the presence of *Mya arenaria* in San Francisco Bay in 1874. Newcomb recognized the species as the familiar sand clam, or soft-shell clam, of the Atlantic coast. Knowing of oyster transfers from Puget Sound, Whitcomb concluded that *Mya* had been introduced from the Pacific Northwest, where he erroneously imagined it was a native. Writing in 1881, Robert E. C. Stearns corrected Newcomb's story by pointing out that *Mya* was an Atlantic species, not native to Puget Sound, and that the San Francisco Bay discovery represented a new introduction of the common Atlantic coast species to the Pacific. Stearns argued that the mollusk was undoubtedly brought in with the frequent (and continuing) rail shipments of live eastern oysters. See Stearns, "*Mya arenaria* in San Francisco Bay."

57.   Ibid., 365.

58.   Weymouth, "Edible Clams, Mussels and Scallops of California," 44–45.

59.   This effort is itself a fascinating topic for historians. For one thing, the Goals Project scientists had to decide on a basic framework for assessing the condition of the bay, and whether the past condition of the bay—say in 1800—or the present condition of the bay—in 2000—should be the benchmark upon which to measure success in maintaining species and habitat levels. The project members were conscious of the question: "restore to what?" Furthermore, they wondered, how should ecological health be defined? The project's Science Review Group chairman, renowned hydrologist Luna B. Leopold, asked whether selected species should be used to indicate habitat conservation goals, and whether those goals should be recorded on maps. Luna B. Leopold to Mike Monroe and Carl Wilcox, co-chairs, Resource Managers Group, San Francisco Bay Area Wetlands Ecosystem Goals Project, March 1, 1999, reprinted in Goals Project, *Baylands Ecosystem Habitat Goals.*

60.   Goals Project, *Baylands Ecosystem Habitat Goals,* 56–58.

61.   Wilentz, *Chants Democratic.*

62. Stasz, *Jack London's Women*, 28. The following picture of London's youth is drawn from several biographical accounts, of which the best is Stasz's. See also Kershaw, *Jack London*; Kingman, *Pictorial Life of Jack London*; and Stone, *Sailor on Horseback*. Stone's biography, which dominated the field until Stasz's and Kershaw's archival work, exemplifies the problems that afflict histories of Jack London: it is often hard to tell what is fact and what is fiction in his life, as Stone implicitly acknowledged in a second edition of the book, which carried the subtitle "A Biographical Novel."

63. Stasz, *Jack London's Women*, 23–25.

64. Jane Disard Wright, cited in Lasartemay and Rudge, *For Love of Jack London*, 132.

65. Stasz, *Jack London's Women*, 27–28. See also Atherton, *Jack London in Boyhood Adventures*, 26–41, 50–62.

66. Stone, *Sailor on Horseback*, 31–32. See also London's own version of this important moment and its consequences for his life in *John Barleycorn*.

67. London's writing always contained autobiographical elements, and at times it is hard to tell what is carefully reconstructed fact and what is fictional embellishment. His books on San Francisco Bay are particularly hard to classify, given their combination of romantic story with superb and accurate detail about working life. London, *Cruise of the Dazzler* and *Tales of the Fish Patrol*.

68. London is an irresistible figure for scholars interested in gender and the creation of manliness in the early twentieth century. Among other studies, see Stasz, *Jack London's Women*; and Auerbach, *Male Call*.

69. Jack London to Houghton Mifflin & Co., January 31, 1900, Box 1, Folder 2, Jack London Papers M77, Special Collections, Stanford University Libraries.

70. The H-West online listserv community discussed the prevalence of canned and fresh oysters throughout the American West on November 8 and 9, 2000. For consumption of canned oysters by Native American miners during California's gold rush, see Hammond and Morgan, *Captain Charles M. Weber*.

71. Fitch, *Common Marine Bivalves of California*, 21.

72. Brief investigation turned up several dozen citations on the nutritional value of shellfish. For oysters as treatment for anemia (iron deficiency), see Levine, Remington, and Culp, "Value of the Oyster in Nutritional Anemia." Recent research has confirmed and expanded the food value of shellfish. Researchers found that Pacific oysters—a different but similar species to those eaten in nineteenth-century California—contain a very high ratio of protein to fat. Researchers also found that the relatively high level of cholesterol in shellfish is mostly the "good" cholesterol that helps prevent heart disease. Recent literature is summarized in Dong, *Nutritional Value of Shellfish*. See also Childs et al., "Effects of Shellfish Consumption," 31.

73.   For nearly 150 years, taxonomists knew the native oyster of the northeast-ern Pacific as *Ostrea lurida,* which translates roughly as the "pale yellow" or "ghastly" oyster. The animal was known popularly as the "Olympia oyster" or "native oyster." Taxonomists have recently moved *O. lurida* to a new genus, *Ostreola conchaphila.* This translates roughly as "mussel-like (or seashell-like) shell-loving oyster," a reference to the mollusk's need for a rocky or shell substrate.

74.   Duflot de Mofras, *Port de San Francisco dans la Haute Californie.* David Rumsey provides this map in his magnificent collection of San Francisco Bay maps available online at http://davidrumsey.com. It is not clear if Duflot de Mofras was describing live oysters or empty shells. Timothy Babalis points out that San Francisco Bay's native oyster population had declined some centuries prior to European arrival. It is certainly true that native oyster shells dominate the lower levels of Bay Area shellmounds, decreasing in percentage over time. Greengo, "Molluscan Species in California Shell Middens." San Francisco Bay's native oyster population appears to have been much smaller in the 1850s than it had been in the mound builders' time. Babalis, "Critical Review." See also Babalis, "Restoring the Past."

75.   Laura Jones, Stanford University staff archaeologist, pers. comm., October 21, 2000.

76.   Bocek, "Hunter-Gatherer Ecology and Settlement Mobility," 315–329.

77.   Twain, "The Old Thing," 335. This and many other Mark Twain articles can be found online at www.twainquotes.com. Andrew Beahrs has also written about Twain and oysters in San Francisco. See Beahrs, *Twain's Feast.*

78.   Norris, *McTeague,* 4. Sean Wilentz has described a similar landscape in New York's working-class Bowery district: Wilentz, *Chants Democratic,* 257.

79.   Bureau of the Census, U.S. Department of Commerce and Labor, *Fisheries of the United States,* 26–29, 42, 66–68, 86.

80.   Ibid., 26–29, 42, 66–68, 86. Despite the tremendous importance of the oys-ter industry nationally, "oyster" turns up only one time in my search of congres-sional debates between 1833 and 1875. That single reference was an unsuccessful bill to suspend taxation of Virginia oysters in the first session of the Forty-First Congress. On menhaden and its importance, see Matthew McKenzie's excellent book *Clearing the Coastline.*

81.   Barrett, *California Oyster Industry,* 21–26.

82.   Ibid., 30. See also Barrett, "Oyster Industry of California."

83.   Twain, "Another Enterprise," 415.

84.   *Daily Alta California,* October 22, 1869.

85.   Ingersoll, *History and Present Condition of the Fishery Industries,* 202.

86.   Barrett, *California Oyster Industry,* 20, 24–25.

87.   The finely detailed maps of the U.S. Coast and Geodetic Survey (USCGS) convey south bay communities' dependence on tidal creeks. In the 1850s, USCGS

surveyors mapped and individually labeled navigable sloughs and hamlets, such as "Hayward's Landing," "Mowry's Landing," and "Eden Landing." See U.S. Coast and Geodetic Survey, "T-Sheet 635," available online at the San Francisco Estuary Institute's historical ecology site, http://maps.sfei.org/tSheets/viewer.htm (accessed December 6, 2012).

88.   Bancroft, *History of California*, 7:83.

89.   For copper smelter, see Bain, "Mines and Mining," 69. For oil refineries, see R. Arnold, "Petroleum Resources and Industries of the Pacific Coast."

90.   Ted Grosholtz, Department of Environmental Science and Policy, UC Davis, pers. comm., October 2, 2003.

91.   Skinner, *Historical Review of Fish and Wildlife Resources*, 42–44, and figure 20, "Comparative Landings of Oysters for the State and San Francisco Bay Area 1916–1958," 44.

92.   Chestnut, "Oyster Reefs," 198.

93.   Newspaper headlines and feature stories attest to the continued popularity of the idea of a tragedy of the commons concept among many journalists and the general public. Scholars are far more critical. *Science* magazine ran a thoughtful special issue on the thirtieth anniversary of this important concept or, perhaps we might say, literary trope. *Science*, December 11, 2003.

94.   For production figures, see Barrett, "Oyster Industry of California," 5–6, 10–11; and Gilliam, *San Francisco Bay*, 172. Experts on declining oyster populations in Chesapeake Bay and Long Island Sound say that oysters stressed by pollution, low oxygen levels, or simply changes in sediment, salinity, and temperature become more susceptible to existing oyster pests and new diseases. Whitman Miller, ecologist, Smithsonian Environmental Research Center, pers. comm., October 22, 2003; Ted Grosholz, Professor of Environmental Science and Policy, University of California-Davis, pers. comm., October 2, 2003.

95.   For watery oysters, see Bonnot, "California Oyster Industry," 67. For claim that pollution was to blame, see Barrett, "Oyster Industry of California," 19–20.

96.   "San Francisco Bay Oysters."

97.   The three studies were Kennedy, "Sanitary Survey of Oyster Beds"; Sumner, "Report Upon the Physical Conditions in San Francisco Bay"; and Miller, Ramage, and Lazier, "Study of the Physical and Chemical Conditions of San Francisco Bay."

98.   In *The Sanitary City*, Martin Melosi notes that investment in sewage disposal technology far outstripped sewage treatment technology; the widespread adoption of the water closet in the early twentieth century ensured that America's waterways became open sewers. While sewage was the primary concern for early twentieth-century scientists, heavy metals and other toxic discharges from

industrial plants around San Francisco Bay certainly fouled the bay, as contemporaries recognized. See, for example, discussions of actual and feared pollution from copper and lead smelters. For a description of Bay Area industrial waste dischargers in 1915, see Bain, "Mines and Mining," 68–69. For pollution from the Selby lead smelter near Benicia, see Holmes, Franklin, and Gould, *Report of the Selby Smelter Commission*; and LeCain, "The Limits of 'Eco-Efficiency.'" For concerns about a proposed copper smelter near San Mateo, see R. E. Swain to Stanford University Board of Trustees, January 24, 1907, Box 2, Folder 3, Horace Davis Papers SC028, Stanford University Archives, Stanford University Libraries. For the impact of Prohibition-era moonshiners on tidal streams south of San Francisco, see *Spirit of Independence*, 7.

99. Heath, "Investigation of the Clams of California," 27.

100. On the history of sewage treatment, see Melosi, *Sanitary City*. For a fine description of the waste history of one San Francisco Bay community, see Elkind, *Bay Cities and Water Politics*, 31–32, 145–155.

101. Committee of East Bay Engineers, *Preliminary Report Upon Sewage Disposal*, 8–9. See also Elkind, *Bay Cities and Water Politics*, 146.

102. Miller, Ramage, and Lazier, "Study of the Physical and Chemical Conditions of San Francisco Bay."

103. Conn, "Outbreak of Typhoid at Wesleyan," 243.

104. Ibid., 243.

105. Ibid., 264.

106. Connecticut Board of Health, "Table VII."

107. Sinclair, "What Life Means to Me."

108. Food historians recognize a fundamental shift in the American diet that took place during the Progressive era, partly in response to muckraking journalists' exposure of risks from industrially processed foods and partly following newly authoritative (if sometimes sadly wrong) medical science. This is the era that gave us hygiene, home economics, and baby formula. A good introduction to this fascinating literature is Levenstein, *Revolution at the Table*.

109. Heath, "Investigation of the Clams of California." Mitchell Postel argues that pollution from industry and city sewers killed the oyster industry, and that regulators ignored this evidence in their obsession with alleged overfishing by Chinese shrimp fishers. Postel, "Lost Resource."

110. Weymouth, "Life History of the Dungeness Crab," 32. See also Postel, "Lost Resource," 26–41.

111. Gilliam, *San Francisco Bay*, 144, 172–173.

112. Samuel Hays put forth a similar point long ago: in the postwar era, Americans shifted from seeing the world as a place for production to a place for consumption. See Hays, *Beauty, Health, and Permanence*. My argument here complicates Hays's formula in the sense that San Francisco Bay went from being a

place of consumption (literally) to a place to dump sewage and industrial wastes, and to produce industrial salt and chemicals. Those extractive industries took off as people stopped eating out of the bay. Furthermore, to some extent, industrial users benefited from foragers' loss. Had the bay remained a place for people to eat, wastes might have been more deeply resented and perhaps regulated. Now bay users find themselves attempting to overcome nearly one hundred years of history in which waste and industrial use has trumped foraging and fishing.

113.   Levenstein, *Revolution at the Table.*

114.   Dredgers removed approximately thirty million tons of oyster shells for cement between 1924 and 1967. Goldman, *Salt, Sand and Shells,* 10–19.

115.   Since 2002, a small group has been working to restore the native oyster in San Francisco Bay. See Sculati, "Still Hanging On." See also Paul Rogers, "In Restoring Oysters, Scientists See New Hope for the Bay," *San Jose Mercury News,* June 8, 2004. Yet native oysters may have not been widespread. Andrew Cohen, pers. communication.

CHAPTER 5

1.   For Redwood Shores and Berkeley Marina, see histories produced by the respective city libraries: Redwood City Public Library, "Redwood City History: Redwood Shores," www.redwoodcity.org//library/info/localhistoryroom.html (accessed November 29, 2012); and Charles Wollenberg, "A Kind of Peace," http://berkeleypubliclibrary.org/system/Chapter8.html (accessed March 5, 2005). See also "Leslie Tells Land Policy," *Redwood City Tribune,* February 3, 1966; and "Leslie Claims $200,000 Monthly Loss on Redwood Shores Delay," *Palo Alto Times,* November 7, 1969.

2.   California State Division of Mines, "Salt," 3; for evaporation, see Ver Planck, *Salt in California,* 43.

3.   On the history of San Francisco Bay salt making, see Brown, "Salt for the Scraping." See also Sandoval, *Mt. Eden.* For a superficial but tantalizing discussion of salt in California Indian cultures, see Kroeber, "Culture Element Distributions."

4.   Sullivan, *Travels of Jedediah Smith,* 52.

5.   Farley, "Salt-Making in Alameda."

6.   Brown, "Salt for the Scraping," 118, 120.

7.   Kurlansky, *Salt,* 281–287. Kurlansky says that gold rush–era salt makers largely employed Chinese laborers.

8.   Ver Planck, "Salines in the Bay Area."

9.   Brown, "Salt for the Scraping," 118.

10. The poor quality of General Land Office maps of the shoreline, and the implication of corruption, is evident through a comparison. The intricately detailed maps of south bay marshlands drawn in the 1850s by U.S. coast surveyors—men whose concern was to accurately map the meandering sloughs for navigation—contrast sharply with the straight lines and minimal detail on General Land Office maps of the shoreline boundaries of Mexican land grants. Historical ecologist Robin Grossinger has demonstrated that coast survey maps and charts were astonishingly accurate. Some 1850s charts of bay sloughs closely match recent satellite photographs. Grossinger, Askevold, and Collins, *T-Sheet User Guide;* and Robin Grossinger, San Francisco Estuary Institute, pers. comm., February 12, 2003.

11. The real estate speculator and journalist J. Ross Browne spent the last years of his life promoting various development schemes for tidal "swamplands" in the south bay. It is clear that some of these lands, particularly the massive "Beard tract" near present-day Dumbarton Bridge, ended up as salt ponds. See E.S. Beard to J. Ross Browne, August 21, 1872, J. Ross Browne Correspondence and Papers, BANC MSS 78/163c, Bancroft Library, University of California, Berkeley.

12. Brown, "Salt for the Scraping," 118, 120.

13. On salt as food preservative, see Laszlo, *Salt: The Grain of Life,* 1–11; and Kurlansky, *Salt: A World History,* particularly 91–105, 109–161.

14. On salt and human history generally, see the entertaining work by Mark Kurlansky, *Salt: A World History.* For a chemist's appreciation of salt in human history, see Pierre Laszlo's often witty and occasionally profound *Salt: The Grain of Life.* At first, most salt for table use was imported from Liverpool as ship's ballast; nineteenth-century San Francisco Bay salt was considered cruder, less refined, and destined for ore refining rather than food preservation. Hubert Howe Bancroft reported in 1890, however, that "the [San Francisco Bay] Cal. salt is improving so much as to supplant the Lower Californian and English supplies." Bancroft, *History of California,* 7:87.

15. Ralph L. Phelps, "Salt Industry" folder, Ralph L. Phelps Papers, BANC MSS C-D 5048, Folder 11, Number 1, Bancroft Library, University of California, Berkeley.

16. For descriptions of bittern and its precipitates, see Kurlansky, *Salt,* 294–298; and Laszlo, *Salt,* 108–111.

17. For Dow process, see Laszlo, *Salt,* 109–129; see also Kurlansky, *Salt,* 291–308.

18. California State Division of Mines, "California Chlorine-Caustic Industry," 3–4.

19. Goldman, *Salt, Sand and Shells,* 22–24.

20. Gilliam, *San Francisco Bay,* 170.

21. California State Division of Mines, "California Chlorine-Caustic Industry," 3.

22. Ver Planck, *Salt in California*, 107–111.

23. Ibid., 9.

24. Bill Cronon describes a similar process in which land became capital in nineteenth-century Chicago's hinterlands. See Cronon, *Nature's Metropolis*, 148–206.

25. Lopez, *Report on Leslie Salt Company Properties*, 12.

26. During the 1910s and 1920s, land speculator-cum-utopian Charles Weeks laid out a new subdivision in the marshes near the small town of Menlo Park, California. "Runnymede" was supposed to provide residents with "one acre and independence": both housing and income through egg farming. The area is now part of one of San Francisco Bay's poorest communities, East Palo Alto. See Steve Staiger, "East Palo Alto's Early Seeds of Utopia," *Palo Alto Weekly*, November 19, 1999. In 1934, developers near Long Beach, California, advertised "semi-sustaining garden homes" on large lots. See Waldie, *Holy Land*, 62, 68–71. Richard White describes how Depression-era urbanites from Seattle attempted to survive by moving to nearby rural areas and running dairy or egg farms. See White, *Land Use, Environment, and Social Change*, 128–141.

27. Goldman, *Salt, Sand and Shells*, 26.

28. Such dams would have been perhaps the greatest calamity ever to befall San Francisco Bay. As critics dating back to Grunsky and his nineteenth-century proposal pointed out, damming the tidal estuary would destroy fisheries, interfere with navigation, reduce tidal flushing of pollutants, contaminate water supplies, increase mosquito habitat, diminish ecological productivity, increase damage to port facilities by wood-boring mollusks, create vast areas susceptible to earthquakes, require complex sewer and drainage systems, destroy existing property values, foul up the local climate by reducing the cooling effect of wind on open water, and introduce a whole series of other predictable and unimagined problems. In 2007, the Bay Conservation and Development Commission studied new proposals to dam the bay, this time to prevent sea level rise. Their report underlined the immense cost and catastrophic risks of such projects. See San Francisco Bay Conservation and Development Commission, *Analysis of A Tidal Barrage*.

29. Office of Area Development, U.S. Department of Commerce, *Comprehensive Survey*; and U.S. Army Corps of Engineers, San Francisco District, *Areas Susceptible of Reclamation in San Francisco Bay Area*.

30. Gilliam, *San Francisco Bay*, 215.

31. In their own way, industrialists shared a similar view of the salt ponds. For Leslie Salt Company executives, as for many in the business community, the salt ponds represented a kind of reservoir of undeveloped space, a land reserve,

and a space pregnant with potential. Where conservationists focused on emptiness as a positive value, builders could see it as rich potential. For another view of the history of the concept of open space, see Rome, *Bulldozer in the Countryside.*

32. San Francisco Bay Conservation and Development Commission, *Ownership*, 4–14; for forty-four thousand acres, see Ver Planck, *Salt in California*, 42.

33. San Francisco Bay Conservation and Development Commission, *Ownership*, 12–14.

34. *San Francisco Chronicle*, February 12, 1969. See also *San Francisco Chronicle*, March 2, 1968; February 26, 1969; and May 8, 1969. Leslie officials previously fought creation and confirmation of the bay commission. See *San Francisco Chronicle*, January 17, 1965; November 7, 1965; and December 9, 1965. For a description of salt harvest on Leslie properties, see *San Francisco Chronicle*, November 1, 1965.

35. For a history of the idea of "open space," see Rome, *Bulldozer in the Countryside.*

36. M. Scott, *Future of San Francisco Bay*, 68–70.

37. San Francisco Bay Conservation and Development Commission, *Recreation on and around San Francisco Bay*, 9.

38. Ibid., 38.

39. Ibid., 44.

40. Ibid., 5–7.

41. Spangle and Associates, *Municipal, State and Federal Programs Affecting San Francisco Bay*, 40.

42. Alameda County Regional Small Craft Harbor Study Committee, *Preliminary Feasibility Report, Coyote Hills Aquatic Park.*

43. Ibid.; for a narrative history of these plans, see M. Scott, *Future of San Francisco Bay*, 77–78.

44. Santa Clara County Planning Commission, *Plan for Parks, Recreation and Open Space*, 20–21.

45. Ibid., 20–21. Searching for these materials is a reminder that nothing is more quickly forgotten or discarded than an outdated planning document. Files are scattered in libraries around San Francisco Bay, including Stanford University's collection of local planning documents.

46. Peter Alagona has written thoughtfully about the particular role of wildlife discourse in California history in *After the Grizzly.*

47. Hays, "From Conservation to Environment," 23.

48. R. Andrews, *Managing the Environment*, 202.

49. Richard Walker describes how local environmental activists used federal authority and money to create many of the Bay Area's conservation areas. See Walker, *Country in the City.*

50.   Essential reading for understanding federal efforts to acquire land for open space and wildlife refuges is Fairfax et al., *Buying Nature,* especially 133–169.

51.   R. Andrews, *Managing the Environment,* 202–205.

52.   For suburbs and open space, see Rome, *Bulldozer In The Countryside.* For Seattle, see Klingle, *Emerald City;* and for San Francisco, see Walker, *Country in The City.* For a larger discussion of environmental responses to urban pollution, see Rothman, *Greening of A Nation?,* 24–31, 55. Rothman argued that urban development had little to do with the rise of environmental thinking: "In most cases, 'environmentalists' of the 1950s and early 1960s took little notice of urban sprawl and pollution except in the most peripheral of ways. Environmentalism had expanded the reach of the conservation movement and had created a new and broader constituency for it, but it had not increased the range of issues that concerned its adherents" (55). Rothman saw no real connection between suburban development and the demand for a clean, beautiful environment. But more recent work has shown quite the opposite. In *The Bulldozer in the Countryside,* Adam Rome demonstrates that postwar suburban development was a central issue inspiring environmental concerns nationwide. Pollution in Seattle's Lake Washington and the debate over San Francisco Bay's tidelands demonstrate that postwar civic activism all along the West Coast was closely connected to environmental problems caused by postwar growth in the region. On Lake Washington, see Klingle, *Emerald City.* See also Booker, "'Metro is *Not Only* Sewers!'"

53.   The League of Women Voters may be the best example of the link between traditional efforts to address urban problems and their extension to new postwar environmental problems such as pollution and disappearing open space. Mrs. Ward Duffy, chairman of the Leagues of Women Voters of the San Francisco Bay Area, expressed a typical sentiment in 1964, when speaking in favor of a new state agency. She said, "The public interest is complex and complicated and demands coordination and cooperation among all levels of government and among all private interests in order to achieve the greatest good for all the inhabitants of the Bay Area." See Mrs. Ward Duffy, public testimony, November 10, 1964, in San Francisco Bay Conservation Study Commission, *Report to the California Legislature.*

54.   Lehrer, "Pollution." In a November 18, 2004, posting to the H-Environment listserv, Patrick Gavin Duffy of Marinwood Station pointed out this connection.

55.   In 1963, California's lower legislative house overwhelmingly passed a bill that would have allowed cities and counties to reclaim state tidelands for development. The bill died in the state senate. "Bay Reclamation Bill," *San Francisco Chronicle,* June 4, 1963.

56.   For bay commission purpose and values, see McAteer-Petris Act, Cal. Public Law S.B. 309 (1965), the updated act in 1969, and the Bay Conservation and

Development Commission Plan in 1969. Historians note that the Bay Conservation and Development Commission inspired coastal protection efforts throughout California; Stanley Scott credits the bay commission with directly inspiring the California Coastal Commission, responsible for protecting the natural features of California's ocean coast since the 1970s. See S. Scott, *Governing California's Coast*, 9–11.

57.   McAteer-Petris Act, Cal. Public Law S. B. 309 (1965).

58.   Courts sustained the bay commission's regulatory power over bay fill as justifiable actions in the public interest. For power to permit fill by cities, see San Francisco Bay Conservation and Development Commission v. Town of Emeryville, 69 Cal. 2d 533 (S. F. No. 22591. In Bank. Nov. 13, 1968). For power to permit fill by private owners, see Candlestick Properties, Inc. v. San Francisco Bay Conservation and Development Commission 11 Cal. App. 3d 557, 89 Cal. Rptr 897 (Civ. No. 26216. Court of Appeals of California, First Appellate District, Division Three. September 24, 1970). But disputes over the bay commission's jurisdiction continue. See Littoral Development Co. v. San Francisco Bay Conservation and Development Commission 24 Cal. App. 4th 1050, 29 Cal. Rptr. 2d 518 (No. A061428. First Dist., Div. Five. May 2, 1994).

59.   The case was unusual for, among other things, never coming to trial. For one party's version of the issues at stake, see Briscoe, "Some Legal Problems of Tidal Marshes." See also "Fighting to Save San Francisco Bay," *Time Magazine*, July 5, 1968.

60.   Shaw and Fredine, *Wetlands of the United States*, 9.

61.   Robert M. Wilson explores this tension at great length in his excellent study of Pacific flyway wildlife refuges, *Seeking Refuge.*

62.   Historian Richard Andrews notes, "The tensions between proponents of preservation and recreational development intensified as both outdoor recreation demand and other economic pressures continued to mount. These pressures focused on the parks and on other natural lands of all kinds, particularly on the remaining seashores, lakeshores, and other open-space lands near urban areas." R. Andrews, *Managing the Environment*, 191.

63.   Ibid., 191–193. Andrews argues that these national seashores were intended to do three things: protect the seashore areas, "meet burgeoning recreational demand," and, finally, take pressure off of national parks "by providing additional opportunities for mass recreation nearer to urban areas."

64.   Statement of Arthur L. Ogilvie, Recording Secretary, South San Francisco Bay Lands Planning Conservation and National Wildlife Refuge Committee, in *The Nation's Estuaries*, 223–227.

65.   G. Douglas Hofe, Director, Bureau of Outdoor Recreation, United States Department of the Interior, to Roger Morton, Secretary of the Interior, "Memo: Proposed San Francisco Bay National Wildlife Refuge," July 16, 1971, San Francisco Bay National Wildlife Refuge Archives, Newark, California.

66. Bureau of Outdoor Recreation, *Proposed San Francisco Bay National Wildlife Refuge*, 31.

67. Ibid., 32–33.

68. The refuge gradually expanded; by 1979 Congress had appropriated money to expand the refuge to some eighteen thousand acres, and in the 1980s Congress promised to ultimately fund as many as forty-three thousand acres. For a visualization of refuge growth, see M. Booker, "Visualizing San Francisco Bay's Forgotten Past."

69. Hofe to Morton, "Memo."

70. The national wildlife refuge system has long served varied economic masters. Sometimes intended to produce waterfowl for sport hunters, refuges in California have also served as wastewater basins for irrigated agriculture. See Wilson, *Seeking Refuge*, 96–98; and Garone, *Fall and Rise of Wetlands*, 209–236. The Don Edwards San Francisco Bay National Wildlife Refuge now covers almost twenty-six thousand acres. Spanning twelve cities and three counties, it is the largest urban wildlife refuge in the United States. By 1979, the refuge had acquired eighteen thousand acres of land, of which fifteen thousand were obtained from the Leslie Salt Company. In the 1980s, Congress authorized the refuge to expand, should subsequent appropriations appear, to as many as forty-three thousand acres. This acreage and the refuge's proposed expansion areas are exactly coincident with Leslie Salt Company's properties.

71. M. Scott, *San Francisco Bay Area*, 310. Richard Walker celebrates conservation successes in *The Country in the City*.

CONCLUSION

1. PCBs are a continuing source of concern and of study in San Francisco Bay. Accessible and chilling maps of PCB concentrations in the bay over time are found in the San Francisco Estuary Institute's annual summaries of research, "The Pulse of the Estuary," www.sfei.org/rmp/pulse (accessed December 3, 2012). See also Daum et al., *Sediment Concentration in San Leandro Bay*.

2. Much of the mercury dumped in Sierra rivers during the gold rush is now trapped beneath San Francisco Bay. This sediment lies dormant and largely harmless in the oxygen-free mud but could reenter the food chain if disturbed by, for example, efforts to restore tidal scour to salt ponds. The same hydraulic miners who added this extraordinary load of toxins to the bay also, ironically, provided the sediment that has kept the mercury buried and out of the food chain. The U.S. Environmental Protection Agency published a special report on the use of sand and gravel in mercury-contaminated sites, advocating essentially the

same methods used unconsciously by the miners. See U.S. Environmental Protection Agency, *Sand and Gravel Overlay.*

3. See "Reclaiming the Salt Ponds for People and Nature," a special issue of *Bay Nature* 4, no. 4 (July 2004). See also Patton, *Turning Salt into Environmental Gold.*

4. Unnamed scientist quoted in Stuart Leavenworth, "Toxic Dilemma: Plans to Restore Delta and Bay Wetlands Could Create a Deadlier Form of Mercury Passed Up the Food Chain," *Sacramento Bee,* October 20, 2003. The problems with methyl mercury and the consequences of reopening baylands to the tides are both uncertain and great, a recipe for controversy. The present restoration effort in south bay salt ponds is somewhat cautiously considering this question in its stakeholder meetings. Monitoring of restored ponds is under way to determine if methyl mercury levels have increased. As of late 2012, that remains unclear. See South Bay Salt Pond Restoration Project, www.southbayrestoration.org /monitoring (accessed December 3, 2012). The Regional Monitoring Program of the San Francisco Estuary Institute gives annual reports of ongoing studies on mercury in San Francisco Bay sediments. See www.sfei.org/rmp/current_psss (accessed December 3, 2012). Other useful summaries of mercury in the bay include the mercury-themed 2008 report by the San Francisco Estuary Institute, *Pulse of the Estuary.* On methyl mercury generally, see Goyer et al., *Toxicological Effects of Methyl Mercury.* On methyl mercury in San Francisco Bay, see the prescient study by Olson, "Methylation of Mercury Compounds by San Francisco Bay Sediments."

5. This description of the competing values of two kinds of restorationists derives from my observation of South Bay Salt Pond Restoration Group meetings, conversations with agency personnel, and discussions with biologists associated with resource agencies and nonprofit environmental organizations.

6. In 1995 the refuge was renamed Don Edwards San Francisco Bay National Wildlife Refuge to honor Congressman Edwards. Laura Watt has written perceptively on the conflicting goals of restorationists. See Watt, "Conflicting Restoration Goals in the San Francisco Bay"; and Watt, Raymond, and Eschen, "On Preserving Ecological and Cultural Landscapes."

7. For projected sea level rise around San Francisco Bay, see Knowles, "Potential Inundation due to Rising Sea Levels"; California Climate Change Center, *Impacts of Sea-Level Rise*; and San Francisco Bay Conservation and Development Commission, *San Francisco Bay Scenarios for Sea Level Rise.* Also see reports by the San Francisco Bay Conservation and Development Commission: *Sea Level Rise; Living with A Rising Bay;* and *Revised Staff Report and Staff Recommendation for Proposed Bay Plan Amendment.*

8. The South Bay Salt Pond Restoration Project website provides action updates, access to ongoing scientific studies, and a calendar of public meetings.

www.southbayrestoration.org/ (accessed December 4, 2012). For an introduction to the extraordinary historical ecology informing the project, see San Francisco Estuary Institute, "Sound Bay Salt Pond Landscape Synthesis Report," www.sfei .org/SBSPLandscapeSynthesisReport (accessed December 4, 2012).

9. There is a parallel here to Thomas Andrews's concept of "workscapes," ever-evolving places like San Francisco Bay's oyster beds and salt ponds "that are shaped by the interplay of human labor and natural processes." T. Andrews, *Killing for Coal*, 125.

10. Amy Hutzl of the California Coastal Commission used the "front yard" metaphor at a South Bay Salt Pond Restoration Group planning meeting, Palo Alto, California, April 9, 2003.

11. Thanks to Robin Grossinger of the San Francisco Estuary Institute for his contribution to this paragraph.

12. See the July 2004 special issue of *Bay Nature*, "Reclaiming the Salt Ponds for People and Nature," particularly Baye and Grossinger, "Once and Future Bay."

Bibliography

ARCHIVES AND MANUSCRIPT COLLECTIONS

Alviso Branch Library, San Jose Public Library
Bancroft Library, University of California, Berkeley
    1906 Earthquake and Fire Digital Collection
    California Land Grants, Land Warrants, and Other Land Tenure Materials,
        1860–1909, MSS C-I 31
    George Davidson Papers, 1845–1911, MSS C-B 490
    George D. Roberts Correspondence, 1871–1877, MSS C-B 466
    Grunsky Family Papers, 1830–1869, MSS C-B 557
    Hubert Howe Bancroft Collection, MSS C-D 834
    John Ross Browne Correspondence and Papers, MSS 78 / 163c
    John Wilson Correspondence and Papers, C-B 420
    Letters to Gwendolyn C. Steinbeck and Other Papers, MSS 71 / 40c
    Notebook Relating to California Land Claims, MSS C-I 16
    Official Documents Relating to Early San Francisco, 1835–1857, MSS
        C-A 370
    Papers Relating to Property Known as the Alameda Marsh, in the Oakland
        Estuary, 1916–1921, MSS 80 / 74 c

Ralph L. Phelps Papers, MSS C-D 5048
Save San Francisco Bay Association Records, 1953–2004, MSS 87 / 29c
Stephen Watts Kearny Papers, MSS C-B 633
Thomas Oliver Larkin Papers, 1839–1856, MSS C-B 37–45
William Chapman Ralston Correspondence, MSS C-B 77 / 88c
William Squire Clark Collection, MSS C-D 245
California Room, San Jose Public Library
California State Archives, Sacramento
    Governor's Office, Land Office Papers
    William Hammond Hall Correspondence and Papers
    William Hammond Hall Papers, State Engineering Field Books
California State Historical Society, North Baker Library
Earth Sciences and Map Library, University of California, Berkeley
Holt-Atherton Special Collections, University of the Pacific Library,
    Stockton, CA
    Cannon-Walker Family Papers, MSS 255
    Grunsky Family Vertical Files
Huntington Library, San Marino, California
Map Collections, Branner Earth Sciences Library, Stanford University
National Archives and Records Administration, San Bruno, CA
    Bureau of Land Management, RG 49
    Records of the California State Office, 1853–1985
    Records of the Regional Office, SF, 1866–1951
    Records of Surveyor General of CA, 1873–1921
Oakland History Room, Oakland Public Library
San Francisco Bay National Wildlife Refuge Archives, Newark, California
Special Collections, Crown Law Library, Stanford University
Special Collections, Sacramento Public Library
Special Collections, San Jose State University Library
Special Collections, Stanford University Libraries
    Adolph Sutro Papers, J004
    Edward F. Ricketts Papers, M0291
    Jack London Papers, M077
    Pacific Slope Scrapbooks, M0211
    William Bierlie Hyde Papers, MS 267
University Archives, Stanford University Libraries
    Horace Davis Papers, SC028
United States Geological Survey Photographic Library, Denver, Colorado
Water Resources Library, University of California, Berkeley

OTHER SOURCES

Alagona, Peter S. *After the Grizzly: Endangered Species and the Politics of Place in California.* Berkeley: University of California Press, 2013.

Alameda County Regional Small Craft Harbor Study Committee. *Preliminary Feasibility Report, Coyote Hills Aquatic Park.* Hayward: Alameda County Regional Small Craft Harbor Study Committee, 1961.

Alexander, Gregory S. *Commodity and Propriety: Competing Visions of Property in American Legal Thought, 1776–1970.* Chicago: University of Chicago Press, 1997.

Allardt, George F. *Map No. 1 of Tidelands: To Be Sold at Auction by the Order of the Board of Tide Land Commissioners by Talbert & Leet, Auctioneers.* 1:6000. San Francisco: Geo. H. Baker, 1869. Earth Sciences Library, University of California, Berkeley.

Anderson, Byron. "Biographical Portrait: Spencer Fullerton Baird (1823–1887)." *Forest History Today* (Fall 2002): 31–33.

Anderson, M. Kat. "Native Californians as Ancient and Contemporary Cultivators." In *Before the Wilderness: Environmental Management by Native Californians,* edited by Thomas C. Blackburn and M. Kat Anderson, 151–174. Menlo Park, CA: Ballena Press, 1993.

Andrews, Richard, N. L. *Managing the Environment, Managing Ourselves: A History of American Environmental Policy.* New Haven, CT: Yale University Press, 1999.

Andrews, Thomas. *Killing for Coal: America's Deadliest Labor War.* Cambridge, MA: Harvard University Press, 2008.

Arnold, Anthony. *Suisun Marsh History: Hunting and Saving a Wetland.* Marina, CA: Monterey-Pacific Publishing, 1996.

Arnold, Ralph. "Petroleum Resources and Industries of the Pacific Coast." In *Nature and Science on the Pacific Coast: A Guide-Book for Scientific Travelers in the West,* edited by the American Association for the Advancement of Science, Pacific Coast Committee, 75–87. San Francisco: Paul Elder, 1915.

Astro, Richard. *John Steinbeck and Edward F. Ricketts: The Shaping of a Novelist.* Minneapolis: University of Minnesota Press, 1973.

Atherton, Frank Irving. *Jack London in Boyhood Adventures. Jack London Journal* 4 (1997): 16–172.

Atwater, Brian Franklin. "Ancient Processes at the Site of Southern San Francisco Bay: Movement of the Crust and Changes in Sea Level." In *San Francisco Bay: The Urbanized Estuary,* edited by T. J. Conomos, 31–45. San Francisco: American Association for the Advancement of Science, Pacific Division, 1979.

Atwater, Brian Franklin, Susan G. Conard, James N. Dowden, Charles W.

Hedel, Roderick L. MacDonald, and Wayne Savage. "History, Landforms, and Vegetation of the Estuary's Tidal Marshes." In *San Francisco Bay: The Urbanized Estuary*, edited by T. J. Conomos, 347–386. San Francisco: American Association for the Advancement of Science, Pacific Division, 1979.

Auerbach, Jonathan. *Male Call: Becoming Jack London*. Durham, NC: Duke University Press, 1996.

Babalis, Timothy. "Critical Review: A Historical Perspective on the National Research Council's Report 'Shellfish Mariculture in Drakes Estero.'" Unpublished paper, National Park Service, Pacific West Regional Office, Oakland, August 11, 2009.

———. "Restoring the Past: Environmental History and Oysters at Point Reyes National Seashore." *The George Wright Forum* 28, no. 2 (2011): 199–215.

Bain, H. Foster. "Mines and Mining." In *Nature and Science on the Pacific Coast: A Guide-Book for Scientific Travelers in the West*, edited by the American Association for the Advancement of Science, Pacific Coast Committee, 65–74. San Francisco: Paul Elder, 1915.

Bakken, Gordon Morris. *Practicing Law in Frontier California*. Lincoln: University of Nebraska Press, 1991.

Bakker, Elna S. *An Island Called California: An Ecological Introduction to Its Natural Communities*. 2nd ed. Berkeley: University of California Press, 1984.

Bancroft, Hubert Howe. *History of California*. Vol. 6, *1848–1859*. San Francisco: History Company, 1888.

———. *The History of California*. Vol. 7, *1860–1890*. San Francisco: History Company, 1890.

———. *Works*. Vol. 38, *Essays and Miscellany*. San Francisco: History Company, 1890.

Barlow, John P., Carl J. Lorenzen, and Richard T. Myren. "Eutrophication of a Tidal Estuary." *Limnology and Oceanography* 8, no. 2 (April 1963): 251–262.

Barrett, Elinore Magee. *The California Oyster Industry*. Resources Agency of California, Department of Fish and Game, Fish Bulletin 123. Sacramento: State Printing Office, 1963. www.oac.cdlib.org/ark:/13030/kt629004n3/?brand=oac4 (accessed December 7, 2012).

———. "The Oyster Industry of California." MA thesis, University of California, Berkeley, 1961.

Barry, John M. *The Great Mississippi Flood of 1927 and How It Changed America*. New York: Simon and Schuster, 1998.

Bates, Mrs. D. B. *Incidents on Land and Water, or Four Years on the Pacific Coast*. Boston: E. O. Libby, 1858.

Bay Institute. *From the Sierra to the Sea: The Ecological History of the San Francisco Bay-Delta Watershed*. Novato, CA: Bay Institute of San Francisco, 1998.

Baye, Peter R., Phyllis M. Faber, and Brenda Grewell. "Tidal Marsh Plants of the San Francisco Bay Estuary." In *Baylands Ecosystem Species and Community Profiles*, by Goals Project, 9–33. Oakland: San Francisco Estuary Institute / San Francisco Bay Regional Water Quality Control Board, 2000.

Baye, Peter, and Robin Grossinger. "Once and Future Bay: Lessons from History for Revitalizing the Bay." *Bay Nature* 4, no. 4 (July 2004): 22–27.

Beahrs, Andrew. "The Decades-Long Comeback of Mark Twain's Favorite Food." *Smithsonian* 42, no. 6 (June 2012): 62–69.

———. *Twain's Feast: Searching for America's Lost Foods in the Footsteps of Samuel Clemens*. New York: Penguin, 2010.

Bean, Lowell John, ed. *The Ohlone Past and Present: Native Americans of the San Francisco Bay Region*. Menlo Park, CA: Ballena Press, 1994.

Beardsley, Richard K. *Temporal and Areal Relationships in Central California Archaeology—Part One*. Reports of the University of California Archaeological Survey 24. Berkeley: University of California, 1954.

Beechey, F. W. *Narrative of a Voyage to the Pacific and Beering's Strait, To Cooperate with The Polar Expeditions: Performed in His Majesty's Ship Blossom, Under the Command of Captain F. W. Beechey, R.N. FRS & c. In the Years 1825, 26, 27, 28*. 2 vols. London: Henry Colburn and Richard Bentley, 1831.

Beller, Erin, Micha Salomon, and Robin Grossinger. *Historical Ecology of Western Santa Clara Valley*. Oakland: San Francisco Estuary Institute, 2010.

Benneman, William, ed. *A Year of Gold and Mud: San Francisco in Letters and Diaries, 1849–1850*. Lincoln: University of Nebraska Press, 1999.

Bidwell, John. "Life in California Before the Gold Discovery." *Century Illustrated Magazine* 41, no. 2 (December 1890): 163–183.

Blackburn, Thomas C., and M. Kat Anderson, eds. *Before the Wilderness: Environmental Management by Native Californians*. Menlo Park, CA: Ballena Press, 1993.

———. "Managing the Domesticated Environment." In *Before the Wilderness: Environmental Management by Native Californians*, edited by Thomas C. Blackburn and M. Kat Anderson, 15–26. Menlo Park, CA: Ballena, 1993.

Bocek, Barbara. "Hunter-Gatherer Ecology and Settlement Mobility Along San Francisquito Creek." PhD diss., Stanford University, 1987.

Bolton, Herbert Eugene, ed. and trans. *Anza's California Expeditions*. Vol. 3, *The San Francisco Colony*. Berkeley: University of California Press, 1930.

Bonnett, Wayne. *San Francisco by Land and Sea: A Transportation Album*. Sausalito, CA: Windgate Press, 1997.

Bonnot, Paul. "The California Oyster Industry." *California Fish and Game* 1, no. 1 (1935): 65–80.

Booker, Matthew Morse. "'Metro is *Not Only* Sewers!': Environment and Politics in Postwar Metropolitan Seattle." Unpublished manuscript, 1997.

————. "Real Estate and Refuge: An Environmental History of San Francisco's Tidal Wetlands, 1846–1972." PhD diss., Stanford University, 2005.

————. "Visualizing San Francisco Bay's Forgotten Past." *Journal of Digital Humanities* 1, no. 3 (Summer 2012). http://journalofdigitalhumanities. org/1-3/visualizing-san-francisco-bays-forgotten-past-by-matthew-booker/ (accessed December 7, 2012).

Booker, Matthew, Michael De Groot, and Kathy Harris. "From Salt Ponds to Refuge in San Francisco Bay." Stanford, CA: Spatial History Project, Stanford University, 2010. www.stanford.edu/group/spatialhistory/cgi-bin/site/pub.php?id=49 (accessed November 30, 2012).

Booker, Matthew, and Alec Norton. "Visualizing Sea Level Rise and Early Bay Habitation, 6000 B.P. to Present: The Emeryville Shellmound." Stanford, CA: Spatial History Project, Stanford University, 2009. www.stanford.edu/group/spatialhistory/cgi-bin/site/pub.php?id=9 (accessed December 7, 2012).

Booker, Patricia. [Map of the Sacramento-San Joaquin Delta]. Scale not given. In *Delta West: The Land and People of the Sacramento-San Joaquin Delta,* by Roger Minick and Dave Bohn, 17. Berkeley: Scrimshaw, 1969.

Bray, R.N., A.D. Bates, and J.M. Land. *Dredging: A Handbook for Engineers.* 2nd ed. London: Arnold, 1997.

Brechin, Gray. *Imperial San Francisco: Urban Power, Earthly Ruin.* Berkeley: University of California Press, 1999.

Brewer, William. *Up and Down California in 1860–1864.* 3rd ed. Edited by Francis P. Farquhar. Berkeley: University of California Press, 1966. First published 1930 by Yale University Press.

Briscoe, John. "Some Legal Problems of Tidal Marshes." In *San Francisco Bay: The Urbanized Estuary,* edited by T.J. Conomos, 387–400. San Francisco: American Association for the Advancement of Science, Pacific Division, 1979.

Brook, James, Chris Carlsson, and Nancy J. Peters, eds. *Reclaiming San Francisco: History, Politics, Culture.* San Francisco: City Lights Publishers, 2001.

Brown, Alan K., ed. and trans. *A Description of Distant Roads: Original Journals of the First Expedition into California, 1769–1770, by Juan Crespi.* San Diego: San Diego State University Press, 2001.

————. "Salt for the Scraping: Origin of the San Francisco Bay Salt Industry." *California Historical Quarterly* 39 (Winter 1960): 117–120.

Browne, J. Ross. "Agricultural Capacity of California: Overflows and Droughts." *Overland Monthly* 10, no. 4 (April 1873): 297–314.

————. "Reclamation and Irrigation." In *Report of the Commissioner of Agriculture,* by the U.S. Department of Agriculture. Washington, DC: U.S. Department of Agriculture, 1873.

Bryant, Edwin. *What I Saw in California: Being the Journal of a Tour, by the Emigrant Route and South Pass of the Rocky Mountains, across the Continent of North America, the Great Desert Basin, and through California.* New York: D. Appleton, 1848.

Buffum, Edward Gould. *Six Months in the Gold Mines: From a Journal of Six Months Residence in Upper and Lower California, 1847–8–9.* Philadelphia: Lea and Blanchard, 1850.

Bureau of the Census, U.S. Department of Commerce and Labor. *Special Reports: Fisheries of the United States, 1908.* Washington, DC: Government Printing Office, 1921.

Bureau of Outdoor Recreation. *Proposed San Francisco Bay National Wildlife Refuge.* San Francisco: U.S. Department of the Interior, 1971. SFBNWR Archives, Newark, CA.

California Board of Fish Commissioners. *Biennial Reports of the Commissioners of Fisheries.* Sacramento: Superintendent of State Printing, 1871–1890.

California Board of State Harbor Commissioners. *Biennial Report for the Two Fiscal Years Commencing July 1, 1896, and Ending June 30, 1898.* Sacramento: Superintendent of State Printing, 1899.

California Board of Tide Land Commissioners. *Report of the Board of Tide Land Commissioners and the State Board for the Year Ending November 1, 1869.* San Francisco: State Board, 1869. California Pamphlets Vol. 9, Bancroft Library, University of California, Berkeley.

California Climate Change Center. *The Impacts of Sea-Level Rise on the California Coast.* Oakland: Pacific Institute, 2009.

California Constitutional Convention. *Debates and Proceedings of the Constitutional Convention of California, 1878–1879.* 3 vols. Sacramento: J.D. Young, State Printer, 1880.

California Department of Public Works, Division of Water Resources. *San Joaquin River Basin.* Bulletin 29. Sacramento: Division of Water Resources, 1931.

———. *Variation and Control of Salinity in Sacramento–San Joaquin Delta and Upper San Francisco Bay.* Bulletin 27. Sacramento: Division of Water Resources, 1930.

California Legislature, Assembly Committee on the Bulkhead. *Testimony against the Necessity of a Bulkhead or Seawall in San Francisco.* Sacramento, CA: [1859?].

"California Oysters." *The Manufacturer and Builder* 7, no. 8 (August 1875).

California State Division of Mines. "The California Chlorine-Caustic Industry." *Mineral Information Service* 3, no. 4 (April 1950).

———. "Salt." *Mineral Information Service* 11, no. 7 (July 1958).

California State Earthquake Investigation Commission. *The California Earthquake of April 18, 1906: Report of the State Earthquake Investigation Commission.*

Carnegie Publication 87. Washington, DC: Carnegie Institution of Washington, 1908–1910.

———. *Map of Portion of San Francisco, Showing 1906 Apparent Earthquake Intensity* [map]. 1:40,000. In *The California Earthquake of April 18, 1906*. Washington, DC: Carnegie Institution of Washington, 1908–1910.

California State Joint Committee on Public and State Lands. *Report of the Joint Committee to Inquire into and Report upon the Condition of the Public and State Lands Lying within the Limits of the State*. Sacramento: T. A. Springer, State Printer, 1872. California Pamphlets, Vol. 10, Bancroft Library, University of California, Berkeley.

California State Land Commission. *Report of the State Land Commission to the Legislature of the State of California*. Sacramento: State Office, F. P. Thompson, Superintendent State Printing, 1877.

Carlton, J. T. "Biological Invasions and Cryptogenic Species." *Ecology* 77, no. 6 (1996): 1653–1655.

Carson, Rachel. *The Edge of the Sea*. New York: New American Library, 1955.

Catton, Theodore. *Inhabited Wilderness: Indians, Eskimos, and National Parks in Alaska*. Albuquerque: University of New Mexico Press, 1997.

Center for Land Use Interpretation. *Back to the Bay: Exploring the Margins of the San Francisco Bay Region*. Culver City, CA: Center for Land Use Interpretation, 2001.

Chan, Sucheng. *This Bittersweet Soil: The Chinese in California Agriculture, 1860–1910*. Berkeley: University of California Press, 1986.

Chatard, Thomas M. "Salt Making Processes in the United States." In *Seventh Annual Report of the United States Geological Survey to the Secretary of the Interior 1885–86*, by J. W. Powell, Director, 497–535. Washington, DC: Government Printing Office, 1888.

Chestnut, A. F. "Oyster Reefs." In *Coastal Ecological Systems of the United States*, edited by H. T. Odum, B. J. Copeland, and E. A. McMahan, 2:171–203. Washington, DC: Conservation Foundation, 1974.

Chiang, Connie. *Shaping the Shoreline: Fisheries and Tourism on the Monterey Coast*. Seattle: University of Washington Press, 2008.

Childs, M. T., C. S. Dorsett, A. Failor, L. Roidt, and G. S. Omenn. "Effects of Shellfish Consumption on Cholesterol Absorption in Normolipidemic Men." *Metabolism* 36 (1987): 31–35.

Chin, John L., Florence L. Wong, and Paul R. Carlson. *Shifting Sands and Shattered Rocks: How Man Has Transformed the Floor of West-Central San Francisco Bay*. U.S. Geological Survey Circular 1259. Reston, VA: U.S. Geological Survey, 2004.

Clark, Walter Van Tilburg, ed. *The Journals of Alfred Doten, 1849–1903*. Reno: University of Nevada Press, 1973.

Cohen, A. N., and J. T. Carlton. "Accelerating Invasion Rate in a Highly Invaded Estuary." *Science* 279 (1998): 555–558.

———. "Nonindigenous Aquatic Species in a United States Estuary: The Case Study of the Biological Invasions of the San Francisco Bay and Delta." Washington, DC: U.S. Fish and Wildlife Service, 1995.

Committee of East Bay Engineers. *Preliminary Report upon Sewage Disposal for the East Bay Cities of Alameda, Albany, Berkeley, El Cerrito, Emeryville, Oakland, Piedmont, San Leandro, and Richmond to the East Bay Executive Association.* Oakland: Committee of East Bay Engineers, 1938.

Commonwealth Club of San Francisco. *The Population of California.* San Francisco: Parker Printing, 1946.

Conlin, Joseph. *Bacon, Beans and Galantines: Food and Foodways on the Western Mining Frontier.* Reno: University of Nevada Press, 1986.

Conn, H. W. "The Outbreak of Typhoid Fever at Wesleyan University." In *Seventeenth Annual Report of the State Board of Health of the State of Connecticut,* by the Connecticut Board of Health, 243–264. New Haven: Tuttle, Morehouse and Taylor, 1895.

Connecticut Board of Health. "Table VII: Nosological Arrangement by Counties, with Comparative Mortality for Ten Years." In *Seventeenth Annual Report of the State Board of Health of the State of Connecticut,* 120. New Haven: Tuttle, Morehouse and Taylor.

Conomos, T. John, ed. *San Francisco Bay: The Urbanized Estuary: Investigations into the Natural History of San Francisco Bay and Delta with Reference to the Influence of Man.* San Francisco: American Association for the Advancement of Science, Pacific Division, 1979.

Cook, Sherburne F., and Robert F. Heizer. "The Physical Analysis of Nine Indian Mounds of the Lower Sacramento Valley." *University of California Publications in American Archaeology and Ethnology* 40 (1956): 281–312.

Cook, Sherburne F., and A. E. Treganza. "The Quantitative Investigation of Indian Mounds, with Special Reference to the Relation of Physical Components to the Probable Material Culture." *University of California Publications in American Archaeology and Ethnology* 40 (1956): 223–262.

Cooper, Arthur W. "Salt Marshes." In *Coastal Ecological Systems of the United States,* edited by H. T. Odum, B. J. Copeland, and E. A. McMahan, 2:55–98. Washington, DC: Conservation Foundation, 1974.

Country Club of Washington Township Research Committee. *History of Washington Township.* 2nd ed. Niles, CA: Country Club of Washington Research Committee, 1950. First published 1904.

Coy, Owen C. *Guide to the County Archives of California.* Sacramento: California Historical Survey Commission / California State Printing Office, 1919.

Cronise, Titus Fay. *The Natural Wealth of California . . . Together with a Detailed Description of Each County.* San Francisco: H. H. Bancroft, 1868.

Cronon, William. *Changes in the Land: Indians, Colonists, and the Ecology of New England.* New York: Hill and Wang, 1983.

———. "Commentary: Reading the Palimpsest." In *Discovering the Chesapeake: The History of an Ecosystem,* edited by Philip D. Curtin, Grace S. Brush, George W. Fisher, 355–73. Baltimore: Johns Hopkins University Press, 2001.

———. *Nature's Metropolis: Chicago and the Great West.* New York: W. W. Norton, 1991.

Crosby, Alfred W. *The Columbian Exchange: Biological and Cultural Consequences of 1492.* Westport, CT: Greenwood, 1972.

———. *Ecological Imperialism: The Biological Expansion of Europe, 900–1900.* Cambridge: Cambridge University Press, 1986.

Crowder, William. *Between the Tides.* New York: Dodd, Mead, 1931.

Cutter, Donald C. "Some Musings on the Gold Rush and Its Hispanic Heritage." *Western Historical Quarterly* 30, no. 4 (Winter 1999): 429–433.

Dana, Richard Henry. *Two Years Before the Mast: A Personal Narrative of Life at Sea.* New York: Harper, 1840.

Darleth, Charles, Jr. "The Destructive Extent of the California Earthquake of 1906; Its Effect upon Structures and Structural Materials, within the Earthquake Belt." In *The California Earthquake of April 18, 1906,* edited by David Starr Jordan, 79–212. San Francisco: A. M. Robinson, 1907.

Dasmann, Raymond. *The Destruction of California.* New York: Macmillan, 1965.

Daum, T., S. Lowe, R. Toia, G. Bartow, R. Fairey, J. Anderson, J. Jones. *Sediment Concentration in San Leandro Bay, California.* Oakland: San Francisco Estuary Institute, 2000. www.sfei.org/sites/default/files/finalslbay.pdf (accessed December 7, 2012).

Davies, Andrea Rees. *Saving San Francisco: Relief and Recovery after the 1906 Disaster.* Philadelphia: Temple University Press, 2011.

deBuys, William, and Joan Myers. *Salt Dreams: Land and Water in Low-Down California.* Albuquerque: University of New Mexico Press, 1999.

De Groot, Michael, and Matthew Booker. "The Struggle for Ownership of the San Francisco Bay Area, 1769–1972." Spatial History Project, Stanford University, 2009. www.stanford.edu/group/spatialhistory/cgi-bin/site/pub.php?id=15 (accessed December 13, 2012).

DeLay, Brian. *War of a Thousand Deserts: Indian Raids and the U.S.-Mexican War.* New Haven, CT: Yale University Press, 2008.

Delgado, James P. *To California by Sea: A Maritime History of the Gold Rush.* Columbia: University of South Carolina Press, 1990.

Dill, William A., and Almo J. Cordone. *History and Status of Introduced Fishes in California, 1871–1996.* Resources Agency of California, Department of Fish and Game, Fish Bulletin 178. Sacramento: State Printing Office, 1963. www. oac.cdlib.org/ark:/13030/kt8p30069f/?brand=oac4 (accessed December 7, 2012).

Dong, Fay M. *The Nutritional Value of Shellfish*. Seattle: Washington Sea Grant/University of Washington School of Fishery Sciences, 2001.

Dow, Gerald. "Bay Fill in San Francisco." MA thesis, California State University, San Francisco, 1973.

Dreyfus, Philip J. *Our Better Nature: Environment and the Making of San Francisco*. Norman: University of Oklahoma Press, 2008.

Duflot de Mofras, Eugene. *Port de San Francisco dans la Haute Californie* [map]. In *Exploration de l'Territoire de l'Oregon, des Californies et de la Mer Vermeille, Executee Pendant les Annees 1840, 1841 et 1842 par M. Duflot de Mofras*, vol. 3, map no. 16. Paris: A. Bertrand, 1844. David Rumsey Historical Map Collection, http://davidrumsey.com (accessed December 3, 2012).

Duhaut-Cilly, Auguste Bertrand. *Voyage autour du monde, principalement a la Californie et aux Iles Sandwich, pendant les annees 1826, 1827, 1828, et 1829*. Translated by Charles Franklin Carter and reprinted as *Duhaut-Cilly's Account of California in the Years 1827–28. California Historical Society Quarterly* 8, nos. 2–4 (June–December 1929): 131–166; 214–250; 306–336.

Eads, James B. *Report of James B. Eads, Consulting Engineer, in Relation to Proposed Improvement to Promote Rapid Drainage, and to Improve the Navigation of the Sacramento River*. Sacramento: J.D. Young, Superintendent State Printing, 1880.

Eastwood, Alice, ed. "Menzies' California Journal." *California Historical Society Quarterly* 2, no. 4 (January 1924): 265–340.

Eaton, Joe. "Still Waiting for the Book." Review of *Before California: An Archaeologist Looks at Our Earliest Inhabitants*, by Brian Fagan. *Faultline: California's Environmental Magazine*, May 23, 2003. www.faultline.org/fmag/bookstore/2003/05/fagan.html (accessed November 9, 2012).

Eddy, William. *Official Map of San Francisco Compiled from the Field Notes of the Official Re-Survey Made by Wm. Eddy*. Scale not given. New York: F. Michelin, 1849. Bancroft Library, University of California, Berkeley.

Edmondson, W. T. *The Uses of Ecology: Lake Washington and Beyond*. Seattle: University of Washington Press, 1996.

Elkind, Sarah. *Bay Cities and Water Politics: The Battle for Resources in Boston and Oakland*. Lawrence: University Press of Kansas, 1998.

Ellickson, Robert C. *Order without Law: How Neighbors Settle Disputes*. Cambridge, MA: Harvard University Press, 1994.

Elton, Charles. *The Ecology of Invasions by Animals and Plants*. London: Methuen, 1958.

Enos, John Summerfield, California Commissioner of Labor Statistics. *The Condition of the Laborers Employed by Contractors on the Seawall at San Francisco, etc under Senate Resolution of March 3, 1885*. Sacramento: James J. Ayers, Superintendent State Printing, 1886.

Esser, Kimberly. "'Notoriously Swampy and Overflowed': An Inland Maritime Landscape of the California Delta." MA thesis, Sonoma State University, 1999.

Eyer, Marguerite. *Vancouver in California*. Los Angeles: Glen Dawson, 1953.

Faber, Phyllis. *Common Wetland Plants of Coastal California: A Field Guide for the Layman*. 2nd ed. Mill Valley, CA: Pickleweed Press, 1996.

Fagan, Brian. *Before California: An Archaeologist Looks at Our Earliest Inhabitants*. Oxford: Rowman and Littlefield, 2003.

Fairfax, Sally K., Lauren Gwin, Mary Ann King, Leigh Raymond, and Laura A. Watt. *Buying Nature: The Limits of Land Acquisition as a Conservation Strategy, 1780–2004*. Cambridge, MA: MIT Press, 2005.

Farley, Judson. "Salt-Making in Alameda." *Overland Monthly* 6 (February 1871): 105–112.

Fiege, Mark. *Irrigated Eden: The Making of an Agricultural Landscape in the American West*. Seattle: University of Washington Press, 1999.

Fisher, Colin. "Race and US Environmental History." In *A Companion to American Environmental History*, edited by Douglas Cazaux Sackman, 99–115. Malden, MA: Blackwell, 2010.

Fitch, John E. *Common Marine Bivalves of California*. Fish Bulletin 90. Sacramento: State of California Department of Fish and Game Marine Fisheries Branch, 1953.

Foote, A.D. "The Redemption of the Great Valley of California." *Transactions of the American Society of Civil Engineers* 66 (March 1910): 229–245.

Fremont, John Charles. *A Report of the Exploring Expedition to The Rocky Mountains in the Year 1842, and to Oregon and North California in the Years 1843–44.* Washington, DC: Gales and Seaton, 1845.

Fritz, Christian G. *Federal Justice in California: The Court of Ogden Hoffman, 1851–1891*. Lincoln: University of Nebraska Press, 1991.

Fritzsche, Bruno. "San Francisco, 1846–1848: The Coming of the Land Speculator." *California Historical Quarterly* 51, no. 1 (Spring 1972): 17–34.

Fry, Kathleen Whalen. "Farming the Water: Japanese Oyster Laborers in Washington State and the Creation of a Trans-Pacific Industry." PhD diss., Washington State University, 2011.

Galloway, Devin, David R. Jones, and S.E. Ingebritsen, eds. *Land Subsidence in the United States*. U.S. Geological Survey Circular 1182. Washington, DC: U.S. Geological Survey, 1999.

Galloway, Devin, and Francis S. Riley. "San Joaquin Valley, California: Largest Human Alteration of the Earth's Surface." In *Land Subsidence in the United States*, edited by Devin Galloway, David R. Jones, and S.E. Ingebritsen,

23–34. U.S. Geological Survey Circular 1182. Washington, DC: U.S. Geological Survey, 1999.

Garone, Philip. *The Fall and Rise of the Wetlands of California's Great Central Valley.* Berkeley: University of California Press, 2011.

Gates, Paul Wallace. *The Farmer's Age: Agriculture, 1815–1860.* New York: Holt, Rinehart and Winston, 1960.

———. *History of Public Land Law Development.* Washington, DC: U.S. Government Printing Office, 1968.

George, Henry. *Our Land and Land Policy.* New York: Doubleday and McClure, 1902.

———. "What the Railroad Will Bring Us." *Overland Monthly* 1, no. 4 (October 1868): 297–306.

Gifford, E. "Composition of Californian Shell Mounds." *University of California Publications in American Archaeology and Ethnology* 12, no. 1 (1916): 1–29.

Gilbert, Grove Karl. "Hydraulic Mining Debris in the Sierra Nevada." Professional Paper 105. Washington, DC: U.S. Geological Survey, 1917.

Gilbert, Grove Karl, et al. *The San Francisco Earthquake and Fire of April 18, 1906, and Their Effects on Structures and Structural Materials: Reports.* Department of the Interior, U.S. Geological Survey, Bulletin 324, Series R, Structural Materials. Washington, DC: General Printing Office, 1907.

Gilliam, Harold. *San Francisco Bay.* Garden City, NY: Doubleday, 1957.

Goals Project. *Baylands Ecosystem Habitat Goals: A Report of Habitat Recommendations Prepared by the San Francisco Bay Area Wetlands Ecosystem Goals Project.* Oakland: U.S. Environmental Protection Agency / San Francisco Bay Regional Water Quality Control Board, 1999.

———. *Baylands Ecosystem Species and Community Profiles: Life Histories and Environmental Requirements of Key Plants, Fish and Wildlife.* Oakland: San Francisco Bay Estuary Institute / San Francisco Bay Regional Water Quality Control Board, 2000.

Goldman, Harold. *Salt, Sand and Shells: Mineral Resources of San Francisco Bay.* San Francisco: Bay Conservation and Development Commission, 1967.

Goodwin, Cardinal. *The Establishment of State Government in California, 1846–1850.* New York: Macmillan, 1914.

Goyer, R., V. Aposhian, L. Arab, D. Bellinger, T. Burbacher, J. Jacobson, L. Knobeloch, et al. *Toxicological Effects of Methyl Mercury.* Washington, DC: National Academy Press, 2000.

Greengo, Robert. "Molluscan Species in California Shell Middens." *Reports of the University of California Archaeological Survey* 13 (December 10, 1951): 1–29.

Grivas, Theodore. *Military Governments in California 1846–1850, with a Chapter on Their Prior Use in Louisiana, Florida and New Mexico.* Glendale: Arthur H. Clark, 1963.

Grossinger, Robin M. "Documenting Local Landscape Change: The San Francisco Bay Area Historical Ecology Project." In *The Historical Ecology Handbook: A Restorationist's Guide to Reference Ecosystems,* edited by Dave Egan and Evelyn A. Howell, 425–442. Covelo, CA: Island Press, 2001.

———. "Seeing Time: An Historical Approach to Restoration." *Ecological Restoration* 17, no. 4 (1999): 251–252.

Grossinger, Robin M., and Ruth A. Askevold. *Napa Valley Historical Ecology Atlas: Exploring a Hidden Landscape of Transformation and Resilience.* Berkeley: University of California Press, 2012.

Grossinger, Robin M., Ruth A. Askevold, and Joshua N. Collins. *T-Sheet User Guide: Application of the Historical U.S. Coast Survey Maps to Environmental Management in the San Francisco Bay Area.* SFEI Report No. 427. Oakland, CA: San Francisco Estuary Institute, 2005.

Grossinger, Robin M., Ruth Askevold, Charles J. Striplen, Elise Brewster, Sarah Pearce, Kristen Larned, Lester J. McKee, and Joshua N. Collins. *Coyote Creek Watershed Historical Ecology Study: Historical Condition, Landscape Change and Restoration Potential in the Eastern Santa Clara Valley, California.* Oakland: San Francisco Estuary Institute, 2006.

Grossinger, Robin M., Erin Beller, Micha Solomon, Alison Whipple, Ruth Askevold, Charles J. Striplen, Elise Brewster, and Robert Leidy. *South Santa Clara Valley Historical Ecology Study.* Oakland: San Francisco Estuary Institute, 2008.

Guard, B. Jennifer. *Wetland Plants of Oregon and Washington.* Auburn, WA: Lone Pine, 1995.

Hagwood, Joseph J., Jr. *A Commitment to Excellence: A History of the Sacramento District U.S. Army Corps of Engineers, 1929–1973.* Sacramento: U.S. Army Engineer District, 1976.

Hahn, Jonathan, and Jonathan Prude, eds. *The Countryside in the Age of Capitalist Transformation.* Chapel Hill: University of North Carolina Press, 1985.

Haight, H. H. "Governor's Message." In *Journal of the Assembly during the Eighteenth Session of the Legislature of the State of California, 1869–1870,* 38–57. Sacramento: D. W. Gelwicks, State Printer, 1870.

Hamalainen, Pekka. *The Comanche Empire.* New Haven: Yale University Press, 2009.

Hammond, George P., and Dale L. Morgan. *Captain Charles M. Weber: Pioneer of the San Joaquin and Founder of Stockton, California.* Berkeley: Friends of the Bancroft Library, 1966.

Hansen, Gladys, and Emmet Condon. *Denial of Disaster: The Untold Story and Photographs of the San Francisco Earthquake and Fire of 1906.* San Francisco: Cameron and Company, 1989.

Hart, John, and David Sanger. *San Francisco Bay: Portrait of an Estuary.* Berkeley: University of California Press, 2003.

Harte, Bret. "Neighborhoods I Have Moved From." *The Californian* 1, no. 2 (June 4, 1864).

Hartog, Hendrik. *Public Property and Private Power: The Corporation of the City of New York in American Law, 1730–1870.* Chapel Hill: University of North Carolina Press, 1983.

Hattori, Eugene M., and Jerre L. Kosta. "Packed Pork and Other Foodstuffs from the California Gold Rush." In *The Hoff Store Site and Gold Rush Merchandise from San Francisco, California,* edited by Allen G. Pastron and Eugene M. Hattori, 82–93. Society for Historical Archaeology Special Publication 7. San Francisco: Society for Historical Archaeology, 1990.

Hays, Samuel P. *Beauty, Health, and Permanence: Environmental Politics in the United States, 1955–1985.* New York: Cambridge University Press, 1987.

———. *Conservation and the Gospel of Efficiency: The Progressive Conservation Movement, 1890–1920.* Cambridge, MA: Harvard University Press, 1959.

———. "From Conservation to Environment: Environmental Politics in the United States Since World War II." *Environmental Review* 6, no. 2 (Fall 1982): 14–41.

Heath, Harold. "Investigation of the Clams of California." In State of California Fish and Game Commission, Fish Bulletin 1, 27–28. Sacramento: State Superintendent of Printing, 1913.

Hedgpeth, Joel W., ed. *The Outer Shores Part 1: Ed Ricketts and John Steinbeck Explore the Pacific Coast.* Eureka, CA: Mad River Press, 1978.

———"San Francisco Bay: The Unsuspected Estuary, a History of Researches." In *San Francisco Bay: The Urbanized Estuary,* edited by T. J. Conomos, 9–30. San Francisco: American Association for the Advancement of Science, Pacific Division, 1979.

Heizer, Robert Fleming, ed. *The Destruction of California Indians: A Collection of Documents from the Period 1847–1865 in Which are Described Some of the Things that Happened to Some of the Indians of California.* Santa Barbara, CA: Peregrine Smith, 1974.

———. "Salt in California Indian Culture." In *Salt in California,* California Bureau of Mines, Bulletin 175, by William Ver Planck. San Francisco: Bureau of Mines, 1958.

———, ed. *Smithsonian Handbook of the North American Indian.* Vol. 8, *California.* Washington, DC: Smithsonian Institution, 1978.

———. *They Were Only Diggers: A Collection of Articles from California Newspapers, 1851–1866, on Indian and White Relations.* Ramona, CA: Ballena Press, 1974.

Heizer, Robert Fleming, and Theodora Kroeber. *Ishi, the Last Yahi: A Documentary History.* Berkeley: University of California Press, 1979.

Helm, Michael, ed. *City Country Miners: Some Northern California Veins.* San Francisco: City Miner Books, 1982.

Hibbard, Benjamin H. *A History of the Public Land Policies.* Madison: University of Wisconsin Press, 1924.

Hill, C. L., and C. A. Kofoid, eds. *Marine Borers and their Relation to Marine Construction on the Pacific Coast. Final Report of the San Francisco Bay Marine Piling Committee.* San Francisco: San Francisco Bay Marine Piling Committee, 1927.

Hittell, John S. *A History of the City of San Francisco; and Incidentally of the State of California.* San Francisco: A. L. Bancroft, 1878.

Historical Atlas Map of Santa Clara County, California. San Francisco: Thompson and West, 1876.

Historical Atlas Map of Solano County, California. San Francisco: Thompson and West, 1878.

Holliday, J. S. *The World Rushed In: The California Gold Rush Experience.* New York: Simon and Schuster, 1981.

Holmes, Beatrice Bert. *A History of Federal Water Resources Programs, 1800–1960.* Washington, DC: U.S. Department of Agriculture Economic Research Service, 1972.

Holmes, J. A., Edward C. Franklin, and Ralph E. Gould. *Report of the Selby Smelter Commission.* U.S. Bureau of Mines, Bulletin 98. Washington, DC: General Publishing Office, 1915.

Horne, Alexander J., and Charles R. Goldman. *Limnology.* 2nd ed. New York: McGraw-Hill, 1994.

Horwitz, Morton J. *The Transformation of American Law, 1780–1860.* Cambridge: Harvard University Press, 1977.

Hurtado, Albert. *Indian Survival on the California Frontier.* New Haven, CT: Yale University Press, 1988.

Igler, David. "Diseased Goods: Global Exchanges in the Eastern Pacific Basin, 1770–1850." *American Historical Review* 109, no. 3 (June 2004): 693–719.

———. *Industrial Cowboys: Miller and Lux and the Transformation of the Far West, 1850–1920.* Berkeley: University of California Press, 2001.

———. "Longitudes and Latitudes." *Environmental History* 10, no. 1 (January 2005): 44–46.

Ingebritsen S. E., and Marti E. Ikehara. "Sacramento-San Joaquin Delta: the Sinking Heart of the State." In *Land Subsidence in the United States,* U.S. Geological Survey Circular 1182, edited by Devin Galloway, David R. Jones, and S. E. Ingebritsen, 83–94. Washington, DC: U.S. Geological Survey, 1999.

Ingersoll, Ernest. *The History and Present Condition of the Fishery Industries: The Oyster-Industry.* Washington, DC: U.S. Government Printing Office, 1881.

Isenberg, Andrew C. *Mining California: An Ecological History.* New York: Hill and Wang, 2005.

Issel, William, and Robert W. Cherny. *San Francisco, 1865–1932: Politics, Power, and Urban Development.* Berkeley: University of California Press, 1986.

Jackson, Robert H., and Richard Castillo. *Indians, Franciscans, and Spanish Colonization: The Impact of the Mission System of California Indians.* Albuquerque: University of New Mexico Press, 1995.

Jacoby, Karl. *Crimes against Nature: Squatters, Poachers, Thieves, and the Hidden History of American Conservation.* Berkeley: University of California Press, 2001.

James, L. Allan. "Sustained Storage and Transport of Hydraulic Gold Mining Sediment in the Bear River, California." *Annals of the Association of American Geographers* 79, no. 4 (December 1989): 570–592.

Johnson, David Alan. *Founding the Far West: California, Oregon, and Nevada, 1840–1890.* Berkeley: University of California Press, 1992.

Jones, William Carey. *Report on the Subject of Land Titles in California.* Vol. 3, Senate Executive Doc. 18, 31st Cong., 2nd Sess., 2–136. Washington, DC: General Printing Office, 1850.

Jordan, David Starr. "Spencer Fullerton Baird and the U.S. Fish Commission." *The Scientific Monthly* 17 (August 1923): 97–107.

Josselyn, Michael. *The Ecology of San Francisco Tidal Marshes: A Community Profile.* Washington, DC: U.S. Fish and Wildlife Service, Division of Biological Services, 1983.

Judd, Richard. *Common Lands, Common People: The Origins of Conservation in Northern New England.* Cambridge, MA: Harvard University Press, 1997.

Keiner, Christine. *The Oyster Question: Scientists, Watermen, and the Maryland Chesapeake Bay since 1880.* Athens: University of Georgia Press, 2010.

Kelley, Robert. *Battling the Inland Sea: Floods, Public Policy, and the Sacramento Valley.* Berkeley: University of California Press, 1989.

Kelman, Ari. *A River and Its City: The Nature of Landscape in New Orleans.* Berkeley: University of California Press, 2003.

Kemble, John Haskell. *San Francisco Bay: A Pictorial Maritime History.* Cambridge, MD: Cornell Maritime Press, 1957.

Kennedy, Clyde C. "A Sanitary Survey of the Oyster Beds of San Francisco Bay." MS thesis, University of California, Berkeley, 1912.

Kershaw, Alex. *Jack London: A Life.* London: HarperCollins, 1997.

King, T. Butler. "Report of T. Butler King to John M. Clayton, Secretary of State, Washington, March 22, 1850." In *Eldorado, Or, Adventures in the Path of Empire, Comprising A Voyage to California, Via Panama; Life in San Francisco and*

Monterey; Pictures of the Gold Region; and Experiences of Mexican Travel, by Bayard Taylor, 2:333–360. London: Henry G. Bohn, 1850.

Kingman, Russ. *A Pictorial Life of Jack London.* New York: Crown, 1979.

Kinsey, Darin S. "The Fish Car Era in Nebraska." *Railroad History* 177 (Autumn 1997): 43–67.

———. "Seeding the Water as the Earth: The Epicenter and Peripheries of a Western Aquacultural Revolution." *Environmental History* 11, no. 3 (July 2006): 527–566.

Klingle, Matthew. *Emerald City: An Environmental History of Seattle.* New Haven: Yale University Press, 2007.

Knowles, Noah. "Potential Inundation due to Rising Sea Levels in the San Francisco Bay Region." *San Francisco Estuary and Watershed Science* 8, no. 1 (2010): 1–19.

Kroeber, A. L. "Culture Element Distributions: XV Salt, Dogs, Tobacco." *Anthropological Records* 6, no. 1 (February 18, 1941): 1–6.

Krone, Ray B. "Sedimentation in the San Francisco Bay System." In *San Francisco Bay: The Urbanized Estuary,* edited by T. J. Conomos, 85–96. San Francisco: American Association for the Advancement of Science, Pacific Division, 1979.

Kurlansky, Mark. *Salt: A World History.* New York: Penguin Putnam, 2002.

Langston, Nancy. *Where Land and Water Meet: A Western Landscape Transformed.* Seattle: University of Washington Press, 2003.

Lasartemay, Eugene P., and Mary Rudge. *For Love of Jack London: His Life with Jennie Prentiss—A True Love Story.* New York: Vantage Press, 1991.

Laszlo, Pierre. *Salt: The Grain of Life.* New York: Columbia University Press, 2001.

LeCain, Timothy. "The Limits of 'Eco-Efficiency': Arsenic Pollution and Cottrell Electrical Precipitator in the U.S. Copper Smelting Industry." *Environmental History* 5, no. 3 (July 2000): 336–351.

Lee, Gabriel, Alec Norton, Andrew Robichaud, and Matthew Booker. *Morgan Oyster Company's Bay Holdings, 1930* [map]. 2008. Scale not given. Spatial History Project, Stanford University. www.stanford.edu/group/spatialhistory/cgi-bin/site/viz.php?id=109 (accessed December 3, 2012).

———. *San Mateo County Bay Ownership, 1877–1927* [map]. 2008. Scale not given. Spatial History Project, Stanford University. www.stanford.edu/group/spatialhistory/cgi-bin/site/viz.php?id=25& (accessed December 3, 2012).

Lehrer, Tom. "Pollution." *That Was The Year That Was.* WB#6175. Warner Brothers, 1965.

Leonard, John, R. *The Fish Car Era of the National Hatchery System.* Washington, DC: U.S. Fish and Wildlife Service, 1979.

Levenstein, Harvey. *Revolution at the Table: The Transformation of the American Diet.* New York: Oxford University Press, 1988.

Levine, Harold, Roe E. Remington, and F. Bartow Culp. "The Value of the Oyster in Nutritional Anemia." *Journal of Nutrition* 4 (1931): 469.

Lightfoot, Kent G., and Otis Parrish. *California Indians and their Environment: An Introduction.* Berkeley: University of California Press, 2009.

Limerick, Patricia Nelson. *The Legacy of Conquest: The Unbroken Past of the American West.* New York: W. W. Norton, 1987.

Lockington, W. N. "Rambles Round San Francisco." *American Naturalist* 12, no. 6 (June 1878): 347–354.

London, Jack. *The Cruise of the Dazzler.* New York: Century, 1902.

———. *John Barleycorn: Alcoholic Memoirs.* London: Mills and Boon, 1914.

———. *Tales of the Fish Patrol.* New York: Macmillan, 1905.

Lopez, Claire. *Report on Leslie Salt Company Properties.* San Francisco: Leslie Salt Company, 1973.

Lounsbury, Ralph G. "Records of Mexican Land Claims in California." In *California Indians IV: American Indian Ethnohistory California and Basin-Plateau Indians,* edited by David A. Horr, 201–297. New York: Garland, 1974.

MacGinitie, G. E. "Some Effects of Fresh Water on the Fauna of a Marine Harbor." *American Midland Naturalist* 21, no. 3 (May 1939): 681–686.

Malamud-Roam, Frances, Michael Dettinger, B. Lynn Ingram, Malcolm K. Hughes, and Joan L. Florsheim. "Holocene Climates and Connections between the San Francisco Bay Estuary and its Watershed." *San Francisco Estuary and Watershed Science* 5, no. 1 (February 2007): 1–28.

Manning, Harvey. *Walking the Beach to Bellingham.* Seattle: Madrona, 1986.

Margolin, Malcolm. *The East Bay Out: A Personal Guide to the East Bay Regional Parks.* Berkeley: Heyday Books, 1974.

———. *The Ohlone Way: Indian Life in the San Francisco-Monterey Bay Area.* Berkeley: Heyday Books, 1978.

McCay, Bonnie J. *Oyster Wars and the Public Trust: Property, Law, and Ecology in New Jersey History.* Tucson: University of Arizona Press, 1998.

———. "The Pirates of Piscary: Ethnohistory of Illegal Fishing in New Jersey." *Ethnohistory* 31, no. 1 (Winter 1984): 17–37.

McEvoy, Arthur. *The Fisherman's Problem: Ecology and Law in the California Fisheries, 1850–1980.* New York: Cambridge University Press, 1986.

McKenzie, Matthew. *Clearing the Coastline: The Nineteenth-Century Ecological & Cultural Transformation of Cape Cod.* Hanover: University Press of New England, 2010.

McPhee, John. *Assembling California.* New York: Farrar, Straus and Giroux, 1993.

McWilliams, Carey. *Factories in the Field: The Story of Migratory Farm Labor in California.* Boston: Little, Brown, 1939.

———. *Small Farm and Big Farm.* New York: Public Affairs Committee, 1945.

Meehan, Betty. *Shell Bed to Shell Midden.* AIAS New Series No. 37. Canberra: Australian Institute of Aboriginal Studies, 1982.

Melosi, Martin. *The Sanitary City: Urban Infrastructure in America from Colonial Times to the Present.* Baltimore: Johns Hopkins University Press, 2000.

Menzel, Dorothy. *The Archaeology of Ancient Peru and the Work of Max Uhle.* Berkeley: R. H. Lowie Museum of Anthropology, 1977.

Merchant, Carolyn, ed. *Green Versus Gold: Sources in California's Environmental History.* Covelo, CA: Island Press, 1998.

Merrell, James H. *The Indians' New World: Catawbas and their Neighbors from European Contact through the Era of Removal.* New York: W. W. Norton, 1991.

Merrill, Michael. "Cash is Good to Eat: Self-Sufficiency and Exchange in the Rural Economy of the United States." *Radical History Review* 3 (1977): 42–71.

Miller, A. Whitman. "Assessing the Importance of Biological Attributes for Invasion Success." PhD diss., University of California, Los Angeles, 2000.

Miller, Robert C., W. C. Ramage, and Edgar L. Lazier. "A Study of Physical and Chemical Conditions of San Francisco Bay, Especially in Relation to Tides." *University of California Publications in Zoology* 31, no. 11 (1928): 201–267.

Milliken, Randall. *A Time of Little Choice: The Disintegration of Tribal Culture in the San Francisco Bay Area, 1769–1810.* Menlo Park, CA: Ballena, 1995.

Minick, Roger, and Dave Bohn. *Delta West: The Land and People of the Sacramento-San Joaquin Delta.* Berkeley: Scrimshaw, 1969.

Molhausen, Baldwin. *Diary of a Journey from the Mississippi to the Coasts of the Pacific with a United States Government Expedition.* 2 vols. London: Longman, Green, Brown, Longman, and Roberts, 1858.

Montoya, Maria. *Translating Property: The Maxwell Land Grant and the Conflict Over Land in the American West, 1840–1900.* Berkeley: University of California Press, 2002.

Moore, H. F. "Oysters and Methods of Oyster-Culture." In *A Manual of Fish-Culture, Based on the Methods of the United States Commission of Fish and Fisheries, with Chapters on the Cultivation of Oysters and Frogs,* by the U.S. Bureau of Fish and Fisheries, 263–340. Washington, DC: Government Printing Office, 1897.

Morrison, Rev. Harry B., and A. Greger. *Mission and Rancho Lands of Mission San Jose.* Scale not given. Fremont: Old Mission San Jose, 1997.

Moss, Madonna. "Shellfish, Gender, and Status on the Northwest Coast of North America: Reconciling Archeological, Ethnographic and Ethnohistorical Records of the Tlingit." *American Anthropologist* 95, no. 3 (1993): 631–652.

Moyle, Peter B. "Introductions in California: History and Impact on Native Fishes." *Biological Conservation* 9 (1976): 101–118.

Muir, John. "The Bee Pastures." In *The Mountains of California*, 340–342. New York: Century, 1894.

Murdock, C.A. *A Backward Glance at Eighty; Recollections & Comment: Massachusetts 1841, Humboldt Bay 1854, San Francisco 1864*. San Francisco: P. Elder, 1921.

Nash, Gerald. *State Government and Economic Development: A History of Economic Policies in California, 1849–1933*. Berkeley: Institute of Governmental Studies, 1964.

Nash, Linda. "Finishing Nature: Harmonizing Bodies and Environments in Late-Nineteenth-Century California." *Environmental History* 8, no. 1 (January 2003): 25–52.

———. *Inescapable Ecologies: A History of Environment, Disease and Knowledge*. Berkeley: University of California Press, 2007.

———. "Transforming the Central Valley: Body, Identity, and Environment in California, 1850–1970." PhD diss., University of Washington, 2000.

The Nation's Estuaries: San Francisco Bay and Delta, Calif. Hearing Before a Subcommittee of the Committee on Government Operations House of Representatives. 91st Cong., 1st Sess., May 15, 1969. Washington, DC: Government Printing Office, 1969.

Neasham, Vernon Aubrey. *Wild Legacy: California Fishing and Hunting Tales*. Berkeley: Howell-North Books, 1973.

Nelson, N.C. "The Ellis Landing Shellmound." *University of California Publications in American Archaeology and Ethnology* 7, no. 5 (1910): 357–426.

———. "Shell Mounds of the San Francisco Bay Region." *University of California Publications in American Archaeology and Ethnology* 7, no. 4 (1909): 309–348.

Nesbit, D.M. *Tide Marshes of the United States*. Misc. Spec. Report 7. Washington, DC: Department of Agriculture, 1885.

Norris, Frank. *McTeague: A Story of San Francisco*. New York: Grosset and Dunlap, 1899.

Odum, H.T., B.J. Copeland, and E.A. McMahan, eds. *Coastal Ecological Systems of the United States*. 4 vols. Washington, DC: Conservation Foundation, 1974.

Office of Area Development, U.S. Department of Commerce. *Comprehensive Survey of San Francisco Bay and Tributaries, October 1959*. Washington, DC: U.S. Department of Commerce, 1959.

Official and Historical Atlas Map of Alameda County, California. Oakland: Thompson and West, 1878.

Olmstead, Roger, and Nancy Olmstead. *San Francisco Waterfront: Report on Historical Cultural Resources for the North Shore and Channel Outfalls Consolidation Projects*. San Francisco Wastewater Management Program. San Francisco: Techni-Graphics, 1981.

Olson, Betty Haak. "Methylation of Mercury Compounds by San Francisco Bay Sediments." PhD diss., University of California, Berkeley, 1974.

Ostrom, Eleanor. *Governing the Commons: The Evolution of Institutions for Collective Action.* Cambridge: Cambridge University Press, 1990.

Painter, Nell Irvin. *Standing at Armageddon: The United States, 1877–1919.* New York: W. W. Norton, 1987.

Patton, Cynthia. *Turning Salt into Environmental Gold: Wetland Restoration in the South San Francisco Bay Salt Ponds.* Oakland: Save San Francisco Bay Association, 2002.

Pearson, Michael N. "Littoral Society: The Case for the Coast." *The Great Circle* 7 (1985): 1–8.

———. "Littoral Society: The Concept and the Problems." *Journal of World History* 17, no. 4 (December 2006): 353–373.

Perez, Crisotomo. *Land Grants in California: A Compilation of Spanish and Mexican Private Land Claims in the State of California.* Rancho Cordova, CA: Landmark Enterprises, 1996.

Peterson, Richard H. "The Failure to Reclaim: California State Swamp Land Policy and the Sacramento Valley, 1850–1866." *Southern California Quarterly* 56 (Spring 1974): 45–60.

Pisani, Donald J. "Beyond the Hundredth Meridian: Nationalizing the History of Water in the United States." *Environmental History* 5, no. 4 (October 2000): 466–482.

———. *From the Family Farm to Agribusiness: The Irrigation Crusade in California, 1850–1931.* Berkeley: University of California Press, 1984.

———. *To Reclaim a Divided West: Water, Law, and Public Policy, 1848–1902.* Albuquerque: University Press of New Mexico, 1992.

———. *Water, Land, and Law in the West: The Limits of Public Policy, 1850–1920.* Lawrence: University Press of Kansas, 1996.

Polk, James K. *The Diary of James K. Polk during His Presidency, 1845 to 1849.* Chicago: A. C. McClurg, 1910.

Pollock, Leland W. *A Practical Guide to the Marine Animals of Northeastern North America.* New Brunswick, NJ: Rutgers University Press, 1998.

Postel, Mitchell. "A Lost Resource: Shellfish in San Francisco Bay." *California History* 67 (March 1988): 26–41.

President's Water Resources Commission. *Report of the Commission.* Vol. 3, *Water Resources Law.* Washington, DC: President's Water Resources Commission, 1950.

Press, Daniel. *Saving Open Space: The Politics of Local Preservation in California.* Berkeley: University of California Press, 2002.

Prince, Hugh. *Wetlands of the American Midwest: A Historical Geography of Changing Attitudes.* Chicago: University of Chicago Press, 1997.

Purkitt, J. H. *A Letter on the Water Front Improvement Addressed to the Hon. James Van Ness, Mayor of San Francisco*. San Francisco: Whitton, Towne, Printers, 1856.

Pyne, Stephen. *Grove Karl Gilbert: A Great Engine of Research*. Austin: University of Texas Press, 1980.

Raphael, Ray, and Mark Livingston. *An Everyday History of Somewhere: Being the True Story of Indians, Deer, Homesteaders, Potatoes, Loggers, Trees, Fishermen, Salmon and Other Living Things in the Backwoods of Northern California*. New York: Alfred A. Knopf, 1974.

Rawls, James J. *Indians of California: The Changing Image*. Norman: University of Oklahoma Press, 1984.

"Returned." *The Overland Monthly* 1, no. 1 (July 1868): 100.

Rhode, Paul. "Learning, Capital Accumulation, and the Transformation of California Agriculture." *Journal of Economic History* 55, no. 4 (1995): 773–800.

"Rice Growing in California." *The California Farmer and Journal of Useful Sciences* 27, no. 2 (January 1867): 2.

Rick, Torben C., and Jon M. Erlandson. *Human Impacts on Ancient Marine Ecosystems: A Global Perspective*. Berkeley: University of California Press, 2008.

Ricketts, Edward F., and Jack Calvin. *Between Pacific Tides: An Account of the Habits and Habitats of Some Five Hundred of the Common, Conspicuous Seashore Invertebrates of the Pacific Coast between Sitka, Alaska, and Northern Mexico*. Stanford: Stanford University Press, 1939.

Roberts, Allen, and Matthew Booker. *Shell Mounds in San Francisco Bay Area* [map]. 2009. Scale not given. Spatial History Project, Stanford University. www.stanford.edu/group/spatialhistory/cgi-bin/site/viz.php?id=23& (accessed November 27, 2012).

Roberts, Doyle Loman. "Reclamation of California Delta Lands." MA thesis, University of the Pacific, 1951.

Robbins, Roy M. *Our Landed Heritage: The Public Domain, 1776–1936*. Princeton, NJ: Princeton University Press, 1942.

Robinson, J. P. *Report upon the Condition and Requirements of the City Front of San Francisco Made to the San Francisco Dock and Wharf Co., January 25, 1859*. Sacramento: H. S. Crocker, Printers, 1859.

Robinson, W. W. *Land in California*. Berkeley: University of California Press, 1948.

Rodger, Katherine. *Renaissance Man of Cannery Row: The Life and Letters of Edward F. Ricketts*. Tuscaloosa: University of Alabama Press, 2002.

Rohrbaugh, Malcolm J. *The Land Office Business: The Settlement and Administration of American Public Lands, 1789–1837*. New York: Oxford University Press, 1968.

Rome, Adam. *The Bulldozer in the Countryside: Suburban Sprawl and the Rise of American Environmentalism*. Cambridge: Cambridge University Press, 2001.

Rose, Carol M. "The Comedy of the Commons: Custom. Commerce, and Inherently Public Property." *University of Chicago Law Review* 53, no. 3 (Summer 1986): 711–781.

———. *Property and Persuasion: Essays on the History, Theory, and Rhetoric of Ownership*. Boulder, CO: Westview, 1994.

Rothman, Hal K. *The Greening of A Nation? Environmentalism in the United States Since 1945*. Fort Worth, TX: Harcourt Brace, 1998.

———. *The New Urban Park: Golden Gate Recreation Area and Civic Environmentalism*. Lawrence: University Press of Kansas, 2004.

Royce, Josiah. *California: From the Conquest in 1846 to the Second Vigilance Committee in San Francisco*. New York: Alfred A. Knopf, 1948. First published 1886 by Houghton Mifflin.

Royster, Charles. *The Destructive War: William Tecumseh Sherman, Stonewall Jackson, and the Americans*. New York: Alfred A. Knopf, 1991.

———. *The Fabulous History of the Great Dismal Swamp: A Story of George Washington's Times*. New York: Alfred A. Knopf, 1999.

Rubin, Jasper. *A Negotiated Landscape: The Transformation of San Francisco's Waterfront since 1950*. Chicago: Center for American Places, 2011.

Rubissow, Okamoto Ariel, and Kathleen M. Wong. *Natural History of San Francisco Bay*. Berkeley: University of California Press, 2011.

Sackman, Douglas Cazaux. *Wild Men: Ishi and Kroeber in the Wilderness of Modern America*. Oxford: Oxford University Press, 2010.

Sandoval, John. *Mt. Eden, Cradle of the Salt Industry in California*. Mt. Eden, CA: Mt. Eden Historical Publishers, 1988.

San Francisco Bay Conservation and Development Commission. *Analysis of A Tidal Barrage at the Golden Gate*. San Francisco: Bay Conservation and Development Commission, 2007. www.bcdc.ca.gov/pdf/planning/Golden_Gate_Dam_Report.pdf (accessed November 29, 2012).

———. *Living with A Rising Bay: Vulnerability and Adaptation and On the Shoreline*. San Francisco: Bay Conservation and Development Commission, 2009. www.bcdc.ca.gov/BPA/LivingWithRisingBay.pdf (accessed December 7, 2012).

———. *Ownership: Part of a Detailed Study of San Francisco Bay*. San Francisco: Bay Conservation and Development Commission, 1968.

———. *Recreation on and around San Francisco Bay*. San Francisco: Bay Conservation and Development Commission, 1968.

———. *Revised Staff Report and Staff Recommendation for Proposed Bay Plan Amendment 1–08 Concerning Climate Change*. San Francisco: Bay Conservation

and Development Commission, 2011. www.bcdc.ca.gov/proposed_bay_
plan/10–01Recom.pdf (accessed December 7, 2012).

———. *San Francisco Bay Plan.* San Francisco: Bay Conservation and
Development Commission, 1969. www.bcdc.ca.gov/laws_plans/plans/
sfbay_plan.shtml (accessed December 12, 2012).

———. *San Francisco Bay Scenarios for Sea Level Rise* [maps]. Scale not given.
www.bcdc.ca.gov/planning/climate_change/index_map.shtml (accessed
November 4, 2011).

———. *Sea Level Rise: Predictions and Implications for San Francisco Bay.* San
Francisco: Bay Conservation and Development Commission, 1987. www.
bcdc.ca.gov/pdf/planning/cc_slr_rpt_1988.pdf (accessed December 7,
2012).

San Francisco Bay Conservation Study Commission. *A Report to the California
Legislature.* San Francisco: San Francisco Bay Conservation Study
Commission, 1965.

"San Francisco Bay Oysters." *California Fish and Game* 2, no. 4 (October 1916): 208.

San Francisco Board of Supervisors. *Municipal Reports.* San Francisco: City of
San Francisco, 1868–1910.

San Francisco Estuary Institute. *The Pulse of the Estuary: Monitoring and
Managing Water Quality in the San Francisco Estuary.* SFEI Contribution 559.
Oakland: San Francisco Estuary Institute, 2008.

Santa Clara County Planning Commission. *A Plan to Fulfill the Needs of a
Growing Metropolitan Community for: Parks, Recreation and Open Space.* San
Jose, CA: Santa Clary County Planning Commission, 1959.

Schenk, W. "The Emeryville Shellmound: Final Report." *University of California
Publications in American Archaeology and Ethnology* 23 (1926): 147–282.

Scofield, W. L. *California Fishing Ports.* Sacramento: California Department of
Fish and Game, 1954.

Scott, Mel. *The Future of San Francisco Bay.* Berkeley: University of California
Institute of Governmental Studies, 1963.

———. *San Francisco Bay Area: A Metropolis in Perspective.* Berkeley: University
of California Press, 1985.

Scott, Stanley. *Governing California's Coast.* Berkeley: University of California
Institute for Governmental Studies, 1975.

Sculati, Christine. "Still Hanging On: The Bay's Native Oysters." *Bay Nature* 4,
no. 4 (July 2004): 34–38.

Seasholes, Nancy S. "Gaining Ground: Boston's Topographical Development in
Maps." In *Mapping Boston,* edited by Alex Krieger and David Cobb, 118–145.
Boston: MIT Press, 1999.

———. *Gaining Ground: A History of Landmaking in Boston.* Boston: MIT Press,
2003.

Shaler, Nathaniel S. "Beaches and Tidal Marshes of the Atlantic Coast." In *The Physiography of the United States: Ten Monographs,* edited by the National Geographic Society, 137–168. New York: American Book Company, 1896.

Shalowitz, Aaron L. *Shore and Sea Boundaries: With Special Reference to the Interpretation and Use of Coast and Geodetic Survey Data.* 2 vols. Coast and Geodetic Survey, U.S. Department of Commerce, Publication 10–1. Washington, DC: U.S. Government Printing Office, 1962.

Sharpsteen, William Crittenden. "Vanished Waters of Southeastern San Francisco: Notes on Mission Bay and the Marshes and Creeks of the Potreros and Bernal Rancho." *California Historical Society Quarterly* 21, no. 2 (June 1941): 113–126.

Shaw, Samuel P., and C. Gordon Fredine. *Wetlands of the United States: Their Extent and Their Value to Waterfowl and Other Wildlife.* Circular 39. Washington, DC: U.S. Fish and Wildlife Service, 1956.

Sher, Sandra. "The Native Legacy of Emeryville." *The Journal of the Emeryville Historical Society* 5, no. 2 (Summer 1994) and no. 3 (Autumn 1994).

Sherman, William Tecumseh. *Memoirs of General William T. Sherman.* New York: D. Appleton and Company, 1875.

Shipek, Florence. *Pushed into the Rocks: Southern California Indian Land Tenure, 1769–1986.* Lincoln: University of Nebraska Press, 1988.

Shoup, Lawrence H., and Randall T. Milliken. *Inigo of Posolmi: The Life and Times of a Mission Indian.* Novato, CA: Ballena, 1999.

Shumate, Albert. *Rincon Hill and South Park: San Francisco's Early Fashionable Neighborhood.* Sausalito, CA: Windgate, 1988.

Sinclair, Upton. "What Life Means to Me." *Cosmopolitan* 41 (October 31, 1906): 591–595.

Skinner, John E. *An Historical Review of the Fish and Wildlife Resources of the San Francisco Bay Area.* Water Resources Branch Report No. 1. Sacramento: California Department of Fish and Game, 1962.

Solnit, Rebecca. *Infinite City: A San Francisco Atlas.* Berkeley: University of California Press, 2010.

Soulé, Frank. "The Earthquake and Fire and Their Effects on Structural Materials." In *The San Francisco Earthquake and Fire of April 18, 1906 and Their Effects on Structures and Structural Materials,* by the U.S. Geological Survey, 131–158. Washington, DC: Government Printing Office, 1907.

Soulé, Frank, John H. Gihon, and James Nisbet. *The Annals of San Francisco; Containing a Summary of the History of California and a Complete History of Its Great City: To Which are Added, Biographical Memoirs of Some Prominent Citizens.* New York: Appleton, 1855.

"Sowing Rice—Reaping Shipworms." *Pacific Marine Review* 17 (September 1920): 105–106.

Spangle, William, and Associates, City and Regional Planners. *Municipal, State and Federal Programs Affecting San Francisco Bay, Part of a Detailed Study of the Bay.* Jointly with Paul Sedway and Associates, City and Regional Planning. San Francisco: San Francisco Bay Conservation and Development Commission, 1966.

Special Committee of the California State Assembly. *The Entire Official Testimony and the Report of the Committee as to the Necessity of a "Bulkhead or Sea-wall," on the Water Front of the City of San Francisco, Taken Before a Special Assembly Committee of 1859.* Sacramento: Daily Standard Office, 1860.

Spence, Mark David. *Dispossessing the Wilderness: Indian Removal and the Making of the National Parks.* Oxford: Oxford University Press, 2000.

A Spirit of Independence: Brisbane Before Incorporation. Brisbane: City of Brisbane, 1996.

Stasz, Clarice. *Jack London's Women.* Amherst: University of Massachusetts Press, 2001.

State Harbor Commissioners. *Biennial Report, 1906–1908.* Sacramento: W.W. Shannon, Superintendent of State Printing, 1908.

Stearns, Robert E. C. "Exotic Mollusca in California." *Science* 11, no. 278 (April 27, 1900): 655–659.

———. "*Mya arenaria* in San Francisco Bay." *American Naturalist* 15, no. 5 (May 1881): 362–366.

Steinberg, Theodore. *Nature Incorporated: Industrialization and the Waters of New England.* Amherst: University of Massachusetts Press, 1991.

———. *Slide Mountain, or the Folly of Owning Nature.* Berkeley: University of California Press, 1995.

Stoll, Steven. *The Fruits of Natural Advantage: Making the Industrial Countryside in California.* Berkeley: University of California Press, 1998.

Stone, Irving. *Sailor on Horseback: The Biography of Jack London.* Boston: Houghton Mifflin, 1938.

Street, Richard Steven. *Beasts of the Field: A Narrative History of California Farmworkers, 1769–1913.* Stanford: Stanford University Press, 2004.

Striplen, Chuck, and Sarah DeWeerdt. "Old Science, New Science: Incorporating Traditional Ecological Knowledge into Contemporary Management." *Conservation in Practice* 3, no. 30 (Summer 2002): 1–7.

Sullivan, Maurice S. *The Travels of Jedediah Smith: A Documentary Outline Including the Journal of the Great American Pathfinder.* Santa Ana, CA: Fine Arts Press, 1934.

Sumner, F. B. "A Report Upon the Physical Conditions in San Francisco Bay, Based upon Operations of the U.S. Fisheries Steamer 'Albatross' during the Years 1912–1913." *University of California Publications in Zoology* 14, no. 1 (1914): 1–198.

Taylor, Bayard. *Eldorado, Or, Adventures in the Path of Empire, Comprising A Voyage to California, Via Panama; Life in San Francisco and Monterey; Pictures of the Gold Region; and Experiences of Mexican Travel*. Vol. 2. London: Henry G. Bohn, 1850.

Taylor, Joseph. *Making Salmon: An Environmental History of the Northwest Fisheries Crisis*. Seattle: University of Washington Press, 1999.

Taylor, Paul S. "Statement to House Government Operations Committee Subcommittee on Conservation and Natural Resources, August 20 and 21, 1969." In *The Nation's Estuaries: San Francisco Bay and Delta, Calif. Hearing Before a Subcommittee of the Committee on Government Operations House of Representatives*, 229–233. 91st Cong., 1st Sess., May 15, 1969. Washington, DC: Government Printing Office, 1969.

Taylor, Paul S., and Dorothea Lange. *American Exodus: A Record of Human Erosion*. New York: Reynal and Hitchcock, 1939.

Theberge, Albert E., Jr. *150 Years of Tides on the Western Coast: The Longest Series of Tidal Observations in the Americas*. Washington, DC: U.S. Dept. of Commerce, National Oceanic and Atmospheric Administration, 2005. http://oceanservice.noaa.gov/topics/navops/ports/150_years_of_tides.pdf (accessed June 7, 2012).

Thompson, E. P. *The Making of the English Working Class*. New York: Vintage, 1963.

Thompson, John. "Early Reclamation and Abandonment of the Central Sacramento–San Joaquin Delta." *Sacramento History: Journal of the Sacramento Historical Society* 6, no. 1–4 (2006): 41–72."

———. "The Settlement Geography of the Sacramento-San Joaquin Delta." PhD diss., Stanford University, 1957.

Thompson, John, and Edward Dutra. *The Tule Breakers: The Story of the California Dredge*. Stockton: Stockton Corral of Westerners, 1983.

Tide Land Reclamation Company. *Fresh Water Tide Lands of California*. San Francisco: M. D. Carr, 1869.

Tobriner, Stephen. *Bracing for Disaster: Earthquake-Resistant Architecture and Engineering in San Francisco, 1838–1933*. Berkeley: Heyday Books, 2006.

Towle, Jerry C. "Authored Ecosystems: Livingston Stone and the Transformation of California Fisheries." *Environmental History* 5, no. 1 (January 2000): 54–74.

Twain, Mark [Samuel Clemens]. "Another Enterprise" (Virginia City *Territorial Enterprise*, December 26–27, 1865). In *The Works of Mark Twain: Early Tales and Sketches*, 2:413–415. Berkeley: University of California Press, 1981.

———. "The Old Thing" (Virginia City *Territorial Enterprise*, November 18, 1865). In *The Works of Mark Twain: Early Tales and Sketches*, 2:332–335. Berkeley: University of California Press, 1981.

―――. *The Works of Mark Twain: Early Tales and Sketches*. Vol. 2, *1864–1865*. Berkeley: University of California Press, 1981.

Twain, Mark [Samuel Clemens], and Bret Harte. *Sketches of the Sixties: Being Forgotten Material Now Collected for the First Time from The Californian, 1864–1867*. San Francisco: John Howell, 1926.

Tyrrell, Ian. "Beyond the View from Euro-America: Environment, Settler Societies, and Internationalization of American History." In *Rethinking American History in a Global Age*, edited by Thomas Bender, 168–191. Berkeley: University of California Press, 2002.

―――. *True Gardens of the Gods: Californian-Australian Environmental Reform, 1860–1930*. Berkeley: University of California Press, 1999.

Uhle, Max. "The Emeryville Shell Mound." *University of California Publications in American Archaeology and Ethnology* 7, no. 1 (1907): 1–84.

United States. *The Statutes at Large and Treaties of the United States from December 1, 1845 to March 3, 1851*. Edited by George Minot. Vol. 9. Boston: Little, Brown, 1862.

U.S. Army Corps of Engineers, San Francisco District. *Areas Susceptible of Reclamation in San Francisco Bay Area* [map]. 1:250,000. San Francisco: U.S. Army Corps of Engineers, 1959.

U.S. Coast and Geodetic Survey. *San Francisco Bay, Southern Part*. 1:40,000. Washington, DC: National Ocean Service, 1882.

U.S. Congress. *Report of the Joint Special Committee to Investigate Chinese Immigration*. 41st Cong. 2nd sess., Senate, Report 689. Washington, DC: General Printing Office, 1877.

U.S. Environmental Protection Agency. *Sand and Gravel Overlay for Control of Mercury Sediments*. Water Pollution Research Control Series 16080 HVA 01 / 72. Washington, DC: U.S. Environmental Protection Agency, 1972.

Uzes, Francois D. *Chaining the Land: A History of Surveying in California*. Sacramento: Landmark Enterprises, 1977.

Valencius, Conevery Bolton. *The Health of the Country: How American Settlers Understood Themselves and Their Land*. New York: Basic Books, 2002.

Vance, Jay. *Geography and Urban Evolution in the San Francisco Bay Area*. Berkeley: Institute of Governmental Studies, 1964.

Ver Planck, William E. "Salines in the Bay Area." In *Geologic Guidebook of the San Francisco Bay Counties*, California Division of Mines, Bulletin 154, 219–222. San Francisco: California Division of Mines, 1951.

―――. *Salt in California*. California Division of Mines, Bulletin 175. San Francisco: California Division of Mines, 1958.

Vileisis, Ann. *Discovering the Unknown Landscape: A History of America's Wetlands*. Covelo, CA: Island Press, 1997.

Von Langsdorff, Georg H. *Voyages and Travels in Various Parts of the World During the Years 1803, 1804, 1805, 1806, and 1807.* London: Henry Colburn, 1813–1814. Special Collections, Stanford University Libraries.

Waldie, D. J. *Holy Land: A Suburban Memoir.* New York: St. Martins, 1996.

Waldorf, Dolores. "Gentleman from Vermont: Royal H. Waller." *California Historical Quarterly* 22, no. 2 (June 1943): 110–118.

Walker, Richard. *The Country in the City: The Greening of the San Francisco Bay Area.* Seattle: University of Washington Press, 2007.

Warren, Louis, S. *The Hunter's Game: Poachers and Conservationists in Twentieth-Century America.* New Haven, CT: Yale University Press, 1997.

Watkins, Eleanor. "The San Francisco Earthquake: A Personal Account." *California Geology* 34, no. 12 (December 1981): 260–266.

Watson, Elizabeth Burke. "Changing Elevation, Accretion, and Tidal Marsh Plant Assemblages in a South San Francisco Bay Tidal Marsh." *Estuaries* 27, no. 4 (August 2004): 684–698.

Watt, Laura A. "Conflicting Restoration Goals in the San Francisco Bay." In *Restoration and History: The Search for a Usable Environmental Past,* edited by Marcus Hall, 218–220. New York: Routledge, 2010.

Watt, Laura A., Leigh Raymond, and Meryl L. Eschen. "On Preserving Ecological and Cultural Landscapes." *Environmental History* 9, no. 4 (October 2004): 620–647.

Weber, David J. *Bárbaros: Spaniards and Their Savages in the Age of Enlightenment.* New Haven, CT: Yale University Press, 2005.

———. *The Spanish Frontier in North America.* New Haven, CT: Yale University Press, 1992.

Wennersten, John R. *Oyster Wars of Chesapeake Bay.* Centerville, MD: Tidewater Publications, 1981.

West, Elliott. *The Contested Plains: Indians, Goldseekers, and the Rush to Colorado.* Lawrence: University Press of Kansas, 1998.

Weymouth, Frank. "The Edible Clams, Mussels and Scallops of California." *California Fish and Game Commission Bulletin* 4 (1921).

———. "Investigation of the Life History of the Dungeness Crab (*Cancer magister*)." In State of California Fish and Game Commission, Fish Bulletin 1, 29–34. Sacramento: State Superintendent of Printing, 1913.

Wheeler, Alfred. *Land Titles in San Francisco and the Laws Affecting the Same, with a Synopsis of All Grants and Sales of Land within the Limits Claimed by the City.* San Francisco: Alta California Steam Printing Establishment, 1852. Schedule A. Held in Special Collections, Crown Law Library, Stanford University.

Whipple A. A., R. M. Grossinger, D. Rankin, B. Stanford, and R. A. Askevold. *Sacramento-San Joaquin Delta Historical Ecology Investigation: Exploring Pattern and Process*. Richmond, CA: San Francisco Estuary Institute-Aquatic Science Center, 2012.

White, Richard. "From Wilderness to Hybrid Landscapes: The Cultural Turn in Environmental History." *The Historian* 66 (2004): 557–564.

———. *"It's Your Misfortune and None of My Own": A History of the American West*. Norman: University of Oklahoma Press, 1991.

———. *Land Use, Environment, and Social Change: The Shaping of Island County, Washington*. Seattle: University of Washington Press, 1980 (1992).

———. *The Organic Machine: The Remaking of the Columbia River*. New York: Hill and Wang, 1995.

———. *Railroaded: The Transcontinentals and the Making of Modern America*. New York: W.W. Norton, 2011.

Whitney, Josiah C. *Map of the Region Adjacent to the Bay of San Francisco*. 1:126,720. Sacramento: California Geological Survey, 1873.

Wilentz, Sean. *Chants Democratic: New York City and the Rise of the American Working Class, 1788–1850*. New York: Oxford University Press, 1984.

Williams, Raymond. *Keywords: A Vocabulary of Culture and Society*. New York: Oxford University Press, 1976.

Wilson, Robert M. "Directing the Flow: Migratory Waterfowl, Scale and Mobility in Western North America." *Environmental History* 7, no. 2 (April 2002): 247–266.

———. *Seeking Refuge: Birds and Landscapes of the Pacific Flyway*. Seattle: University of Washington Press, 2010.

Worster, Donald. *Rivers of Empire: Water, Aridity and the Growth of the American West*. New York: Oxford University Press, 1985.

Wyman, Jeffries. "An Account of Some Kjoekkenmoeddings, or Shell-heaps, in Maine and Massachusetts." *American Naturalist* 1, no. 11 (1868): 561–584.

Index

Page numbers in italics refer to figures and maps.